Mora

ALEXANDRA ORME was born in Warsaw, Poland. But, says she, "I'm not a Pole by blood but by sheer frantic habit. Once you start being a Pole, it's terribly hard to stop. Try it; hopeless struggle."

She was brought up in Poland, Switzerland, Germany and England and maintains she had no education whatsoever — a highly doubtful statement since she speaks and writes four languages fluently and can keep up a conversation in four others.

In 1931 Alexandra Orme married for the first time. To escape the Germans and the Russians in 1939, they crossed the border into Hungary, where her husband died. Then, in 1944, she married a Hungarian — the Jumbo of this book; claims his decision to propose was the direct result of his release from Gestapo Headquarters. "Everything was sunshine to him," she says.

What happened then is the subject of COMES THE COMRADE! — one of the most uniquely devastating bits of autobiography we have ever read.

Comes the Comrade!

By ALEXANDRA ORME

Comes the Comrade!

WILLIAM MORROW & COMPANY
NEW YORK, 1950

Translated from the Polish by M. A. Michael and L. Meyer.
The sketches and the endpaper were drawn by the author.
Published in Great Britain under the title
From Christmas to Easter.
Copyright 1949 by William Morrow and Company, Inc.
Printed in the United States of America.
By H. Wolff, New York.

Cast of Characters

LIDA	Narrator; a Polish citizen staying with her Hungarian husband's brother at Mora Manor.
JUMBO	Lida's husband; a large man, good-natured, and the link between his family and the Polish group.

The Hungarians of the Manor House:

TACITUS	lord of Mora Manor; stern, silent and very lordly.
MARIETTA	wife of Tacitus, and a Countess in her own right.
FRANZI	nineteen-year-old son of Tacitus and Marietta.
ELSIE and nine-year-old ALEC	cousins of Marietta who fled Budapest.

The Hungarians at the Dower House:

RUDI	brother to Marietta. A Count with holdings in Southern Hungary.

v

DOLLY   Rudi's wife and MUKI, their six-year-old son with his nurse, HONONO.

The Polish group:

FIFI   dear friend of Lida's who came with her from Poland.

JACK   a nephew of Lida's.

LINA and MATHILDA   Two Hungarian cooks.

Some of the Russian soldiers:

NICOLAS   the thoughtful one, to be distinguished from Nicholas, the Hooligan.

VICTOR   later known as Victor-Chaliapin who came to loot and stayed to sing.

MAJOR SERGIEJ   who cheated at dominoes.

THE TALL MAJOR   who loved to go hunting.

KUZMA   the Tartar who had two pounds of sugar to trade.

MAJOR BLASHCHUK   who liked Banquets at midnight.

WARRANT OFFICER SASHKA   in command of the men at the mill and a "friendly."

KUZNETSOFF   a difficult "liberator."

Comes
the
Comrade!

22nd

December

ELSIE and I had been raking up leaves. We carried them in huge baskets to where the fig trees stood and carefully covered their bare, crooked branches with them, jeering at ourselves the while. Said Elsie, "You'd think there was nothing more important than to cover up the trees so that we shall have figs next year."

"There's nothing like fresh figs," I agreed, and we went on patiently and senselessly carrying our huge baskets full of rotten, sour-smelling leaves. We agreed that we ought to spend the night in the cellar as the front could not be more than two or three miles away from Mora, and there might be fighting in the village itself by morning.

But who was fighting whom? There was not a single German left in the village.

We went back to the Manor. It belonged to my husband's younger brother, whom we called Tacitus. This was not entirely a joke, for he really was very taciturn. He had a wife, Marietta, and a son, Franzi, but to describe his whole family now would be to anticipate. I had better begin at the beginning.

There were three of us Poles: myself, my nephew Jack, and my friend Fifi. Fifi and I had come to Hungary away back in September, 1939, when we fled our country, and there we had remained, so-called emigrés, just like the hundreds of

1

thousands of other Poles dispersed all over the world after the
September disaster. Somehow we had managed to keep alive
during the last five years. We would gladly have fled farther,
but nobody needed us, anywhere. We belonged to no party,
nor were we "endangered," as were half our compatriots; in
short, all the Emigration Departments came to the conclusion
that Poland would lose nothing if I and my Fifi perished, and
that is why we remained stranded in Hungary. During those
five years, we had been doing all kinds of odd jobs, anything
that came our way, just to keep body and soul together. And
we even learnt some Hungarian.

In the spring of 1944, I went so far as to marry a Hungarian, released from a Gestapo prison. Once married we
went to live with Tacitus at Mora. That was in June. Fifi
joined us in July, as companion to my mother-in-law, and
when the old lady died soon afterwards she stayed on in the
Dower House, with the cook and the maid. It was a small
house standing in the middle of a beautiful old park, on the
outskirts of the village. The Manor stood at the head of the
village.

In the autumn I received a letter with the unexpected
news that my nephew had fled from Poland and was then in-
terned at a camp for runaway Poles a hundred and thirty
miles away, and was in danger of being deported to Germany.
After many and complicated endeavours, my husband succeeded in getting him released and brought him to us. Thus,
by a whim of Fate, we all found ourselves together in Mora:
Fifi, Jack and myself. Fifi is a very tiny person. She has dark
hair, round grey eyes, a shapeless nose. She always wore the
same, miserable little coat which made her look like a wise
child of about twelve or thirteen. She had only one pair of
very old shoes, so she was running about in snowboots, looking like a bewildered Mickey-mouse. Mora lies twenty miles
south-west of Budapest, and is populated by peasants whom
I did not know and in whom I had no confidence whatever.
We almost never left the park, being afraid lest our speech

betray our nationality, and, generally, not wishing to draw too much attention to our presence.

So much for the Poles. Chief of the Hungarians and lord of Mora was Tacitus. Tacitus is a tall, very handsome man with a greying beard specially grown for the war. He always dressed as though he were going out shooting. I need not describe his character, as it will emerge sufficiently in the pages of this book. So we come to Marietta, his wife. She also is tall, very slim and beautiful, every inch an aristocrat. She is about forty-five, but looks younger. She has a son of nineteen, Franzi.

Franzi is six feet tall; his one and only ambition is to be mistaken for a peasant. By dint of much trying he has achieved his aim, and even his expression is that of a peasant. Considering his parents' breeding it cannot have been an easy thing to accomplish. However, just as his mother is every inch a countess so Franzi is now a boor in all his movements, in everything he says, even in his instincts and in appearance. Both he and his mother have always lived in the shadow of Tacitus, who, like a veritable Zeus, has governed their world and moulded—at least superficially—all their thoughts and actions. (He also has a daughter, but she was at school in Switzerland, and is a replica of her mother).

My husband, nicknamed Jumbo on account of his height and plumpness, for all that he is a big man is not strong, and those weeks spent in a German prison had ruined his health. His dominant trait is even temper and patience. He is a good talker and likes to have an audience.

Then there was Elsie, Marietta's cousin and another refugee from Budapest. She is a tiny, exotic person. Her mother was English, but, owing to a fateful short-circuit in the lighting system of a Paris hotel towards the end of the nineteenth century, there was Malayan blood in her veins.

Elsie is small, frail and has a very dark complexion. Her pupils are large and dark, floating in bluish eyeballs, their expression almost one of anxiety. Her mouth, full and pretty, has a violet tint all through winter and she has to use a darker lipstick to hide it. Her small nine-year-old son Alec resembles the Negro child of "Rosenkavalier." So must have looked in his childhood the famous Zamor of Madame du Barry. Alec is so pretty that it is a pleasure just to look at him. He never stops fidgeting or emitting inarticulate sounds which are supposed to imitate aeroplane engines, machine-guns or falling bombs. To be long under one roof with him was therefore a nightmare, and for a nervous person an impossibility.

Fifi and Jack took their meals at the Dower House, together with Marietta's brother and his family who had recently fled to us from the south. There was Rudi, his wife, Dolly, Muki their son and his nurse, Honono. Dolly was a typical woman, *i.e.*, the better half of a man, but a half only. Honono was completely useless and just a hindrance, while poor Muki was only six and delicate. (How Tacitus used to curse Fate for saddling him with such a family!) They usually came over to the Manor every day after lunch.

Jack would sometimes come over in the morning to exercise the stallion. There were only a few horses left as the Germans had taken most of them, but anyway only Jack was allowed to ride. Tacitus had decreed that in what he called "this time of national mourning" riding and shooting were unsuitable pastimes, if only because the sight of the gentry riding and shooting, when all the young people had been called up and the country itself was being turned into a battle-field, would make a very bad impression on the peasants. Jumbo agreed with him; but I could never see what effect our refraining from eating a few pheasants would have on the peasants. Nor could Fifi. We had our own opinion about the peasants: that the only way we could please them was by ceasing to exist, so why try to make a good impression on them?

For the last few days the front had been approaching closer and closer. Long ago we decided that when the fighting came, we would take to a cellar in the orchard adjoining the Dower House, and there wait till the worst was over. It was a wine cellar, clean and spacious, ten feet by eighteen. It lay beneath a stone tower that stood alone in the shadow of some olive and pine trees. A vaulted gateway and an iron grill led to it. Then there was a kind of open porch and a massive wooden door opening directly on to the steps. Down the steps was another wooden door and behind it, the cellar. Here, for the last week, had lain thirteen paillasses covered with Persian rugs. In one corner stood a bookcase laden with hams, sausages, tinned foods, and jams. In another corner was a shelf with candles and two earthenware jars: one of kerosene, the other of mead. Another corner was occupied by coat-hooks, on which Dolly's furs already hung. Suitcases served as seats. The place looked as luxurious as a Pharaoh's tomb, and the two children were all impatience to be allowed to sleep there. For the last week Muki had been pestering his parents, "If I am good, very good, may we sleep in the cellar?" Maybe, they would say, for we grown-ups, too, were looking forward to the day when we should sleep in the cellar, even though we also dreaded it, for that day was to bring us our liberation.

The papers never used to call the Russians anything but the "Red Hangmen" or the "Perverts," and the local wireless station, which was manned by Germans, never tired of broadcasting accounts of the horrible crimes committed by the Russians in the eastern part of the country, which they had occupied a considerable time before. It was in the east that Jumbo's factory was. His chief mechanic had fled from there to Mora with his wife and their three children. Although this Machick had not seen much because he had run away in good time, he was only too willing to describe the terrible things supposed to have happened there. The servants all listened to him with that awe and admiration of which only the simple are capable, and his tales spread like wildfire all over the village. What with them and the wireless it was obvious that

the Russians were plundering, raping women, tearing the
boots off people's feet, and murdering the innocent without
distinction of sex or age. We did not believe a word of it.
Among ourselves, we would admit the possibility of there
being isolated cases of Russian soldiers getting drunk and
raping a few women who happened to come their way, but
on the whole we had the best possible opinion of the Russian
Army. Tacitus had even announced that he would throw a
party for the first Russian unit to reach Mora. He would
slaughter as many sheep as might be needed for the occasion,
and would supply them liberally with food, hay, and quarters
—if only they would come, if only they would at last come
and liberate us.

Fifi and I had spent all that summer poring over a Russian dictionary which we had found in an old writing-desk.
From it we learned the Russian alphabet, but, alas, we had
no Russian books to read. We spent hours on end writing
down single words and making them up into sentences; we
even conversed in Russian, or at least that was what we
thought. It was easier for me, because my parents had spoken
Russian just as well as Polish, but poor Fifi's knowledge of
Russian was limited to a few words of "Dark Eyes" and "The
Volga Boatmen." Jack had actually seen the Russians in 1939
in Lwow, and we pestered him with questions, wanting to
know everything that would help us to create a mental picture of that unknown nation. Despite the bitter feelings towards the Russians that the centuries have engendered in
the Poles, we were prepared to like them "on principle." If
nothing else, our hatred for the Germans made us almost
ready to take them to our hearts. We saw everything Russian
through rose-coloured spectacles; we forgave them all their
faults, forgot all our wrongs.

Our entire conversation—not only Fifi's and mine, but
that of the whole lot of us—was centred on the Russians.
What were they like? Imagine yourself daily expecting the
advent of an unknown, vast army surging down upon you

from the East. You, too, would be consumed with curiosity.

We would go from one extreme to the other. One evening we would be inclined to think that everything would turn out all right: we would be lucky and there would be no fighting; the Russians would come and we would welcome them with the traditional bread and salt, in their own language; then we would give them food and drink, tell them all about the horrors of the life we had been living for months; we would get along nicely, the best of friends from the word go. I even kept our last litre of vodka for that; good genuine stuff which it was impossible to get in Hungary any more.

The next evening, however, we would have uncomfortable forebodings that it was not going to be so nice and pleasant after all. There was no getting over the fact that Hungary was an enemy country, still officially fighting on the side of the Germans; and we, being Poles, would not be at all welcome to the Russians. On the contrary, they would say we were bloodsuckers, Fascists, treacherous scum, and all the rest of it.

So the evenings would pass, and at the end of the day we knew no more about the Russians than before. Sometimes, as a reaction to some new German crime, one of us would exclaim, "I will kiss the first Russian I see." But then, clearheaded Fifi would remark that no Russian soldier could safely be kissed on account of his filthiness.

Meanwhile, the peasants, reacting instinctively to the experience of the centuries, were busy burying everything they could: corn, bacon, clothes, and even whole carts. They did not stop to worry over what the Russians looked like; they did not even bother about history. To them, war was war, as flood is flood.

Jumbo, too, thought that we ought to spend the night in the cellar, and when we got back to the house from gathering our leaves, we found that he had already summoned his chauffeur to do the packing. We took things calmly, not hurry-

ing, for it was not the first time the Russians had almost
reached us, only to be pushed back again and make us unpack.

Jack stuffed into the suitcases everything that he could
lay hands on. I gazed at our beloved furniture, which we had
brought from Budapest before the air raids began and which
we now had to leave behind; an old Dutch chest-of-drawers
of which every drawer was painted in dark, faded colours, with
a different landscape on each; two stocky antique writing-
desks, finely inlaid; and an old, 17th-century Spanish chest
with lovely chiselled iron bindings. Those pieces of furniture
were like living creatures; their smooth, shiny, polished wood
reflected light like the skin of a well-groomed horse. Their
shapes, so familiar to us, were full of grace and each had its
own expression, the fruit of days when time passed much
slower than it does now. Should the Manor burn that night,
we should never see them again.

On an old bow-legged chest-of-drawers lay a Chinese
porcelain cat. That cat was called Tchang So Lin and was
my private property. Jumbo had given it to me in the days
when I was on the point of starvation, when a piece of sausage
would have made a much more suitable present, but, then,
Jumbo had been "courting" me, as they used to say in the
old days, and in such circumstances men do not give a sausage
to their girls. I kissed Tchang So Lin between his cool porcelain ears and went on packing. In one corner stood a whole
library of gramophone records. They, too, had to be left behind. I went on stuffing the suitcases with all and sundry;
toothpaste and gloves, soap and suspenders, and cigarettes,
cigarettes everywhere where there was space for them. Then
we made bundles of our furs and rugs.

Elsie was the first to start packing and the first to finish.
She slung her rucksack over her shoulder, took her child by
the hand, and set off into the darkness for the Dower House.
We all were to move in there in about an hour's time, all,
that is, except the servants who had elected to stay on in the
Manor.

Night had already fallen. The stars shone brightly and a fresh frost had hardened the mud and covered the puddles with thin, glass-like ice. There was a smell of cold, sharp air. The only sound was the barking and howling of the village dogs. A night, like any other. We crossed the yard, talking only of how heavy our baggage was. In the Dower House, Fifi was busy getting beds ready for us. Dolly was sitting with her arms crossed. This was her natural attitude, but on this occasion meant to express despair because Rudi had not yet come back from a trip to the capital. Alec and Muki had gone quite mad, and were racing round and round the rooms emitting inhuman squeals. Jumbo came and sat in Fifi's cold bedroom. He was exhausted, both physically and mentally, and sat there smoking one cigarette after the other.

It was a strange thing, but in the Dower House we suddenly felt safe. Perhaps it was because the weeks we had spent in that other house had been weeks of anxiety, while here in these small, modestly furnished rooms we had the impression that we ran much smaller risks, as if it would be more difficult for a bomb to hit this small unpretentious roof than the large magnificent one of the Manor. There were four of us sitting in Fifi's bedroom. On the table was a small oil lamp, for the electric light had suddenly failed. We were all excited, like people about to set out on a journey. Fifi began laying the table; in the kitchen, Matilda, the hunchback cook of my late mother-in-law, was cooking supper for the whole family. Outside it was relatively quiet. Suddenly we heard heavy steps in the room next to us, and somebody's raised voice. Franzi had arrived with his parents, all of them loaded like mules. Franzi never spoke in a normal voice, for as he modelled himself on the peasants he always had to roar like a peasant shouting at his horses or cattle.

Tacitus and his wife had started making their beds when the glad tidings spread that Rudi had returned. Dolly and Marietta ran about laughing and crying, bumping against the

furniture in the dark rooms and generally making a great
commotion. Then dinner was served.

We had red wine and white wine. We drank a lot and
smoked cigarette after cigarette as though this were to be our
last supper. Afterwards I went to the cellar with Jack and
Fifi to get things ready there as well, just in case. Outside,
the big guns had opened up again. The gunners had evidently
had their supper, too. We started making up paillasses. Jack
carried down suitcases; Fifi spread rugs and blankets. Since
the gunfire was getting louder, we decided to sleep in the
cellar after all. Then I opened my bottle of vodka that was
to become famous. There was no knowing whether we should
live to see the morning. Best have a drink. Three-quarters
of a bottle would still be enough for the Russians. Oh, there
were so many reasons in favour of opening that bottle, and
open it we did.

We sat in the long, vaulted cellar, lit by its little lamp, and
drank that heavenly liquid straight from the bottle. The Poles
are fond of vodka. People, the West especially, often ask:
how *can* you like it? It has a revolting taste and burns your
tongue and throat. And yet, there are literally millions who
adore that revolting taste. You see, our tongue anticipates
the effect the alcohol will have on our mind; it knows that in
a moment we shall be flooded with bliss and a sense of well-
being, and so it welcomes that well-known taste joyfully,
though our eyes may flood with tears and our faces grimace.

In Eastern Europe, Mother Vodka has had a heavy task to
fulfil for centuries. It is she who has had to patch all the
holes, to warm the people when they were cold, to dry their
tears when they were sad, to delude their stomachs when they
were hungry, and given them that modicum of happiness
which everybody requires for life, and which is so hard to
come by in half-civilized countries. In Eastern Europe, vodka
is theatre, cinema, concert, and circus; it serves as books for
the illiterate, makes heroes of miserable cowards, is the great
comforter that sweeps all trouble from our hearts. Is there

anywhere in the world another ounce of happiness to be bought for a price so low?

Thus, that evening, like true Slavs, we at once thought of our saviour. And we piously drank the sharp, translucent liquid—out of the bottle. We felt the beneficent warmth running down our throats and spreading quickly across our chests, a pleasant feeling, that made me love Jack and Elsie even more. To tell the truth it was only then that I saw them in their proper light; yes, definitely, I had not been doing them justice. And, God willing, everything was going to turn out for the best and not a hair of our heads would be touched; and the war would soon be over.

We went back upstairs and again sat with Jumbo in Fifi's room. All of a sudden the lights went on. Evidently the Germans had repaired the power plant. We took it for a good omen. The windows were shaking and dancing again. Having nothing better to do, Jumbo decided to put on boots, as, he said, his feet would freeze in his shoes in the cellar.

"You had better take your shoes there with you," said Fifi.

But Jumbo put them in a cupboard in the cloakroom. He would not believe that the Russians could steal such things. Fifi's advice, however, sent Jack into a frenzy of activity and he moved everything he could lay hands on to the cellar, like a hamster carrying corn to its hole. On the walls hung the cardboard puppets for a Punch and Judy show which I had made as a Christmas present for Muki. They remained. But apart from them Jack took everything he could carry down to the cellar. When I went down for the second time, Elsie had altered the entire arrangement, out of sheer boredom from having nothing better to do. And I must admit that she had done it better than I.

The dogs were to sleep with us, too. There was my mongrel, Alf, and Franzi's old pointer, Isa; but not Tacitus' long-haired dachshund which had been left behind in the Manor, abandoned to the tender mercies of the Germans. I remember how I despised Tacitus and his wife for betraying an innocent dog and leaving it in the house from which they had fled to save their lives. Alf lay down at once on Elsie's paillasse, which was the only one made up, and had a fur-lined rug on it. There was a shriek, and a flood of curses poured over the dog's head. Elsie could not bear dogs.

"Take your dog from my bed," she shouted. "I won't sleep in the shelter with the dogs, not for a moment. Out you go! Outside! Get off! Get out, I tell you."

It was a foretaste, a nucleus so to speak, of all our future quarrels, and there were to be many of them. I called Alf softly. He got up with the dignity of a wise animal which has learned forbearance, and ran to me.

We made a fresh start on our "beds," which Elsie had moved. You might think it would have been a comparatively simple matter to arrange them, but Jumbo snored and nobody wanted to sleep next to him. Muki fidgeted constantly and would wake up, crying at the slightest noise. The dogs had fleas, and some did not like them as neighbours. Thus, before we had all agreed who should lie beside whom, what he, or she, should use for blankets, and what for a pillow, much time had passed. At last, however, everybody was satisfied and we settled down.

Dolly and Marietta

23rd
December

THE sun was hardly up. I went quietly to the door for a quick look out. The village was empty, for the peasants had sought shelter from the gunfire, and the Germans, too, seemed to have hidden themselves somewhere, for there was not one to be seen. In the shelter, we sat quietly and patiently, pretending that nothing was going on. The air inside a damaged submarine lying on the ocean-bed could not have been much worse than the atmosphere in our shelter. About eleven o'clock, Jack was despatched to the Dower House to find out the prospects for lunch. Matilda was in the kitchen cooking away just as if nothing had happened. Matilda's was the courage of the half-witted. Just as very stupid children are never afraid of ghosts, because they are unable to imagine them, so our Matilda, who had never seen warfare close, was quite incapable of seeing why it should be dangerous for her to remain in the kitchen. Not that we objected to her courage in the least; because of it we should have a hot lunch, for neither threats, nor pleadings could drag her away from the kitchen to the cellar. Such courage is just as distasteful as cowardice; and that kind of hero causes just as much trouble at critical moments as do ordinary cowards. Neither mentality is a good one to have when times are dangerous.

Several hours later, Jumbo and Jack went up the stairs to

the door, which they carefully opened a little way. There was
no doubt about it, there was firing on all sides, and it was all
small-arms fire. But who was shooting? And at whom? The
orchard was empty. They must be firing from fox-holes and
from behind the box hedges. Jack opened the door a bit
farther and they both stepped cautiously outside, like two
small boys playing Red Indians. We could hear shouts coming from the orchard down the slope in front of us. I crept
to the door, followed by Fifi. Jack turned towards us and said
quickly:

"It's the Russians."

"Pooh!" We refused to believe him, but he stood listening again and presently turned to us with a beaming face.

"I heard them. I distinctly heard them shout: 'Davvay,
davvay!' " (Give, give!).

Still we refused to believe him. I even went back from the
door a little way, beginning to feel bored, when suddenly I
heard Jumbo's voice:

"Come! Come quick!"

He had no time to say more, before I was back again.
There, in front of me, stood two Russian soldiers. They
looked as if they had been cut out of a Nazi poster, only their
faces were broad, honest, and gashed by a childish, kind-
hearted smile. It was about one o'clock, perhaps somewhat
later. So they had come. So they really did exist. They had
liberated us and here were two of them, standing in front of
me.

"We're Poles," the two of us cried, and stretched out our
hands. And then, for the first time truly and not for a joke:
"*Zdrastvojtie.*" (Welcome).

This is how they looked, our first two Russian soldiers:
both were in rags, dressed in quilted, inconceivably dirty uniforms, and long greatcoats the colour of bean soup. One of
them also had a piece of tarpaulin with huge patches of brown
and green, that was probably the cover of some small German
gun, draped over his greatcoat. On their heads they had

peaked caps of artificial sheep-skin with ear-flaps tied on top with a piece of tape. One was young, swarthy, thin, and stupid looking; the other, with red hair cropped almost to the skin, was smiling broadly and revealing a big gap in his teeth. We gazed at each other in silence for a while. Then I ran down the steps to break the great news.

"The wine!" I shouted. "And bread. Quick!"

Without any questions being asked, a bottle of red wine, two or three glasses and a loaf of bread were thrust into my hands. I dashed out from the gloom of the cellar back into the daylight. The two Russians had not dissolved into thin air. They stood there exactly as before. Jumbo was giving them cigarettes, shaking their hands, and telling them in the main European languages how glad he was to see them.

The soldiers drank the wine as though they liked it, tossed the last few drops on to the ground and handed back the glasses. And, strange to relate, we understood almost everything they said! They asked if there were any Germans hidden in the shelter under the tower. We burst out laughing.

"No, only women and children; come and look for yourselves."

But they could not be bothered. The older one, the one with red hair, got very talkative. We learned that the dirty tramp standing in front of us was really a civil engineer, that his father had been a famous surgeon in Kiev, before the Germans killed him. He had been seventy-two then. We believed every word they said, and we were enchanted with such a social system that could give a gap-toothed boor like that a university education. Our new friend, after a moment's consideration, gave us back our loaf, assuring us that in the Red Army they had enough bread, that they were not hungry. We gave them a lot of cigarettes, so glad were we that they had come. While we talked, the "Civil Engineer" happened to glance at our hands: we all wore wristwatches as well as wedding and other rings, like any other normal Europeans.

"Take off your watches and rings and bury them," our new

friend advised us. "Among the Russians, for every ten good men there is one wicked man and he will take everything; he'll steal them, do you understand? Bury all that well."

We were touched by his giving this advice and at the same time appalled by such sincerity and lack of solidarity.

"Bury it, hurry up and bury it," he advised us again.

"What are they going on firing for?" we asked a little anxiously.

"It's nothing, nothing," they said, leisurely smoking their cigarettes and knocking off the ash with their little fingers. In the end, however, they, too, came to the conclusion that this was not the most suitable moment for a chat, said good-bye abruptly, and hurried off to fight the Germans.

For a while we stood there exchanging impressions when, suddenly, among the bushes down near the house, we saw a man with a tall sheepskin cap and leather jacket, and revolver. He was the exact image of the Political Commissar of the posters; only Political Commissars had been abolished in Russia. So who was he? A Commissar? That, too, was how they used to look on anti-Soviet propaganda posters. Or, perhaps, an Ogpu man? But that institution had also been abolished. Behind this mysterious figure two more soldiers, automatic pistols in their hands, advanced toward us up the slope, parting the bushes as they came. Seeing muzzles pointing toward us we automatically put up our hands.

"We are Poles," we shouted again, hoping that the word "Pole" would have the same magical effect on these Russians as it had had on the first two.

The hideous creature in the leather jacket came up quite close. His eyes were mere slits; he had a broken nose and a shiny, yellowish face.

"Any Germans about? Where?" he asked, and then, after a closer look at us, he added in a broken Hungarian, "I like jewels." That sentence only Jumbo understood.

We wanted to get rid of him as quickly as possible. We pointed to the village at the foot of the hill, assuring him that there were still Germans there, and the three walked on. We heaved a sigh of relief, and again we began wondering. And there was plenty to wonder about. We had so far met only two lots of Russians. The first told us to hide our jewels, the other already knew how to demand them in the local language. Was the whole Soviet Union full of such contradictions? Was Jumbo right, when he said that the Russian character was sufficiently diverse and elastic to allow for the greatest contradictions being found not only among groups, but in one and the same individual? We should see. Meanwhile, instead of more Russians, we could only see Matilda, and behind her the scared face of little Gisella. We could also hear Russian voices near the Dower House. I quickly ran down the orchard steps and entered the kitchen. All the doors were wide open. A crowd of strange figures in long, tattered greatcoats the colour of bean soup roamed about the cold, empty rooms, poking into everything and turning everything upside down. I went into Jack's room. There, among a litter of cigarette packets and old photographs, stood an officer. In his hand he held a pair of Jack's stirrups. Delicate, thin stirrups from an English saddle. He asked some questions. I explained that the village lay at the foot of the hill; still talking we walked through the front door out on to the terrace. The officer seemed to feel he must find some explanation for the crowd of plundering soldiers that filled the house.

"You ought to have stayed in the house," he said, "and not run away. If you had stayed, they wouldn't have touched a thing, nothing would have been lost."

And, as he said that, he played with Jack's stirrups which glistened in the pale light of the setting sun. He went away abruptly, without saying a word more. I looked at his long, well-cut greatcoat. As he went, he swung his hand in which he held the stirrups, and they jingled at every movement. I sighed and went back to the house. It is not going to be easy to understand this new Russia, I thought.

The house was full of people. Soldiers in dirty quilted

jackets were ransacking all the drawers. Suddenly it occurred
to Jumbo that they might perhaps steal his shoes. He ran to
make sure, and to his great astonishment found the cloakroom empty. In his room everything was upside down, all the
drawers pulled out, cupboards and wardrobes wide open. A
herd of six or eight soldiers were trotting round and round
through all the rooms, looking into every corner.

"What are you looking for?" I asked.

"Apples."

They seemed hardly even to notice me. At any rate, my
presence did not appear to embarrass them in their search. I
must admit, though, that I was weirdly dressed: navy-blue
ski-ing trousers, tucked into winter hunting boots of grey felt,
and a war-weary lumber-jacket. I was to go about dressed like
that for the next few months, and that small part of the Red
Army which passed through Mora will never forget it. I
would have liked to have given those men some apples, but
there were none.

One of the soldiers, with gaping teeth and an unruly lock
of brown hair that would not stay under his cap, began talking
with me. The others called him "our Captain," but to me
he looked just another of the soldiers. In fact, he turned out
to be a Second-Lieutenant, but at that time we did not know
Russian ranks, nor the Russians' fondness for promoting
themselves a couple of steps.

"Captain" Ivan sat down at a marble Louis XVI table in
the hall, his comrades round about in easy chairs and on the
settee, which seemed to gasp under their weight. "Wait," I
said, "I'll bring you something to eat." Glad to have somebody to talk to in that foreign land, they settled themselves
comfortably. I brought bread and sausage on a plate. They
demanded glasses.

"Do you drink spirit, Lida?" I had told him my name was
Lida because it has a Russian sound and is easy to remember.
I adopted it for the whole of the Russian occupation.

"I do, when it's there," I answered, and a water-bottle full of pure spirit was planked down on the table. In the village below they were still fighting the Germans.

Jumbo watched the soldiers filling up their glasses with pure spirit and hardly adding any water, with all the horror of the true Westerner in his eyes. We drank a large glass each and bit at our bread and sausage. And again the vodka began to work its magic. Our conversation grew louder and louder, more and more lively. The soldiers' caps began travelling about their heads at amazing speed: from over the right ear to the left; from over their eyes on to the backs of their heads. For you must know that a Russian soldier's cap is far from being just a covering for his head. If I had to deal with a dumb Russian soldier, I could guess his innermost feelings simply by the movements of his cap. The cap serves to express those feelings for which there are no words in imperfect human speech. The Red Army cap, as we came to realize, has a language of its own. That, no doubt, is why it is taken off only in extreme cases and then only by high-ranking officers who are much less impulsive than the rank and file, and most of whom do seem to find the Russian language, one of the richest in the world, adequate to express their joy, surprise or repulsion. Here is a short lesson in cap-language. Raised with both hands two inches above the head it betokens great excitement. (This may be joy at the sight of a jug of wine, or at the news of a victory.) Pushed slowly back on to the nape of the neck, it expresses weariness or meditation, or it may also mean that its owner wanted to say something but has forgotten what. (Uncovering of the forehead obviously helps the memory.) Pulled down on to the forehead, sometimes so low that the eyes arc scarcely visible, is a clear indication of anger. (During descriptions of the ruin and devastation done to the Ukrainian towns all caps invariably descend over their owners' eyes.) Cocked over one ear, left or right, the cap expresses astonishment, perplexity, shyness, and, sometimes exuberance. When its owner is sober, the cap travels slowly; after a few vodkas, its movements become much more lively.

This explains why the caps of Ivan and his comrades began to travel from their foreheads to the backs of their heads,
and from right ear to left ear, nowhere stopping longer than
the thoughts in the heads they covered. I was enchanted with
my guests. Jumbo looked at these gap-toothed, ragged, garlic-
smelling lads with some surprise. He, too, was offered spirit,
but explained politely that he was ill, that he was forbidden to
drink pure alcohol. He asked me not to drink either, which
incensed the Russians. "What! Doesn't drink himself, and
yet grudges a poor woman a glass!" So I drank on. Suddenly
"Captain" Ivan remembered that the village was, perhaps, not
yet taken, that it would be a good thing to have a look round
for billets; and, generally that the Armistice was still a long
way off. He stood up, his men with him, and they went,
promising to return that night.

I went out on to the terrace, for the air in the room was
heavy with a smell that we were to come to know very well,
for it was to persecute us for several months to come.

Along the path from the gate came a group of men. They
were all high-ranking officers, wearing magnificent greatcoats,
tall Cossack caps, and carrying flat, leather map-cases and
compasses, looking just as if they were coming on parade. All
were clean and carefully shaven, making with even, unhurried
steps straight for the terrace. And on the terrace stood I, all
alone.

The first to reach me was a Colonel of the Cossacks in
an ankle-length black felt cape. We shook hands and greeted
each other rather formally, while the others grouped themselves round us. They had exactly the same kind of faces as
those of the soldiers; there was not one with even a trace of
what in Europe we call breeding. All were of medium height,
or short. Not one could speak any foreign language; they
were not even able to put a few words together in German.
We began talking about billets. On behalf of the master of
the house, I offered them some sheep for the units occupying
our village, but the Colonel replied rather sharply and rudely

that the Red Army was not hungry and had no need of anybody's sheep.

"We are not Germans," he barked. "We have lots of food."

"I beg your pardon," I stuttered in embarrassment. "I thought," I stammered on, desperately combing my mind for the fifty Russian words I was supposed to know, but which had of course left it. "I thought maybe you would accept our sheep:—*khasyain*—and we all here—all this family—we are so very glad at your coming that we wanted to celebrate it somehow."

"There, there, that's all right," intervened a kindly Major. "Keep your sheep, you'll need them later on. They'll come in handy."

"Are there any good billets here?"

"I'll take you at once. Down there is a large house, our house. If the fighting has stopped, we can go there now. It's empty. Quarter yourselves there."

I started off to show them the way through the village. Jumbo and Jack had by now joined me. We walked along in a circle of officers, down through the village that was swarming with Russian horse-carts and soldiers. We entered the great yard. We could see officers already in the steward's house. We went in, and dropped a batch of lieutenants and captains. Then the "Brass Hats," with me at their head, walked on through the park to the Manor. They liked the park; asked me if it was a garden. I said that it was. We passed a group of firs. "Same as ours," remarked the Colonel and stroked a protruding branch, smiling. The others halted, too, and looked at the firs, as though unable to understand how they had got into that artificial garden. The Colonel had a set of metal false teeth. I noticed that most Russians had several silver teeth, or else large gaps. Some had all their teeth made of metal, with just one or two of their own scarcely visible, as had the Colonel. It made you feel uncomfortable. Evidently there are few dentists in Russia. Our forefathers also went about toothless and must have looked just like the Russians of to-day. However, nobody seems to mind it in Russia. On the contrary, as we found out later, front teeth of gold or even silver are considered an ornament and a sort of proof of wealth.

We reached the Manor. In the courtyard stood our car beside that of Tacitus, and over them swarmed soldiers like ants over the dead body of a beetle. The whole courtyard was full of horse-carts, straw, and Russians. It was all very like an ant-heap: those hundreds of figures running hither and thither, the carrying of packages, hay, sacks of fodder, and bundles in and out of the Manor, the paths already worn in the grass and leading in every possible direction. Where were the stables, my officers asked. I led them to the stables. They, too, were already seething with activity. Darkness was falling and the soldiers were in a hurry to make themselves comfortable before night.

I saw a senior officer, went up to him and began asking him to make sure they did not take our car. I said that it belonged to my brother-in-law, had a diplomatic number plate, and that even the Germans did not take such cars.

"Where did you learn to speak Russian?" the officer asked, in surprise.

"I am a Pole. I fled from Budapest with my husband, for the Gestapo were after us. My husband was in prison for several months; they even sent him to Vienna."

The officer listened to what I had to say. "All right, I'll tell them that it's your car and that it must be left alone," he said.

Satisfied, I began looking around for my Cossack Colonel. He was taller than the others, and his long cape made a patch of black against the greenish ones of his companions. I found him at once in the crowd.

"Comrade," I cried, pulling his sleeve, "Comrade Colonel, for how many guests shall we order dinner?"

"Don't bother," mumbled the Colonel, busily engaged talking to someone else.

"Why not come?" I asked, tugging at his sleeve. "Just tell me how many officers there will be."

"Eight," answered a voice beside me.

I ran back to the Manor house through the dusk, meeting Jack and Jumbo on my way. Together, pushing our way through the soldiers, who did not seem even to notice us, we entered the hall. It was so crowded that we could hardly get inside. With great difficulty we made our way to my room. There we found a cocktail party at its worst. Soldiers were lying on both our beds. One was busy throwing everything out of the drawers in my dressing-table on to the floor, another was methodically and skilfully taking our wireless to pieces. On two folding garden chairs, brought from Heaven knows where, sat two Russian girls. They were in modest little civilian overcoats, Cossack caps, and their faces were like those of the village girls in the remotest parts of Eastern Poland. Some other soldiers stood by the window, cleaning their automatic pistols and blocking out what little daylight still remained. Several others were looking through our wardrobes. Every drawer was already on the floor, which was littered with Jumbo's medicine bottles, shoes, cotton-wool and toothpaste, all drenched in his mouth-wash. His belts, stockings and Malta orders, for Jumbo was a Knight of Malta, all were covered with powder like a cake with sugar, to make it look prettier. A few otherwise unoccupied soldiers, leaning carelessly over the furniture, were conducting a lively conversation with the two girls.

I greeted my guests. The two women shook hands reluctantly and looked hostilely at me and my weird get-up. Perhaps they were thinking that ski-ing trousers tucked into felt boots was the latest fashion, which had not yet had time to reach the Soviet Union. I asked how they were; told them that this was my room, and how glad I was that they had come. The men grinned good-humouredly, but the women maintained an embarrassed silence. They were not believing a word I said.

"I have just come for my book," I announced, and triumphantly took from the shelf—Karl Marx's biography. On the cover was a woodcut of the Father of the Revolution. I turned the book so that everybody could see whose picture was on the cover. But nobody seemed impressed. I could not understand it at the time, but now I know that there was not one soldier in the room with even an approximate idea of what Marx looked like. And even if they had, they would not have recognized him from a stylised woodcut. To the majority of Russian soldiers such a woodcut is what a photograph is to a dog: just something black-and-white. Drawings make no impression on the majority of them. Nor do engravings, though colours appeal to them. Paintings, for instance, interested them all; so much so, in fact, that we were forced to conclude that most of them were seeing one for the first time in their lives.

Beside my Marx I also wanted to take Tchang So Lin, but he was no longer on his chest-of-drawers. He had vanished. I went to the drawing-room. There, a horde of Russians was lounging over the tables, in the armchairs, on the chests and chairs. The room was full of them. Through the open door I could see Tacitus' study with soldiers wading knee-deep in documents and papers. Everyone was busily occupied. Their chief occupation, as was immediately obvious, was dismantling things. Some were stripping Franzi's and Tacitus' sporting guns, others dismantling the radiogram in the drawing-room, others taking watches and the barometer to pieces. Here they were, still black with the smoke of battle, still panting from their exertions, and yet already sitting busily dismantling everything that could be taken to pieces. I tried to push my way back to my room. Nobody paid the least attention to me. I felt as though I were in a dream, seeing things, that either they were ghosts, or I invisible. I stood watching them. I was pushed and shoved, for they all just walked in the direction in which they wanted to go, without ever looking round. I got into the hall. Suddenly, I was stopped by an officer in a yellow peaked cap. He wanted to know what I was looking for.

"Nothing," I answered, "this is our house."

It was no use explaining that I had come to order dinner for the officers, for in such conditions it was impossible even to think of dinner. The officer in the yellow cap seemed to find me interesting. We went together to my room, where I found a dumbfounded Jumbo and Jack. Night had set in and the room was in complete darkness. The officer, with a few words sent the soldiers scurrying, drew the armchairs closer together, and the four of us sat down for a chat. At last we had found someone sensible in this bedlam, we thought, and began to pour out our hearts. Only Jack was on his guard, remembering Lwow in 1939.

Jumbo talked and I interpreted. He told the officer who he was, everything, including his being a Knight of Malta. Suddenly the officer asked if I had been in England.

"Of course," I answered gladly.

"What for?"

"I went to school there."

"And you've been in Germany?"

"Yes."

"And in Malta, too?"

I had been: a lovely island. And I started to describe as well as I could in Russian all the charms of Malta, for, the room being in darkness, I could not see the expression on the officer's face.

"And where else have you been?" asked the officer, in a calm, pleasant voice.

"Where else? In Italy, in Turkey, Belgium, Greece," I answered at random, trying to remember all my travels. The officer also wanted to know how many languages we spoke. It turned out that to speak English, French and German be-

sides one's mother tongue is a kind of misdemeanour in Soviet
Russia. We could not see the expression on the officer's face,
as it was dark, but we heard his every word as he slowly
hissed:

"Then you are simply international spies."

We burst out laughing at such an idea. Our laughter must
have sounded sincere, for the officer apologized for what he
had just said.

"I am the representative of death," he added.

At that a shiver ran down our spines. What did he mean?
Perhaps this was not a friendly chat after all, but an interrogation? For the first time since coming in contact with the
Russians, I felt afraid. What did it all mean? Jumbo did
not yet quite understand what was happening, but Jack began
shifting uneasily on his chair. I got up quickly to say good-
bye. The officer, too, stood up. Our farewells were profuse
but insincere. Jack and I were sure that we could smell
sulphur.

I now tried to make my way to the kitchen to give the
cook orders for that wretched supper, the idea of which, being
a naive European, I had not yet abandoned. We of the West
live according to certain rules of conduct: we try to keep our
word, to be punctual, to deliver goods promised, even though
we meet with difficulties. These are sound, business principles without which there can be no organization. So I set
out for the kitchen.

Crowds of soldiers again. Well, they can't very well smash
the furniture or steal the pictures, Jumbo told me as we tried
to comfort ourselves. But what on earth did so many want
to come here for? Surely there was enough room in the village? Where would all the officers eat? What would they
sleep on? All the beds were full of soldiers smoking cigarettes
rolled in pieces of newspapers and spitting the husks of sunflower seeds on to the floor. There was so much mud everywhere that you could not see a sign of the parquet floor. It
was quite dark, with only here and there the stump of a

candle burning, or a paraffin lamp, smoking and stinking
without its chimney. The outside doors were never shut, and
the wind whistled about the rooms. Soldiers kept pouring
in. There wasn't a hope of getting the place in order before
supper. Where was the Staff going to live? Certainly not
here, now. We forced our way forward with greater and
greater difficulty, the nearer we got to the kitchen. In the
butler's room off the kitchen some soldiers were busy taking
stacks of snow-white linen out of the cupboards and carrying
them off somewhere. But where? And why? Could it be
possible that they were plundering our house? What could
soldiers want with pillowcases at the front, or with table-
cloths, napkins, kitchen and damask towels? They had already passed through so many countries that surely each must
have had a towel and a napkin by now. And where were they
taking those piles of sheets? We decidedly must go and look
for "our" officers and tell them what was going on. In these
conditions it would be impossible to prepare billets or cook
supper.

At last I managed to reach the kitchen. Our terrified cook
just gazed at me in silence, not daring to open her lips, but
the nasty expression in her little eyes showed that for her the
end of the world had come. Old Lina, who used to be Marietta's mother's lady's maid, stood helplessly in the middle of
the kitchen letting herself be pushed from one side to the
other by the jostling soldiery. From her round, goggling hazel
eyes you would have thought she was in a trance. Understanding nothing of what was happening, she had just given up.
The rest of the servants had fled. I explained to the cook, not
quite believing it myself, that she was to prepare a good supper
for eight officers. My tone was energetic and matter-of-fact,
as much to give myself confidence as her. Then I pounced on
some soldier, a huge ragamuffin who turned out to be a
surgeon: where was the Colonel, I wanted to know. "In the
last room on the left," several voices answered together. The
last one on the left? Ah-ha, that was Elsie's, and again I

pushed my way through a thicket of damp, stinking soldiers'
greatcoats. At last I reached the door. I knocked, a shrill
voice answered me, and I went in. The room was in indescribable disorder, full of smoke, the furniture strewn all over
the place, and at the table, drinking wine, sat an officer with
a red, swollen face and unbuttoned collar. On the table stood
his supper, and on the mahogany chest-of-drawers flickered
a sooty lamp with a broken chimney.

"Well?" said the officer, when his goggling, drunken, blue
eyes caught sight of me.

I began the little speech that I had carefully prepared:
dinner had been ordered for eight officers. I wanted to serve
it in the dining-room, so would it not be possible to have the
soldiers turned out of that room, and of the kitchen, for as
long as they were swarming there, we could not possibly make
a start.

"Ah?" shouted the officer and this time his eyes almost
popped out of his head. "What's that? I am a General! Get
out! Understand? A General!"

I went out, and I did understand. I understood that there
was to be no supper: that there was no need to keep one's
word, and that altogether it was a new life we were beginning. A good thing that the Germans had not burnt the
house and that we had saved our furniture and the car. We
had at least achieved that.

In the corridor, I met my honest ragamuffin surgeon.

"Well," he asked, "is everything settled? Did you get on
all right?"

"No," I answered, "the General said that there would be
no supper."

"Who did you say?" asked several voices together, and
there was a roar of laughter. "What General? There's no
General here."

But I did not want to hear any more. General or no general, it was all the same to me now. My only wish was to get
out of this alien crowd, to return to my own life, to our quiet

and peaceful lair in the shelter. This was war, and that was all there was to it. Anyway, the Germans had been wrong when they said that the Russians destroyed everything. Although they were in an enemy country, they did not smash the furniture, and the next day, or the one after, we would be able to clear up the mess. We would get a dozen women from the village to do the scrubbing, and then we would be able to move in again. Also, we ought not to forget that there were many pleasant, decent fellows among them. Our first Russian, for one, the engineer, then Ivan and his men, and now that officer in the tall Cossack cap, though there was something queer about him. Thus we talked, as we walked back through the park to our shelter.

It was very dark. After looking round carefully to make sure there was no one to hear, Jack started to rebuke me.

"How could you say that you had been abroad? One must never admit that to any Bolshevik, for in their eyes that's a crime."

"What?" I cried. "A crime to be educated abroad? But they themselves send their engineers to the United States to study!"

"That has nothing to do with it," Jack explained. "Those few are but an insignificant fraction of the nation. In Russia you cannot even get letters from abroad without the N.K. W.D. becoming interested in you. I forgot to warn you about it," he added.

"It may have been like that formerly, but not now surely. You cannot keep two hundred million people in chains like that," I said.

"But you can," persisted Jack.

"Well," said I, "what will happen now? Perhaps he was from the N.K.W.D., that representative of death?"

Jumbo implored us to translate our conversation into any decent language such as he could understand, so I repeated it all in French. Jumbo remained unmoved.

"It won't do any harm," he said. "After all we told him

that my brother was a political refugee, that he personally
knows many Soviet politicians, and now in London has become friends with Maisky; that he was our envoy to the
Vatican till the pro-German clique ousted him from our
Foreign Office.

"Diplomats," went on Jumbo patronizingly, "are the same
all over the world, and I see no harm in telling that nice
officer how many times I visited my brother abroad: on the
contrary, it could only have impressed him favourably."

Front-line Troops

23rd-25th
December

WE HEARD steps outside. Somebody was coming down the stairs to our cellar. The door opened and in it appeared two figures silhouetted against the dusk. They were my Ivan, already completely drunk, and an unknown Second-Lieutenant. The latter even had a clean shirt, and there were several medals dangling at his broad chest. We asked both of them to sit down and gave them wine. Ivan's friend was a gunner. He informed us that he was called Victor and that his mother was Hungarian and came from Kechkemet, which latter fact was obviously supposed to impress us. The Hungarians nodded their heads in silent approval. Victor also said that he spoke every language, but that modesty compelled him to confine himself to his own native Russian. We also learnt that he was not, as one might have supposed, a Second-Lieutenant, but really a Captain. That, we came to realize, was the most popular rank in the Soviet Army. Everybody was a Captain, and there just did not seem to be any junior officers or lower ranks in the Red Army.

Victor shouted and lisped. He at once embarked on a long life history, which he interrupted only when he mentioned his wound. Each time that wound cropped up, Victor would seize the hand of the person nearest him and make him feel under his chin where, on the lower jaw, there was

31

a scar. In the light of the lamp, we could see the saliva sputtering from his mouth as he lisped, and his fair, straw-coloured hair kept falling into his blue froggy eyes. He had drenched himself in cheap perfume and the stink of it soon penetrated all over the cellar. Having had his say and recounted his entire life-history, Victor got up and walked out.

It was now time to turn our attention to Ivan who, with the pigheadedness of the drunkard, was quietly but determinedly insisting that we put him up for the night in the cellar. He had taken a liking to us and wanted to sleep with us. How does one get rid of a conquering hero? You cannot just throw him out. Jack and I suggested a walk in the park: fresh air, lovely moon. Ivan let himself be persuaded. Outside the air was really fresh, and it was freezing hard. The moon had climbed above the bare branches of the trees, and the garden was flooded with light. Ivan brushed the unruly lock of hair off his forehead. The smile never left his thick lips, and the gap in his teeth was a yawning black hollow in the darkness of his mouth.

"Lida," he said, "never mind your husband, come and sleep with me. Your husband's old and ill, he will even be glad. Come, come, I have something very important to tell you."

Jack was on the alert at once, and tried to drag Ivan away. I could sense his anger. Ivan, however, just pushed him gently and carelessly aside with a rather unsteady gesture.

"I want to sleep with you all in the cellar," Ivan said plaintively. "And you," suddenly shouting at Jack, "you go away, Jackie-boy! Don't interfere with us. You're in the way, horribly in the way. It's none of your business, what your aunt does. I'll do her no harm, it's warm out here, so off you go, my dear, go back to the cellar. You're not wanted."

Jack did not budge.

"Ivan," I said, "you go and sleep in the Dower House, you will be comfortable there, much better than in the cellar."

"No," answered Ivan slowly, "I don't want to sleep there. I'll sleep with you. I like being with you. I love you all, the whole family!"

Begging Jack to get Ivan somehow to the Dower House, I fled back to the cellar. Jack told us afterwards that the gunners, who had occupied the Dower House, had thrown Ivan out like a dog. He had then gone back to the garden where his men had found him. It was lucky for him that they liked him and had not forgotten about him. We breathed a sigh of relief.

It seemed a small miracle when supper was brought. We ate quickly, glad to be rid of the Russians, but exhausted with all the events and impressions of the day. I drank some wine, and was settling myself comfortably on my paillasse to enjoy a cigarette, when again we heard steps on the stairs. Jack burst in. "The bailiff's brother has come to fetch you," he said from the doorstep. "You must go to some Russians who are quartered in his house; they need an interpreter."

"Very good," I said, and, without saying good-bye, went quickly outside, where the bailiff's brother was waiting for me.

"What's it about?" I asked, but I could not make much sense of what he told me. We walked quickly, crossing fences and passing small groups of soldiers still busied with something or other, and finally entered a small, warm room in which three Russians were sitting round a stove. A paraffin lamp burned brightly on the table. It was cosy and pleasant there in that little room. I was told to sit down; an officer, with his cap on the side of his head, seated himself opposite me, while another, in a round cap, also moved his chair up. "What is your name?" they asked; and I told them: Lida.

"Well, Lida, tell us how long you have been living in the village."

I did my best to tell them our story as accurately and fully as I could. Nevertheless, the young officer with the round cap kept interrupting to tell me in a bored voice that

I was lying. I answered this with a shrug of my shoulders and a smile which was meant to express a sort of tolerant indulgence. But I was afraid.

"Why didn't you escape to the Soviet Union in nineteen thirty-nine? That is what every ally ought to have done."

"But Russia was an ally of the Germans, then, and it was from them that I was escaping."

"We were never allies of the Germans," said the officer. "Everybody knows that; and every decent Pole escaped to Russia, even before nineteen thirty-nine, for Russia never had an alliance with Germany."

I replied that one would hardly have thought that from the papers, or even from the Moscow wireless; that I seemed to remember Ribbentrop being received by Molotov in August, and Cripps sent packing back to England, even though he was the one who looked at the world through pink, if not through red, glasses, while Ribbentrop was Minister of a Fascist country.

The officer in the forage-cap made an attempt to stem the flow of my words, for this was a subject he did not like and he wanted to change it quickly. He admitted that, of course, I could hardly have been expected in 1939 to have foreseen that Russia would go to war with Germany, and then, to change the subject, he asked what Fascists I knew of in Mora. I did not know any, and I began to explain that I did not speak the local language and had had no contact with the village, for, as a Pole, I had had to be very careful; but the young officer boy interrupted as usual and told me that I was lying. I was past being indignant at his continual "You're lying, you're lying!" Obviously they did not intend to believe me, and there was nothing I could do about that.

A summons came for the officer in the forage-cap, and he got up and went out of the room. Then there was silence. I was really afraid and held my hands tightly clasped so that the Russians should not see how they were trembling. Time passed. My eyes strayed round about the room, but I was far from being so gay and easy in my mind as when I had entered it. The third officer, an elderly man with a handsome, swarthy face, a yellow forage-cap and a grey overcoat, was dozing beside the stove. Then the door opened and I myself was summoned.

I was taken to a room where I found the bailiff, his wife and several drunken officers. I was required as interpreter, for the Russians wanted to have the furniture changed round in every room, which the bailiff's young wife was resisting as well as she could. However, there was nothing to be done. The officers insisted, and so we began the senseless job of changing the furniture to suit the Russians' taste, dragging it from one room to the other, and often back to where it had been, only to change it once again. Then I was summoned back to my tormentor.

He now had pencil and paper on the table in front of him, and the officer dozing by the stove had woken up and began taking part in the proceedings, even asking questions himself. My answers were now being written down. Once more they wanted to know who were Fascists in the village. Till then I had always thought that the word "Fascist" applied only to Mussolini's Italians, but to the Russians everybody was a Fascist: the Germans, General Franco's Spaniards, the French collaborationists, the Polish London Government, Churchill, and the peasants in Mora. I defended those poor peasants as best I could. I told them how the police, acting on German orders, had taken four Mora Communists away the previous November, and how my husband had given money to the families thus suddenly deprived of their breadwinners.

"You're lying," said the young officer again, and this time I was too harassed and sleepy even to shrug my shoulders.

Why did nobody come to rescue me, I wondered. Did they imagine I was enjoying myself there? Then a second thought: what a good thing Jumbo did not speak a word of Russian, so that no sentry would ever let him through.

The little officer in the round cap seemed to be tired and

the interrogation hung fire, so I started a polite conversation to try and improve the atmosphere. First, I asked the little swine from what town he came. "From Moscow," he answered, narrowing his brazen little eyes. He had a button of a nose, small and turned up so that you could only see his nostrils and his thick, swollen lips.

"Moscow is a beautiful city, but you'll never see her. Liars like you aren't allowed there. We'll deport you to Siberia, if you don't tell us the truth. Here we are wanting to go to sleep but you go on lying and lying, and we can't get any sense out of you."

There was a sudden commotion at the door, and I could hear Jack's voice. With that, all my old energy returned. I just had to see that Jack did not get involved in this. I now knew that this was the N.K.W.D., but Jack did not, and there he was standing in the doorway, his face beaming, rather like a dog that has run away from home, where it was supposed to stay, in search of its master, and is fearfully proud at having found him. Jack politely wanted to know whether his aunt was ready yet; could she go home now? I signalled to him with my hand: go away. Fortunately the officers threw him out, and I called after him telling him to go home. The door shut and again I was left alone with the three officers. They began asking questions about Budapest. I told them what I knew, all the time explaining that I never bothered with politics, firstly because they were no concern of mine, and, secondly, because I was a foreigner and knew neither the country nor the language.

"You've no lack of imagination anyway, Lida," said the little rascal in the round cap, sarcastically. "We've only just arrived here, yet we already know who are the good people and who are not; we know everything already, and we are only asking these questions to see how long you will go on lying."

"Well," I replied, "it's easy for you, you are specialists; but I am just a stupid person and I don't know anything."

"You know, Lida, you know, only you just don't want to tell us. You'll see, you'll end up in Siberia."

"All right. Send me there. Now, if you like."

Again silence. It was getting very late. I was so tired I could hardly keep my eyes open. The elderly officer beside the stove began quietly groaning. It appeared that he had a bilious attack, and, also, a wound that was hurting him. I grasped at his biliousness as a drowning person grasps at a straw, and began a drawing-room conversation about stomach troubles. I gave him some tips on diet, and the atmosphere improved considerably. We were all four so tired that we were almost tumbling off our chairs. The conversation languished and stopped. After an interval of silence, I plucked up my courage and asked whether I might go home now. I could hardly believe my ears when they said: "Certainly." I shook hands with the officers, not too hurriedly, and pretending to be perfectly calm walked very slowly towards the door. Outside was a dark, wintry night. It must have been very late. There wasn't a sound to be heard in the village, and apparently the Russians were also human and had gone to bed, for there wasn't even a sentry to be seen anywhere.

So ended our first Russian day.

As I lay alongside Fifi that night, she told me how a certain Vassili had tried to pick her up. Almost his first words had been that he wanted to spend the night with her. Fifi had explained, as from one friend to another, that in Europe affairs like that were not arranged quite so quickly as they apparently were in Russia. Vassili had replied that he could have understood her refusal had he been a boor, but that he was a school-teacher, and poor Fifi had had great difficulty in escaping from him. We whispered on for a while yet, for we were all so dazed by this new, unknown world that had so suddenly burst upon us, that none of us felt like sleep. In the end, however, sleep did come and silence reigned in the stuffy dark shelter.

Outside it was freezing, and all the branches were covered with hoar-frost. We ventured down the stone steps leading to the small courtyard in front of the house. The whole place was as silent as the grave, a silence to which we could not accustom ourselves. We crept on towards the house. It was empty.

Matilda maintained that the gunners had left at dawn, anyway there was no one there now, and so we set about plundering our own house. First, we went to Fifi's room. Even before we reached it we could smell the stench of Victor's perfume, and one look around showed that all the blankets had disappeared. So had the puppets I had made for Muki's Punch and Judy show. The puppets did not matter, but it was a pity about the blankets. We searched every room in the house, but there was not one blanket left. And everywhere confusion indescribable, and the stench of cigarette smoke, garlic, and foot-clouts that had not been washed for months. Using our noses and Sherlock Holmes' methods we quickly came to the conclusion that Victor had slept in Jack's room, and in Jack's pyjamas. I, however, had no time to worry about the Dower House, for it was high time we went to the Manor to get the car and put things in order there; so slipping my hand through Jumbo's arm, we set off with Tacitus through the park. We only met a few soldiers, but several of the village boys were sliding on the pond, ruining their last pair of boots. Even though they fled when they saw us, the fact that those peasant children had ventured into the lord of the manor's park was the first sign of the old order giving way.

The sight that confronted us as we walked into the courtyard in front of the Manor was so appalling that we stopped dead: the whole courtyard was covered with heaps of straw, hay and maize, and so littered with papers, bits of china and porcelain, broken pieces of furniture, broken glass, things that had been cushions, that it was hardly possible to make our way through it. The cook burst into tears as we entered the kitchen, and out it all poured, her pent-up tears and her complaints. Everything eatable had been stolen, the ducks and chickens had been slaughtered, the larder broken into and emptied. Poor Lina's face still wore the petrified expression it had had the day before. For her, life was already over.

I wandered through the rooms, jumping over broken furniture. The drawers had been taken out of antique chests and bureaus and used for firewood. A lovely gun-case had served somebody as a bed, and now lay on its back in the bathroom, filled with hay like a trough, as was the bath itself. None of the beds had been used. They stood there stripped of their clothes, just the bare bedstead. The Russians had obviously slept on the floor on mattresses. The pictures still hung on the walls, and our (Jumbo's and mine), bits of furniture, strangely enough, were still intact. In Tacitus' bedroom was a pile of torn photographs. They must have annoyed somebody for him to have taken all that trouble. Having seen the worst, I went back to Tacitus and Jumbo who were already growing impatient, for they wanted me to go with them to the "General" to find out about the car and discuss the state of the house. You see, we were still thinking along European lines, and imagined that it was enough to know Russian to be able to get on with the Russian Army. We were soon to be snubbed and taught a lesson that would serve us in the future, but meanwhile we stepped boldly towards Elsie's room from which we could hear men's voices coming. A soldier we met on the way told us that there were still a few officers there, though most had already left. We knocked and walked in. The room was crowded with Russians and in an indescribable state of filth and disorder. It was hard to believe that it could be possible to make any room so filthy in twenty-four hours without making a special effort to do so. I explained, stammering as I always did when I tried not to make mistakes, that I had come with the owner of the house and his brother to see them about the house and the car. I was hardly allowed to finish. There wasn't a face I knew,

and all their evil eyes were focussed on my face, as in a lens.
"You should not have run from the house!" barked a voice.

A fat, red-faced officer produced the remnants of Jumbo's
uniform of a Knight of Malta, the gold epaulettes, the star
on its ribbon, and waved them under my nose.

"All ruined!" he shouted, as though it were I who had
done it, and not his men. "Who stays at home won't lose
so much as a pin!"

I ventured to remark that I had spent the whole of the
previous afternoon in the house, but the officer obviously
knew very well that he was at fault, and that had made him
lose his temper. Jumbo and Tacitus did not understand a
thing of what was going on, and Jumbo kept on prompting
me:

"What about the car, ask them, quick!"

I did not know how to shut him up. There was something
so alien about the naïveté of his behaviour, that for a moment
those angry Russian officers were closer to me. "Don't fuss,"
I said in French, "there's nothing to be done."

I hastened to take my leave of the Russians, to the great
surprise of my husband and brother-in-law who looked at me
as though I were out of my mind. The officers kept on telling
me we should have stayed in the house and nothing would
have happened, and I preferred to admit that they were right
and get away as quickly as possible, for I could see they were
ashamed and that was making them angry. I understood their
position, and did not want to aggravate it. At last Tacitus
and Jumbo realized that there was nothing to be done, and
we left. Outside we met one of the officers with whom we
had talked the day before, the one I had met at the stables.

"Did they leave your car?" he asked good-naturedly.

You must be new in the Army, poor man, I thought.
"No," I replied, "they have taken it."

The cars had, in fact, vanished.

"It's this blasted war, you know," the good fellow tried
to console me. "We badly need cars, especialy now when we

are pushing forward. We'll give them back after the war. Maybe sooner," he added.

I could see that he was a bit ashamed, too, and trying, by being nice, to make up for what had happened.

"Never mind," I said, with a grateful smile, and ran after Tacitus and Jumbo. All the way home the two of them reproached me for not being firmer. It was unheard of, they said, to take a car with a neutral, diplomatic number plate. I had given in far too easily, and so on. I did not know what to say, but it did seem to me that the Russians had treated me not too badly.

Jumbo still wanted me to try and find one of the officers I had been with the day before, and see if I could learn anything about the car from him. What did he want, exactly? To know whether it had gone north or south, or what? Yet, the Westerners are such queer people, that had Jumbo been given a receipt, just an ordinary slip of paper, if possible with a stamp on it, he would have calmed down at once. In the West tremendous importance is attached to paper that has something written on it, or, at least, it used to be in those now far-off days when a bank note had real value and it was possible to buy, for instance, pork, with such a rainbow-coloured slip of paper. The Russians were not so clever as the Germans; they did not know that it was possible to buy the good opinion of those they robbed with a receipt, with just a small piece of paper. If the Russians needed a car they simply took it without further ado, and here were Jumbo and Tacitus worrying about not having been given a receipt, and working themselves into a dreadful state because the car had vanished without leaving a trace, and they would not know where to look for it. They were quite sure that had the car been taken legally, they would have certainly been given a receipt by the divisional commander or the colonel. How far removed from real life they are, I thought. Accustomed to the abstract, they hover above the earth instead of coming down to it.

Tacitus was sullen and angry. He considered the losses he had borne an injustice on the part not only of the Russian Army but also of God. What had he, God-fearing *pater familias* who all his life had worked honestly to increase his heritage, done to deserve such a blow? Had he ever harmed anyone? Such were the thoughts one could read in his face. Life was hard for Tacitus, for in his conception of the world he was the pivot round which everything revolved. Such as he do indeed have a hard time of it, for what to the ordinary person is just a whim of fate, something unpleasant, to them is a catastrophe; for when something unpleasant happens to the centre of the world it must rank as a catastrophe. Tacitus was unable to say: Well, it's war, and thousands of innocent people must suffer; thousands of women and little children must be killed or crippled; and for years now thousands of decent people have filled prisons and concentration camps just because they were decent and honest, and mothers have lost their sons, senselessly murdered and senselessly murdering; millions have lost their lives, millions have been crippled, millions go about in mourning, millions have lost all their belongings and been rendered homeless. How good is God that He has saved me from all that. Why? Have I deserved it?

That is what Tacitus ought to have said, because one should not bring God into the evil doings of this world. When evil is being done, one should leave Him out of it. It is better that way for Him and for us. But Tacitus was a pious man and would never leave God in peace.

On Christmas Day, the priest came to celebrate Holy Communion, coming to us in our catacomb as in the days of the early Christians. As I watched him scurrying with the Sacrament down the steep steps, glancing anxiously about him in the semi-darkness, I almost felt I ought to draw a fish on the cellar wall.

During Communion I sat in the garden. The whole world

had become an enchanted place, and the garden was made of white coral. From time to time, the grey figure of a Russian soldier in his long, unhemmed greatcoat, an automatic pistol slung around his neck, would flit past through the mist like a fish in an aquarium. One of them, an old Muscovite with long moustaches, came shyly up, and, with a childish, embarrassed smile, pointed to the tree under which I was sitting. "A pine," he said slowly and distinctly, hoping that that would help me to understand him. "They grow in my country, too," he added, and, pointing again at the tree, repeated, "Pine." I know, my friend, I know. They also grow with us; orange-coloured trunk or twisted and crouching with spreading branches and corrugated bark. We used to make little boats of that bark when we were children. And you, how well I know you. I have so often met you in the pages of *War and Peace*; and now you have come to me, yourself. You are such a grand old fellow, and I'm awfully glad to see that you have not changed at all. Then there was a shout of "Timophy! Timophy!" and the old chap turned and dashed away down the garden steps.

Again I was alone, sitting there immersed in the light, silvery mist. It was like sitting at the bottom of a sea, where trees and shrubs are made of white coral and perfect stillness reigns. It was so beautiful, that it was obvious how little man counts in this world. Man goes his way, and God His. What do we matter to Him, that garden seemed to say? With all the beauty of that hoar-frost to look at, perhaps He had fallen under its spell and stopped thinking about us?

After lunch I went with Jumbo and Marietta to the Manor. We walked through the village that was full of soldiers, with none of our former naive confidence that nothing could happen to us. At the home-farm some old moustached veterans shouted to us, "Call a couple of women, Mother, to come and milk the cows!"

"Can't you milk them yourselves?"

"No, we can't. The cows aren't ours. We don't touch

what isn't ours. You should look after your own farm; we
don't want to interfere with your affairs."

Well, well, I said to myself. What a strange people: they
burn your furniture, steal your bed linen, yet they won't milk
your cows, because they belong to somebody else.

The park was littered with paper, mostly family documents, and Jumbo and Marietta were continually stooping to
pick up an ancient charter or a marriage or birth certificate.
What they rescued they hid in a little Grecian temple beside
the pond. "We shan't need those documents for the time
being," said Marietta with a sad smile.

The Manor was in a worse state than ever; in fact, it
seemed that no house could be more thoroughly plundered,
but we were to find out that it could. A Russian sentry at the
door told us that the car had been taken because it belonged
to the Swiss minister. How Swiss? The Vatican was not
Switzerland. No, no, it belonged to the Swiss, and the Swiss
were bad people, Facists the whole lot of them. A fine state
of affairs: taking a car because they thought it belonged to a
neutral diplomat! And what about international law? But
the soldier only wagged his head, and patiently repeated that
it was a Swiss car, as though that were an explanation.

Every room was littered with straw and paper, and broken
glass crunched under our feet. Our gramophone records had
vanished. It was a pity about them, but at the same time it
was comforting to think there must be some cultured Russians; that, if they would steal Mozart, Bach and Chopin,
there must be some among them who were people like us, for
who else, in war time, within a stone's throw of the front,
would steal that particle of culture spell-bound in those records? I forgave them their pathetic little theft, for it was a
pleasant discovery to have made.

In the kitchen we found Lina almost paralyzed with horror, and so appalled and shocked by what was going on that
she could hardly speak. In a quavering voice she told Marietta how the Russians had torn all our photographs to pieces,

how they had burned the furniture in the stoves, and how, the moment they had gone, a mob of peasant children they had collected had rushed in and taken the record albums out to the garden and there smashed the lot, jumping on them with both feet; and old Lina gave a demonstration of how they had done it. After that the mob had returned to the Manor and, like a herd of mischievous monkeys, had destroyed everything still capable of being destroyed. (Oh you dear village children, flower of the peasant nations, if only I could lay my hands on just one of you!)

Tacitus rebuking Village Children in the Park

26th-27th December

ALL the hoar-frost had vanished right after Christmas. We went for a walk in the garden, and there made two acquaintances: Sergeant Myshkowski, and his officer, Grigory. We were afraid of Grigory, for he never smiled. It was he who had suddenly come into the shelter the night before and shone his torch into our frightened, sleepy faces, telling us that he was just making sure that there were no soldiers sleeping in the cellar.

Other officers and other soldiers came to see us. To us they all looked alike, as all Mongols and Negroes do to the average European. The Russian countenance may be described thus: it is like a keg; the lips broad and thick, but quite flat; the nose like a potato, the eyes small. Of course, not every face is like that, but more often than not that description fits them very nicely. The average Russian is of short or of medium height, thick-set, with legs like gate-posts; he radiates health and has the slightly waddling gait of the bear; he is incredibly filthy and untidy, so much so that the normal person cannot even picture it unless he has seen it with his own eyes.

I imagine that as the Russians went unshaven for so many centuries, stubble has now become a symbol of the old order, of the world they have destroyed, while a smooth face is supposed to show that they, too, have European civilization and culture, for nowadays every Russian shaves. It was Peter the Great who started it. He loathed beards and ordered them to be shaved off, as things of the past, and that loathing still seems to persist. Tacitus' beard was a constant source of annoyance and surprise to the Russians. They could not understand why he wore it and were always begging him to remove it.

We had been living with these strange people for three days now. In the evenings we would hear their melancholy songs floating through the frosty air, or their voices roaring and shouting as they drunkenly cursed each other, for they had found Rudi's store of wine in the Dower House. Jumbo and I had our own horde of Tokay wine that I had gone to great pains to rescue from the soldiers. We saved about eleven bottles in all. Some of the bottles we used to keep in the library when we noticed that Russians generally didn't touch books unless they ran out of coal or wood. Later we found out that they hated the stuff, so our supply lasted rather well. We already knew that they lit the stoves with antique furniture or rare books quite indiscriminately. It had also become obvious that complete isolation from Europe, which in spite of everything remains their cultural ideal, has made of present-day Russia a new and completely different world. For them to try and learn about us and the West, was like trying to learn a foreign language by correspondence: it cannot be done, because language is a living thing, and the same can be said about culture. All that age-long tradition and education have given us is non-existent in Russia.

And so, for the past three days we had been living in the midst of those healthy, dirty, merry lads, all of whom, with very few exceptions, were under thirty. Nor could you call the N.K.W.D. so frightful, if you could discuss biliousness during an interrogation. Because they are so primitive and "home-grown" everything about the Russian is simpler, closer to life, less ceremonial. Fifi and I quickly sensed and adapted ourselves to that atmosphere, but the Hungarians are rather like Chinese Mandarins, they live in a world rigid with *rigor mortis*, and that freshness of the Russians, which might perhaps be compared to that of the Americans, shocked and offended them.

At midday, Jumbo, Jack and I walked over to the Manor to see if our furniture was still there, for so far it happened to have been only Tacitus' furniture that had been chopped up and burned. There was no question of moving it, even were it still there, for the whole house now belonged to the Red Army. Our hopes, however, proved vain. Most of our furniture had followed the rest into the stoves, and the floor of our room was littered with ivory leaves and flowers with which one of the tables had been inlaid. By now I had got to know the Russians well enough to realize that they did not burn our furniture out of spite. They burned it because it was there at hand, and also because none of them had the least suspicion that they could have got a whole barrel of vodka for any one of those tables and bureaus they were so heedlessly chopping up. Kitchen stools were not burnt, although they must certainly have been easier to chop up; but then the Russian knows what a kitchen stool is, he has them in his own home and so he respects them.

On our way back we looked into the byre. The cows, which yesterday the soldiers would not even milk "because they belonged to somebody else," had now vanished. The whole herd had been quietly stolen during the night. Now I understood why the Red Army was not hungry, as the Cossack Colonel had assured me that first day, and I also realized how he must have laughed at me when, on behalf of the master of the house, I offered to present them with a paltry dozen or so sheep. Yes, the cows had gone, and, like Jumbo's shoes, the blankets, furniture, cars and so much else, had not even left a little receipt behind them, to the further despair of the Hungarians. Every army evidently has its own methods, but I must admit that those of the Red Army were the simplest.

We were sitting that afternoon in the shelter, talking as usual about the Russians, when we heard steps on the stairs outside and a red-faced, elderly officer walked in. He introduced himself: Chernysheff. We had noticed that only the elderly Russians introduced themselves by their surnames, the younger ones, whether officers or men, only told us their Christian names. Chernysheff had brought a newspaper with him. He opened it, and at our request, began to read aloud. He read with difficulty, as did most Russians. This, of course, was due to lack of practise; and, yet, they all knew the latest Russian books. How? Did they have people to read them aloud in their clubs? Or did they know them from their films? I do not know.

Chernysheff, with a kindly smile, folded up his newspaper and invited the Polish contingent to come and have a glass of wine and a chat in his billet. His landlady was called Teresa, he added, as though afraid that we might not be able to find him. At Chernysheff's there was wine by the gallon; otherwise it was crowded and cosy. He shared the room with a fellow officer, Michail. Teresa, the wife of Tacitus' joiner, stood behind the chairs of the two officers, and, with gestures and looks, gave us to understand that Michail was a good man, and Chernysheff not.

As always, first I, then Fifi, had to recount the story of our lives. Our histories were usually followed by the life-stories of our Russian audience, and, since they mostly lied like troopers, it was often difficult to gather a word of truth, or at any rate in the beginning. Later we became more expert and did quite well. Michail and Chernysheff were amongst the few who did not lie.

Chernysheff told us how by mistake he had spent more than ten years in prison. A fine mistake! I asked him how it was possible for an innocent person to spend more than ten years in prison, and was told, in a tone of surprise, that in Russia thousands of innocent people spent years in prison. "Heavens," he said, "if everybody was to be interrogated and

their statements checked to find out whether they were innocent or not, there wouldn't be time or people to do the more
important work." I then suggested that it was better to risk
one or two guilty people getting off scot-free than to torture
the innocent, for that was what I had been brought up to believe; but placid, honest Chernysheff could not see it. For
him, it was the other way round: less harm to the State if the
innocent spend ten years in gaol than if one harmful person
goes free. So argued Chernysheff, who harboured no grudge
against the regime for robbing him of ten of the best years of
his life, for he considered that they were quite right to have
done it. My arguments offended his sense of law and order,
and in his eyes I was a dangerous individual.

When it came to Michail's turn, he talked like one of the
apostles. He told us that fundamentally everybody is good,
only the conditions in which they find themselves often make
them bad. Everybody is innocent, people don't know that
they are doing wrong. It is only that some individuals are
bad; the masses are good, and, if everybody had good living
conditions evil would disappear from the face of the earth.
Even Hitler was innocent. He was just born like that. He
wasn't evil, only stupid. And it is stupidity that gives birth to
crime, for crime doesn't pay, and so a wise man could not be
bad. Who knew what sort of childhood and youth Hitler
had had to concentrate so much spite in him? A stupid person in unsuitable surroundings can become very dangerous for
the world. Hitler had brought millions of Germans up to be
bad, but was that their fault? Instead of explaining to them
that we were all people and all had the same right to live, the
Germans were told that they were the chosen nation. That
sort of false doctrine must go to anyone's head; and so millions of fundamentally good, innocent people had been made
fools of because one man was stupid enough to believe that
evil paid. If everybody would only try to be good, if only for
a short time as an experiment, he would soon see how much
can be achieved that way. But people are stupid and answer

evil with evil. All that would be changed, as soon as there was enough bread to go round. People will get better; only we must all stick together. The world is indivisible, and the whole of humanity ought to run it together, and together exploit the earth's resources, like being in a huge *Kolchoz* in which we have to live, because we have been put here in the world.

"And I believe," he said, "that that will come about, and then, after this war, the world will become Paradise. In Russia, for example," said Michail sincerely and with the utmost conviction, "a beginning has already been made. There is already just division of goods. And what's all this war about? After a war people are always worse. They don't want to kill each other at all, but they do so in the name of false doctrines. It's a waste of good, innocent people, for at the bottom of his heart everybody is really good."

At this point I had to leave, for a soldier came to tell me that the Major from the Dower House was looking for me. I ran straight there in some anxiety, but it turned out that the Major was only wanting to make us a present of a cow. Lieutenant Boruk told me so formally, in the kitchen. The cook, Washka, and several soldiers gathered round us and nodded their heads approvingly as the Lieutenant made his little speech. The cow was to be fetched at once, so I ran for Jumbo, and he and I and an old soldier with a huge moustache set off for the village to get the cow. She was a heifer and wounded in one of the hind legs.

In all his life Jumbo had never had anything to do with cows. He had seen them through the windows of his car, but that was all and it was not enough. I told him to lead her by the rope I had tied round her horns, and myself encouraged the infuriating animal from behind with a sunflower stalk. Jumbo pulled, but the cow just stood plumb in the middle of the empty village street with every appearance of intending to spend the night there. Jumbo looked as unhappy as the cow, and begged me to relieve him of the rope; so we changed ends. I now tugged and Jumbo was supposed to prod, but he had a softer heart than I, and, instead of shouting and belabouring the brute's revolting behind, he got hold of a wisp of hay from somewhere and waved it in front of her nose, trying in that way to entice her forward. The cow remained unmoved. So we changed ends again.

This time, instead of shouting, I crept up on tip-toe, armed with a proper stick, and dealt the creature two resounding thwacks on the rump. And that set her off! Jumbo leaped aside with the dexterity of a toreador: the cow wound the rope round the next tree and stopped, this time facing away from the Dower House.

We unwound the rope, I cursing the heifer in every language I knew, Jumbo talking to her mildly and diplomatically, and still clutching his hay which he kept thrusting almost into her very mouth. The heifer just turned her head aside in a reproachful gesture. Jumbo again thrust the hay between her damp, thick lips. She shook her head.

"You won't entice a full cow with a wisp of hay," I shouted.

Judging by the expression on the cow's face she agreed with me. Then, turning her head away in disgust, she moved off in the direction of her byre, dragging us after her. We now tried barring her way, leaping from one side of the road to the other, according to the direction in which her horns were pointing. Our united effort succeeded in turning her round to face the Dower House. Jumbo now resignedly took the rope again, and, when I gave the signal, he tugged and I belaboured. I let her have it properly, but the creature had nerves of steel, at any rate where I hit her. Oh God! Why wasn't she a nice delicate, nervous creature? And quite unjustly, we cursed the Russians: *Timeo Danaos et dona ferentes*.

There we stood in the deserted village street gazing at each other helplessly across the back of a cow: I grasping a stout stick, and panting Jumbo a wisp of hay. In silence we made yet another attempt, trying to synchronize our efforts as much as possible. The cow, having taken our measure, now adopted a comfortable defensive position, taking advantage of every inequality in the ground, like the good strategist she was, and keeping all four hooves firmly planted. It must have been a sight to make people weep. In fact, somebody did see us, though he didn't weep. This was a boy from the village, who, thank goodness, happened to come along. With the promise of half his kingdom, Jumbo managed to persuade the boy to lead the cow home for us. He took hold of the rope, gave it a gentle pull and disappeared round the corner with the cow.

It was more than we could do to catch them up. When we reached home, there was the heifer standing in Teresa's yard, looking as mild and innocent as only a cow can. Never believe it, when they look like that!

We returned to the shelter frozen, and were just starting the tale of our appalling afternoon when Grigory arrived with Washka Myshkowski on a visit. We produced a bottle of Tokay, and explaining to gloomy Grigory that it was a hundred years old, filled up the glasses. We were just about to give one to merry, young Washka, when Grigory stopped us.

"The soldier doesn't need it," he said.

For an officer to take this tone with a soldier surprised us; for we had got the impression that in the Red Army it was the officers who were afraid of their men, and not the other way round. Later we came to the conclusion that it all depended on the officer: there were some who managed to keep their men in check, others who were quite unable to cope with them. Whatever authority an officer had, however, it never extended beyond his immediate subordinates, and the most iron disciplinarian was just a windbag as far as the men of any other unit but his own were concerned. It is difficult to conceive how little solidarity there is in the Russian Army. The men are mostly split up into small groups which look after themselves independently of each other. On principle the attitude of one group to the other is hostile, and for an

officer or man to expect to be looked after by a group not
his own, even though it belongs to the same regiment, is to
invite the refusal that ninety-nine times out of a hundred he
will get. Those who have lost their groups wander about like
lone elephants in a hostile jungle, outcasts if ever there were
such.

The Russians organize themselves in packs like wolves,
and it is not the one of the highest rank but he with the
strongest character who is the leader. Theoretically, of course,
it is the superior in rank who is in charge, but we saw several
cases of full Lieutenants going in terror of a Sergeant, or even
an ordinary private. Such well coordinated packs will never
take an outsider into their billet nor give him food; they
much prefer to tell him the most barefaced lies and get rid
of him quickly than to help him. Later we were to see many
struggles between these groups and to exploit them to our
own advantage, using the Russians' own methods which we
were quick to copy.

Grigory was one of those officers who knew how to exact
obedience. Wherever he went, there too went his faithful
Myshkowski, who had been with him for four years and with
whom he would, if need be, share his bundle of straw or his
last crust. We saw many such friendships, and they were
often such that none could have wished for a more faithful
friend. Myshkowski assisted Grigory in everything, and was
as essential to him as his dog is to the shepherd. Grigory was
from the Ukraine. His wife had been murdered by the Germans and the only remaining member of his family was a
young son in an orphanage. As a matter of principle every
Russian from the Ukraine had his entire family in the other
world. We only met one, literally one, for we paid special attention to this, who admitted to having a family unmurdered
and alive, having escaped to Central Asia.

Grigory was not concerned over the loss of his wife. He
would find another after the war, he said. He was a mechanic
by trade, and it was, perhaps, because he was so modest in his

needs that he was so popular with his men. When he refused
to let us give Washka a drink, Washka just growled terrify-
ingly like a dog but never touched the glass. Grigory drank
his off at a gulp and poured the last drop or two on to the
ground; then he smacked his lips, wiped them with the back
of his hand, and graciously pronounced the wine good. We
poured him out a second glass, explaining that Tokay should
be drunk slowly as otherwise you lose the taste and aroma.

"Nonsense!" said Grigory, indignantly. "We always drink
straight off, like this," and a second glass of hundred-year-old
Tokay disappeared down the Lieutenant's throat. Again, he
poured the last few drops on to the ground, kissed the bottom
of the glass and put it back on the table.

Washka kept up a continual angry growl, so like a dog's
that Alf lifted his head and looked round. Grigory just shook
his head and repeated, "Soldiers don't need it," but we were
sorry for poor Washka and slipped him half a glass on the sly.
He did not like it, and half the wine found its way on to the
floor.

After having had to watch his finest wine being treated in
this fashion by our Russian guests, the Soviet Union, as far as
Jumbo was concerned, was finished for ever, and now you can
tell him the most wonderful things about it and he won't believe you.

Jumbo and I paid our first visit to the Dower House since
it was taken over by its present occupiers. We had, it's true,
reconnoitred the kitchen, but never penetrated farther than
that. From the way the remaining furniture had been moved
about it was obvious that the men were sleeping everywhere,
and everywhere was the typical Russian smell: a mixture of
the cheap perfumes for which they have a truly Oriental weakness, stale cigarette smoke, garlic and sweat. The dirt was
fearful, and the disorder worse. I must admit that the present
regime has taught the Russian to wash the upper part of his
body and to shave. This is a colossal achievement, when you

consider their national liking for dirt, and one must suppose
that this new cleanliness of the upper part is due to a Five-
Year Plan. Let us hope that it will be followed by another to
teach them to keep themselves clean all over, for, should Russia ever again occupy Europe, that is a thing that will concern
us all very closely.

Rudi's bedroom had been made to look like a debtor's
prison in the XVIIIth century. It was difficult to see why,
having everything there, the Russians had made themselves
so uncomfortable, and I came to the conclusion that they
were just not accustomed to what we would call normal living conditions. I had noticed that they had managed much
better in the peasants' cottages. Here, however, the loose
covers had been rolled up to serve as pillows, and the pillows
had been put in the chairs; the wire mattresses were leaned
up against the wall as so much useless iron, while the mattresses had been put on the floor; the tables were not covered
with our straw mats, which had been thrown into a corner,
but with the curtains torn from the window; saucers had been
brought from the kitchen to serve as ash-trays, while the ash-
trays themselves lay unused in a dark corner, but arranged in
a complicated design and were obviously supposed to be an
ornament. It was as hot as a Turkish bath. The Russian
soldier will sleep in the snow and twenty degrees of frost without catching cold, but inside he likes his rooms to be tropi-
cally heated, and airing them is a thing he does not recognize.

Some officers, busy chewing sunflower seeds, got up from
the table when they saw us. "Where are you off to?" they
roared, and I told them that I wanted to speak with the Major. We were conducted to Muki's old room, next door,
where sat the Major, a fat, genial, fair-haired man, lounging
in an armchair, and scattered round him, like so many odalis-
ques, were his subordinates, both officers and men, stretched
out in chairs and on mattresses. The Major, whom I already
knew, asked us to sit down and introduced us to another Major lying beside him, who, without getting up, gave us his

hand, as though he had been Madame Recamier. He, in his turn, introduced us to his brother, a young soldier with a shaven head, lying at his feet. This over, we expressed our thanks for the heifer and then, as usual, had to give detailed descriptions first of my life and then of Jumbo's.

The Major showed a sudden interest in the salaries paid to directors of European factories and in costs and prices in the sugar-beet industry. An accountant-lieutenant was summoned and we began laboriously writing down columns and columns of figures. After an hour's work and very heavy translation, the Russians came to the conclusion that in Russia the workmen were paid at least twice as much, and engineers and directors five times as much, as their European counterparts.

"You see," said Jumbo, with a smile, "it's not true that we are bourgeois. We are poorer than you; so it is you who are the bourgeois."

The Russians did not know what to say to this. Here they had been boasting of the differences in their wages and salaries, laughing at us because in Europe engineers were comparatively badly paid, proud that their's earned so much, as though inequality in wages was a wonderful new achievement of socialism, and now they found themselves being called bourgeois! The Major scratched his head:

"Well, with us, people live better than they do here," he said, and that ended the interrogation.

Perhaps wages really are higher in Russia, but what can they get for their money?

The Major asked whether any of our things in the house had disappeared. "Not a thing," we said, though quite unable to know. "You see," the Major went on, "we are leaving to-day. You will be able to move back this afternoon. I'm sorry that you have had to stay underground since the twenty-second, but we're moving out now and you can go back to your house, and live in it undisturbed."

We thanked him, wished them a speedy victory, and said good-bye.

The Hungarians were tremendously excited when they heard the news. The ladies, in particular, could hardly contain their delight at the prospect of sleeping in proper beds again, and of being able to wash and undress at night. We began planning who was to have which room, as we feverishly collected our things and packed.

An hour later I went and had another look at the house. It seemed empty, but at the front door was a small German car. Then the Colonel came out in his dark glasses, the last to leave, and we exchanged a few words standing on the terrace steps. To him I was an exotic figure and he didn't know where to place me in the social scale. At last he, too, left, and the house was empty.

The war was over.

Marietta and Dolly ran quickly through all the rooms, wringing their hands. All that dirt and confusion could not be banished in one day, they decided, so we contented ourselves with opening all the windows wide. The next morning we would get some women from the village to come and scrub.

Now that the Russians had gone, we all poured out of the shelter, like bees out of their hive when spring comes, and sauntered up and down the garden, avoiding the numerous pitfalls left behind by the Russians, for the garden had served several hundred men as water-closets. The garden fence was broken down in many places, and lorries and armoured cars had cut roads through the box hedges. The corpses of several such vehicles, stripped of their wheels, lay on their backs like so many dead animals. This was the first time we had dared walk freely in the garden, and it felt as though the war were over after lasting but a few days, like some strange, unexpected dream. That weird army had descended upon us like a cloud of locusts, we had made friends with them, and now they had disappeared out of our sight for ever. Just like a

dream. So we rubbed our eyes. A flood had come and subsided again, and once more we would go back to our old,
boring life. I had lived at such a tension those last few days
that I did not feel my tiredness at all. And I was, in fact, exhausted, for I had spent half the day in the stuffy, gloomy cellar, at night I had hardly slept at all in my crack between two
paillasses, and I had drunk so much every day that I had
hardly ever been properly sober, and I had talked, talked, and
talked incessantly.

So that was what it was like being behind the Russian
front? Really, we had been extremely lucky that there had
been no proper fighting, and that nothing had happened to
us. Just a few days, and it was all over.

We had lunch in the kitchen, very late but very gay. Even
Lina was radiant and gradually recovering her old self.

That evening Jack and I went out for a walk in the frosty
air. In the courtyard, under a chestnut tree, we met the last
of the Russians: Aram. He was an Armenian. As usual we
had to answer endless questions about ourselves: our names
and ages, how we came there, and all that had happened to
us in our lives. Driver Aram felt duty bound to reciprocate.
Though Aram came from Armenia and not the Ukraine (at
last someone not from the Ukraine!) his life story was just
like the rest: his entire family had been murdered, their house
burned, their cattle driven away, and he alone, a small child,
had escaped with his life, saved by the arrival of some Cossacks. There was, however, one welcome change: all this had
been done by the Turks and not by the Germans!

Oh, those Russians! I knew them first when I was a child.
Those were White Russian émigrés, and now these men of
the Red Army. Despite the intervening twenty years, despite
the fact that whole worlds have crashed and disappeared, the
Russians' stories have not changed at all: at most they differ
in one or two details. Every Russian has always had his entire
family murdered and himself only escaped at the last moment
by a miracle and just in what he stood up in. In the old days

every Russian was either a Prince or a Count; to-day, an engineer or director of a factory, or a professor. In Russia, land of peasants and workers, there do not seem to be any peasants or workers at all. Of all the hundreds I got to know during those months spent under the Red Army, I only met one or two drivers or mechanics and not a single peasant. The corn in Russia seems to grow by itself, and the factories to run without workmen, being manned exclusively by directors. Tsarist Russia was composed of nothing but Counts and Princes, who spent their time at court, and yet the country was there and seemed to get on all right. The only explanation is that centuries ago the Russians discovered the secret of doing without the lower orders. Nevertheless, the European is inclined to be sceptical and to shake his head in disbelief: your *entire* family murdered? The *whole* town burnt to the ground? A Prince? Your brother a Romanov? An engineer? A culinary professor? A mathematician? Director of the Odessa opera? Well, I wonder! And in Russia there always seems to be a reason for murdering people: at first it was that they were Counts or belonged to the Corps of Pages, then it was because they were Mensheviks; or, if not Mensheviks, because their aunt was a Trotskyite, or because their sister-in-law had flirted with Tupolew, or because they were Armenians; and then, although Russian, because they were *Kulaks*; and, finally, just because they were Russians, for by then the Germans had come. There seems no end to this chain of murder, for it still goes on: now it is because they are Volga Germans, or Tartars, or Kirghiz, or Vlassovites. If those who manage to get out of Russia are always the last of the Mohicans, the only surviving representatives of Russian families murdered for one reason or another, who on earth makes up the population of that vast country?

The European wags his head, and no longer believes anything.

Why are the present-day Russians, or at least those in the Red Army, for I did not meet any others, ashamed to admit that they work in a factory, or on a *kolchoz*? The fact remains that they are, and this gave rise to the paradoxical situation that we were always trying to persuade the Russians that we were a sort of peasant, or at any rate working class, and would proudly exhibit our carefully neglected fingers and the blisters that we were at such pains to renew; while they took as much trouble and used the same ingenuity in trying to persuade us that they were soloists in the Leningrad opera, brothers-in-law of some Marshal, or directors of a factory. It was all very strange.

Condoling belatedly with Aram on the loss of his entire family, we took our leave and went back to the shelter. After the house, it seemed a heaven of cleanliness and order.

Staff Officer

28th-31st
December

WE BEGAN scrubbing and cleaning early on the 28th, and we kept at it all day. Six girls came from the village to help, and in two hours stole almost as much as the Russians had. We were highly indignant, never having imagined that the "people" would put that interpretation on Communism. But it was gradually becoming obvious that that was how every peasant imagined Communism to himself: just snatch and plunder, not only from the gentry but from everybody not in a position to defend his property. Those girls even stole a bag and a blouse from under Dolly's very nose, and she has not got over it yet. Elsie, her child, and Rudi moved back to the Dower House.

The following day was another one of perfect peace. We were convinced then that Budapest must have fallen. We were consumed with curiosity as to what was happening in the village and up at the Manor. Were they clear of Russians, too? Jumbo and I set off to find out and to rescue what could still be saved from there.

The village was empty. The whole place was littered with straw and heaps of maize, peas or oats, fed to the horses. Nor were there any signs of sentries round the Manor. Free again! Here, too, we would have to scrub and clean up, for Tacitus wanted to move back as soon as possible and occupy, if only two rooms, so as to show that the house was his property.

As we walked through the deserted rooms, we began laying our plan of campaign: when we should go to Budapest, where start work in the Manor. Not one piece of furniture had survived. The dirt was appalling: straw everywhere and the floors littered with sunflower seeds; the panes in the windows all smashed, and through them came the stench from the guts of slaughtered cattle with which the terrace was covered. From the balustrade the head of a bullock gazed with glazed eyes out over the smiling landscape.

We stood holding hands in that huge empty room, our hearts full of hope for the future. Obviously God was in His heaven, since it had all ended so well; or so we thought, for man is accustomed to believe in the justice of God, especially when he himself has emerged unscathed from oppression. Then we heard the sound of a car driving up to the Manor. What was this? The Russians again?

Into the room where we stood walked an elegant officer in a neat, clean uniform and a yellow cap with a green peak.

"How are you, Lida?" he said, and made straight towards me.

"Good morning," I said in surprise, taking his outstretched hand, "and how do you know that I am called Lida?"

"But we met here one evening not long ago. Don't you remember our chat in the dark?"

Then, suddenly, I did remember. This was the man Jack had made that scene about, telling me that you must never admit to a Russian that you have been abroad.

"I've come in a car to fetch you and your husband. It's waiting for you now."

"Are we going to the Capital? So it has been liberated?" I asked, hopefully and delighted at the prospect.

"Yes," answered the officer, with a smile, "to the Capital. Only hurry, for the car's waiting."

Jumbo and I could hardly contain our delight. Obviously they wanted us to tell them about the Gestapo, the hundreds of Poles that had been deported, the concentration camps, etc. Obviously good psychologists, they knew they could trust us. We hurried to the car and drove to the Dower House to get our things, for the officer said that the trip would last several days. We caused a sensation in the Dower House: Jumbo and his wife going to Budapest! Fifi packed a small suitcase for us in great excitement, throwing in Jumbo's medicines, cigarettes, shaving things, while the officer politely urged us to hurry: Quick! quick! This is very important! Casually we said good-bye to the others, almost bursting with pride at playing such an important role, in the fact that they valued our intelligence and honesty even though we were mere bourgeois.

As the car tore over the bumpy road we talked with the officer. It transpired that only part of the Capital was occupied and that we must thus go a roundabout way to a village about ten miles outside the western suburbs. It was sad-looking country through which we drove: ruined houses, shattered tanks, piles of German helmets with holes through them, dead horses, mile after mile, mile after mile, while overturned telegraph poles and tangles of wire hampered our passage. It was a melancholy sort of day with a heavy leaden sky sunk low above our heads and a wind that whistled through the deserted, devastated vineyards. The nearer we got to our journey's end the more Russian vehicles we passed. There were so many in the actual village itself that we could hardly get through. The sound of gunfire was quite loud, and we could even see the wooded hills where the battle for the city was being fought.

The car stopped suddenly in front of a peasant's cottage in a badly bombed street, and we were told to get out. The officer went into the cottage and came out again in a moment to tell us curtly that here we would spend the night. This was December, and it was already growing dark. Not having had time to eat anything before we left home, we were hungry.

The sudden change in the officer's tone came as a surprise, and when he got into the car and drove away without a word we began to feel apprehensive. An armed guard led us through the porch to a little room on the right, and we heard him say, "Arrested." The blood froze in my veins, but I pretended to myself that I had misheard, and said nothing to Jumbo. Let him remain confident a little longer, and look forward to seeing the city where he was born.

There were two people in that small room, a young Lieutenant with a handsome, Mongolian face, and a little monster in human form, a revolting dirty old Hungarian, with restless, anxious glowing black eyes. I greeted them with a smile and as politely as I knew how in Russian. Silence. Then I asked if I might sit down, trying to talk as though I were free as air and well pleased with the world and myself. Silence. I sat down, and, in French, told Jumbo to do likewise.

"Where did you learn Russian?" suddenly roared the Russian.

That released a flood of words from my lips, and for the umpteenth time I repeated my and Jumbo's story, emphasizing every now and again that I did not speak the local language, for it had suddenly occurred to me that perhaps they were wanting to take me with them up to the front as an interpreter.

"What?" interrupted the old Hungarian, bending down close to my face and blinking his inflamed eyes. "I'll soon teach you to speak. Do you understand what I say? Five years you've been here and you haven't learned the language? We'll soon teach you. We have ways. You'll be singing yet, just you wait."

I moved away, for the old man lisped wetly and stank, so that I felt faint. And I was frightened. Oh God, I thought, give me the strength to keep smiling all the time; let me keep them from seeing how they revolt me and how frightened I am, and I am sure I'll find a way out of this trap.

"I know this kind," said the old man, in Russian, to the officer, "we'll soon finish with them. It will be easy, very easy to find out whether she's lying."

"Oh, how well you speak Russian," I broke in, trying to give my voice the careless, half-bored tone you use at a cocktail party.

"Where do you come from?" suddenly asked Jumbo in Hungarian. "Where did you learn Russian? A very difficult language, that. Did it take you long?"

"Russian literature," I interposed senselessly, turning to the Lieutenant, "is one of the most beautiful."

Our tone was so free and easy, our expressions so innocent and kindly that the atmosphere improved slightly. Even if we are accused of something, I thought, they can't have any proofs, for we are innocent from their point of view.

I do not know how Daniel behaved in the lion's den. In my den I behaved as though my lions were innocent kittens; I called them "nice pussy," and stretched out my hand to scratch them behind the ear. I even pretended to be a mouse, to amuse them, for the gentlest lion always stays a cat, and I tried by every means in my power to show them that not for an instant did I imagine that they had any thought of eating me.

Jumbo took on the old man and I the young officer. We overwhelmed them with questions; never let them get a word in edgeways. I told fantastic tales of a fictitious Russian Major, my great friend; Jumbo told stories of how he had been tortured by the Gestapo; and all this with the ease of experienced people of the world. This technique was quite unknown to the Russians. And how much time you have to waste before you can acquire it! How many years will it be before the Russians acquire this European technique for throwing dust in people's eyes? The Germans living in the centre of Europe never learned how to do it. The Russians have their own methods of diplomacy based on the age-old traditions of the East, but Western Europe with its culture and charm has turned it into a real art, so that the stupidest European who is used to society will lead the best member of the Ogpu up the garden path just by this very adroitness of his tongue that he has learned to wield like an expert fencer his foil. Our tormentors grew so bored with us that they threw us out into a little room on the left of the porch. I can imagine with what relief they saw the door shut behind us. The Germans would without doubt have shot us for such loquacity.

My nerves were so braced, my mind so concentrated, that I had no time left for fear, even though I knew that we were in the hands of the N.K.W.D. The room we were now in was the living-room of the cottage. Half of it was taken up by two box beds full of straw and feathers. On one of these, half-lying, half-sitting, was a young girl with dark hair, and next to her an old man. One or two ragged, unshaven Hungarians sat on stools round about, and there were two Russian soldiers with automatic pistols slung round their necks.

We quickly became acquainted. And once again, with perfect co-ordination and no need to say a word, I took on the Russian and Jumbo his compatriots. The old man proved talkative. He was called Maksym and came from Ruthenia. The girl was a Jewess who had been hiding under false papers in the neighbouring village, and when the Russians had come and freed her she had joined up with them and was now following wherever they went. She lay on the bed powdering her face. This, for her, was life; in fact, Paradise. She was enjoying her liberty like a young animal. Then she got up and, swinging her hips, and throwing devastating glances to every side, walked out of the room. She was a nice girl, though perhaps many people would not agree with that choice of word.

"She's a whore," Maksym whispered to me. "She had ten last night, and now she won't let me have her. Tell her, explain to her, that I love her; that I will reward her. You see, she pretends she doesn't understand. You're a fellow compatriot and you ought to help me. And, if she won't, perhaps

you would like to? I'll give you something for it, too, for
you're on your own. Well, Lida, tell me, would you like to?
You're nobody's and one can talk with you."

Such were the conversations with which we passed the
time till the evening.

At six o'clock—eight o'clock for the Russians—Waska, the
cook, began busying himself with supper. Jumbo, exhausted
with talking to his terrified fellow countrymen, stretched out
on the free bed. The dark-haired girl came back and, leaning
a piece of broken mirror against the sooty paraffin lamp, began carefully painting her face. Into that dreadful room,
where you could actually smell the people's fear, she introduced the fragrance of genuine joy of life. She alone of all
the people there was afraid of nothing, and her carefree attitude was somehow infectious.

The soldiers with the automatic pistols were relieved.
Now and again the disgusting old man from the neighbouring room would come in to inspect Waska's steaming pots
and extract a smoking tit-bit with his fingers that were black
with dirt. Then he would glance gloatingly round the room
and go out. Maksym lay snoring on the second bed next to
Jumbo. We were bored and at the same time rather afraid.
What did it all mean? Those poor, ragged, unshaven devils
had been trailed along for a week already and had no idea
why. Time dragged on. Waska set some pale, un-Russian
beetroot soup on the table, from which he drove the girl who
hastily gathered her paints and powders together, cursing him.
I gave Jumbo his supper where he lay, a few potatoes boiled
in salt water, for Jumbo had no appetite for Waska's beetroot
soup; then I joined the cook at the table. The others were
given nothing to eat.

As usual, I had to relate my life-history. This had changed
with the course of time. Sometimes my mother was Russian,
and she and the entire family were murdered by the Germans
and our house in Warsaw burned, while I escaped in what I
stood up in (this puts you equal with your interlocutor); at

other times, as now, I was a famous painter and, while artists are greatly looked up to in the U.S.S.R., the Hungarians, an uncultured nation, could not appreciate my art, so that for five years I had had to work in a factory in order to make ends meet. In revenge I had refused to learn their language. Waska was greatly moved by this sad story, and told me about himself. He, it turned out, had been so rich that he did not need to work. He had a house, land, cattle, and several large orchards. I expressed surprise that so magnificent a property had not been incorporated in a *Kolchoz*, but Waska explained, not very clearly, that in Russia there is freedom and if someone prefers having his own property to working for a percentage of the profits in a *Kolchoz*, he is at liberty to do so and keep his property. Poor Waska, thirty-five-year-old peasant, was ashamed of those *Kolchozes*, and when I said that it was surprising so many people preferred to work in them, rather than for themselves, he did not know what to say. We drank a little wine, and then I lay down between Jumbo and Maksym and tried to sleep.

About eight o'clock a young Lieutenant I had not seen before came into the room. He had a broken nose and a serious, rather nice, face.

"Please make up the bed properly for these two," he roared, pointing at us, to the guard standing in the doorway. "And culturally, with a pillow and eiderdown; the women must give you sheets. At once, do you understand?"

He turned to us, said good-night, and went out. The arrested peasants relapsed into apathy. Jumbo and I clambered down from our torn paillasse and the terrified woman of the house brought a dirty, streaked eiderdown and an equally dirty pillow to make it "cultured." We preferred the normal straw, but did not dare say so. Once more we stretched out one beside the other on the bed, and, as the unfortunate peasants had meanwhile been led out, we began a whispered conversation.

There seemed to be two schools of thought in the ac-

cursed Ogpu, or N.K.W.D.; one that we were honoured
guests, and the other that we were dangerous spies. Some of
the officers treated us with respect, others as though we were
criminals. We had spent the whole day in unbearable ex-
pectation and nothing had happened. What would come
now? And why had they brought us to within a mile of the
front? It was already very late and we had almost fallen
asleep, cold, exhausted and anxious, when the door suddenly
opened: interrogation.

First they took me. I walked across the dark street to a
house on the opposite side. I went even gladly, for anything
was better than waiting. As I walked I remembered the frightened dumb faces of the arrested peasants out of whom Jumbo
had been unable to get anything. Why had they taken those
poor devils? However, I had no time to worry about that, for
already I was in a tiny, peasant room with a large table in the
centre, around it chairs and in each chair an officer, all of
them looking at me. There was only one pair of eyes I recognized, those of my little tormentor from Mora, the one with
the turned-up nose like a saddle. No doubt he would start his
"you're lying, Lida!" all over again.

"An interpreter is not necessary, Comrade Colonel," said
my friend, and at that an N.C.O. stood up and lazily walked
out of the room, his hands in his pockets. So I was to be interrogated without an interpreter! That wasn't so good. The
accused always has a better chance with an interpreter, and
less responsibility for his own words.

The interrogation began and went on for a long, long
time. I won't describe in detail all the nonsense that was
talked, but it was all about the island of Malta.

"What is Malta?"

"An island in the Mediterranean."

"We know that," roared the Colonel. "I just wanted to
see if you knew it, too. I am a geographer and I know every
island."

Then they wanted to know what I had been doing in

Malta, for they had been informed that I had been there. I
told them that I had just been on a visit. "Aha! just a
tourist," said the Colonel slowly and sneeringly, looking round
at the others who all burst out laughing. What were they
getting at, I wondered. How could I answer them, if I did not
know what they were getting at?

In the pauses I tried to give the conversation a more social
tone. I even recited bits out of Pushkin's *Ruslan and Ludmilla* and *Onegin* that, God knows why, I had once learned
in my youth. One of the officers was visibly impressed by this
proof of my high state of culture, and began first to prompt
me, and then himself took over and declaimed the rest in a
musical, emotional voice. Pushkin must have had in him
some of the qualities of Orpheus, for as his superb lines
flowed out into the hushed room they began to charm, like
a magic spell. The Colonel did not interrupt, but sat there
stolidly with a stony face. "Just you wait, you hangman," I
thought, "I'll teach you not to torment innocent people at
night." But how I was to teach him I did not know. However, I was no longer afraid. It is the entering of the den that
is the worst. Once you are in it, all you can do is to say "nice
pussy" to the lions, and see what happens.

At length the door opened and Jumbo was brought in.
Behind him came the nice N.C.O. who had left the room
when I arrived. He was the interpreter, a Czech. Jumbo was
interrogated through the interpreter, while I was ordered to
sit quiet and not interrupt or join in under any circumstances.
Many things were now to be explained.

The Colonel wanted to know what were the orders and
queer uniforms found in the Manor at Mora. Jumbo explained that they were those of a Knight of Malta. Then the
Colonel asked why the Maltese have uniforms of their own
and why they keep them in cupboards in Hungarians' houses,
when the island belongs to Great Britain. Jumbo explained
that the religious order of the Knights of Malta had nothing
to do with either Great Britain or the inhabitants of Malta,

but was under the protection of the Pope. At that the Colonel wanted to know why the Pope should wish to go against Britain and give asylum to British subjects in Fascist Rome during time of war. Jumbo tried to explain that the Knights of Malta left the island when it was occupied by Napoleon. This the Colonel found hard to swallow and he told the interpreter to tell Jumbo that he could hardly believe that the people of Malta had been sitting all those years in Rome, instead of quietly returning home where things must have been peaceful for at least a century. Jumbo being a patient man, repeated that the Maltese and the Knights of Malta are quite distinct and explained, as simply as he could, that the Order was a sovereign one with its own envoys in many of the European capitals, and that its members were scattered about the world. The Colonel then wanted to know how Jumbo, who had never been in Malta, had suddenly and for no apparent reason become a Maltese. Jumbo sighed an appeal to heaven, and said that he had not become a Maltese, and assuredly never would, but that he was a Knight of Malta which in certain circles in Europe is an honourable distinction. For whom, the Colonel wanted to know; for Jumbo or for the Maltese? Jumbo, with a smile, replied that it was an honour for him.

The Russians now seemed to think that their discovery of the Order of the Knights of Malta had put them on the track of new, hidden enemies of the proletariat, and they continued to torment Jumbo. If it were possible to be a Maltese and not live in Malta, where did Jumbo become one and how was he appointed? Jumbo told him that he was appointed by Rome, for it was a Catholic Order. The whole thing was now clear: the Italians, through their Pope, had been acting against England by giving asylum ever since the days of Napoleon to those citizens of Malta who were dissatisfied with the British Government. These people had created an organization with its own orders and uniforms, which were now active in the Russian rear. These people had never gone back to Malta, just as the White emigrants had never gone back to Russia, and one knew why. It was all as clear as daylight.

During this interminable interrogation, we had learned that the Colonel besides being a geographer was also a professor of history. He had happened not to have learned the history of Europe, but, of course, knew that of every other part of the world very well. This, however, we were unable to confirm. When both parties were exhausted and Jumbo was still as ignorant of what they wanted of him as the Colonel of Malta and the Maltese, they sent us back to our quarters, promising us a further instalment in the morning.

At four o'clock Waska began blowing up the fire in the dark, for to him it was already six o'clock. A moment later the room suddenly filled with children and weeping women. These were the people to whom the cottage belonged. They spent the entire day in cellars because of the closeness of the front, and only emerged just before daybreak to take advantage of the short pause in the battle that always came then, in order to get a hot meal at home. Jumbo tried to comfort the weeping women, but they were beyond comforting. This was not surprising, as we learned from the flood of words they poured out, that the previous evening some drunken Russians had got into the cellar where the whole family was gathered, turned the older women out, forced the owner of the cottage, the only man there, to drink till he was dead drunk and then raped his ten-year-old daughter several times. No one had been able to get help. The soldiers had made such a noise that they had drowned the girl's screams, while others had stood guard over the women outside the cellar. When the girl fainted, they ran away. They had now carried the bleeding girl to her grandmother, and the mother they had brought to us. They would not let her go to her child but tried to soothe her with simple, impressive gestures. It was a scene reminiscent of the Mater Dolorosa of the old paintings of the Middle Ages: those coarse, grave faces framed in kerchiefs, dark shapes surrounding a mother crazed with grief. Despite the horror of what had happened those women never for an instant lost their sense of the theatrical; just such as they must have acted in the Passion plays of the Middle Ages. As I sat there watching this resuscitation of the Gothic spirit, it was as though I were looking at an altar of the Middle Ages that had suddenly come to life: it was a wonderful, very human, and naively realistic performance, its realism framed in art, merged into it and forming an unforgettable whole.

I translated the women's account of the whole affair to Waska, and watched curiously to see what his reaction would be. Waska was a phlegmatic, decent fellow of about forty and he had been soldiering now for four years.

"Damned fools, those women," said Waska slowly, shaking his head. "Why can't they stay in the cottage? They're terrified of bombs and go and hide in holes. And what are we to do? Here am I hard at it the whole day, do you expect me to spend the night as well going round the cellars and keeping guard over little girls? What? With us, in the Ukraine, the Germans raped young girls and then shot them, that's what they did. And our fools saw them and learned what to do, but they never shoot them, not even when they're drunk. The German raped, then out with his revolver, and that was the girl finished. That, you see, is the difference."

I felt that Waska was on the point of telling me how they had massacred his entire family, but luckily Maksym, whom the cries of the women had at last wakened, butted in.

"I've been trying to think what to do about these girls. If the front stays where it is much longer, it will be bad for the girls."

"And bad for you, too," I put in. "What will they think of you? Will the village have pleasant memories of you? You must think of that."

"I am thinking," replied Maksym, "I've just been thinking that one might shut all the young girls up into one room for the night. But that would be bad, too. The lads would find them more easily. And just think how convenient it would be for them to have them all in a bunch. You'd need a whole regiment to guard that lot, for our lads would come from all over the place, if they knew that all the girls were in a bunch. I know the amount of searching it takes to find even an old woman. So, to gather them all into one room, that's not a good idea. You see, I keep thinking about it, but I see there's nothing to be done. It just had to be. When there's war it's better not to have children. They kill your son, wrong your daughter, and whatever you think of it, it's no use."

"Of course, there's nothing to be done," said Waska, looking up from his pots. "I've told her that already."

Waska called me over, as the expert, to taste his morning beetroot soup, then he and I sat down to breakfast. We ate out of one dish, drinking great draughts of wine.

"Eat, Lida, eat!" said good Waska. "Eat as long as we're alive in this mangy world. Mangy it is, there's no denying, but all the same you want to live. That's the way it is."

Maksym came back from outside, where dawn was breaking.

"Is it true, Maksym," I asked, "that the Capital has surrendered?" for I was now beginning to suspect that they had lied to us.

"Who told you that nonsense, Lida? Only part of the town on the other side of the river is ours. On this side things are at a standstill. Oh, no! we're a long way off that, yet."

Now I knew that they had trapped us, and God knows what they intended doing with us.

"Maksym," I said, "I've got a great favour to ask of you. If my husband will have a talk with that girl, you know which, will you come with me across the road to the Colonel?"

"She won't have me," said Maksym gloomily.

"I shan't force her either, but my husband will tell her that you love her."

"That's right, I love her. Let her be told that, for she

understands nothing when you make signs to her. Well, perhaps, I will go with you to your Colonel, or whatever he is."

It took a long time to persuade Maksym, but in the end
we walked together across to the house on the opposite side.
Once there, Maksym disappeared in the twinkling of an eye,
leaving me alone facing the door I knew so well. Braving the
consequences, I went in without knocking. It was a different
room. On a bed stood the Captain, who had taken part in
the interrogation of the night before, dressing. Beside him
lay a fat, pale Jewess, imported from God knows where for she
understood neither Russian nor Hungarian. The Captain
calmly went on pulling up his trousers, paying not the slightest
attention to me. I asked the woman, in Hungarian, if I wasn't
disturbing them. She turned her round eyes on me, shrugged
her shoulders, and rolled her head away. Then I asked in
Russian if we were going to be interrogated yet. The Jewess
looked enquiringly at the Captain, who let go of his trousers,
which sank slowly down over his mistress's face, and looked at
me for the first time, rather surprised. "What's that?" The
woman disentangled her head and looked at me again, as
though she had already seen enough of me. "Run along, run
along," said the Captain. "Can't you see I'm in a hurry, we're
leaving at once. Didn't you know that we were leaving?"

I said "Good-bye," and ran back to Jumbo with the news.
Jumbo, however, who was sitting by the window chatting with
the Jewish girl, had already heard from her that the Russians
were leaving the village. There was feverish activity in the
street, which looked more like a flight than anything. Little
carts and horses were standing in front of the house, cars
laden with the bedding of the N.K.W.D. people drove up,
collected their women, and immediately drove off. I went
outside, for there hadn't been a guard on the door since last
evening, and there I met our little tormentor from Mora.

"You stay here," he ordered. "I'll have you sent later to
the next village."

We'll fall into the hands of the Germans yet, I thought.

Then they were all in front of the cottage, saying good-bye—Waska, the nice young Jewess, and the revolting old interpreter—and suddenly we found ourselves alone in the deserted village with just a young Mongol to guard us. Heavens, supposing the Germans were to arrive! I had no delusions about the peasants; they would say that I was a Russian spy. Luckily a cart drove up to the house and we were ordered into it. I didn't know whether I was glad or sorry; it all seemed very much the same. Hastily packing our wretched case, Jumbo and I got in and we drove off towards the north-west, the young driver with an automatic pistol slung round his shoulders urging on his emaciated horses, and an icy wind blowing in our faces.

Our driver was most untalkative. He didn't know where he was taking us. After ten miles, anxious and frozen to the marrow, we reached a large village filled with soldiers, and a search began for the H.Q. to which we were to be handed over. The horses continually stumbled, for they were so thin that they could scarcely pull even our light cart. The driver stopped every other minute, got down and, asking us politely not to escape in the meantime, went into the cottages to ask questions of the soldiers there; then we would drive on again. As we were to discover, a Russian H.Q. is one of the most elusive things in the world; to find it quickly in any inhabited place is impossible, to find it at all a feat.

It was not till the afternoon that our driver discovered the house in which the H.Q. was. There, presumably, our tormentors had installed themselves, and there the further interrogation we had been promised was to take place. Not a bit of it! There was not a face we recognized. We were conducted into a pleasant, clean room that used to be the home of a railwayman, and there we sat, feeling alternately horribly bored and unpleasantly apprehensive. However, this was a change of surroundings for the better and it did us good and raised our hopes. People of our kind, you see, always think that nothing can happen to them, if they are innocent. (A sentence and a sentiment that many will read with a sigh.)

In came a young Major, thirty years old at the most. We fell upon him. What was going to happen to us? What did they want with us? Where were we to spend the night? And, most of all, when would they let us go? The Major very politely explained that we were to have a talk with one of his fellow-officers, also a Major but a more important one, and that if we could give him the information he needed, the Red Army would be very grateful and would send us back home in a carriage as soon as the interview was over. If, however, it should by then be too late, they would find us good, comfortable quarters for the night. Emboldened by this, we explained that we had tasted nothing since dawn and were immediately sent some fried potatoes.

Then a Woman-Lieutenant came into the room and we began a normal, pleasant conversation: about the Trans-Siberian Railway. Jumbo asked how much a ticket cost. The two Russians laughed and asked if we wanted to go to Vladivostock. Suddenly there was an uproar and a tremendous commotion. An orderly burst into the room, and the Major and the woman disappeared without a word. Surprised, I went and looked out of the window and saw the morning's scene being repeated in what was either panic flight or a rapid advance: overloaded lorries and carts full of officers were tearing off down the road. The whole lot were leaving as fast as they could; only our cart still stood in the rapidly emptying road, the driver leaning, yawning against the horse, and clutching a large grey envelope with the documents in which, I suspected, we were described as a couple of dangerous Maltese spies.

A moment later we were summoned to continue our journey and climbed back on to the cart. Jumbo was already dreadfully tired and had stomach cramp. I asked our idiot driver where we were going, and he mentioned the name of a village a good thirteen miles away but only eight miles from home. That, at least, was something to the good, we consoled ourselves; yet, why were they taking us there? Why had they not interrogated us? That we could not answer, and, as before, we neither knew what it was all about, nor whether we were guests or prisoners. And so we drove, frozen to the marrow, eastwards along a road full of holes and craters, and, as we jogged along and blew into our frozen hands, we repeated to ourselves: it's nearer home, getting nearer home!

We drove into the village and the usual search for the H.Q. began. Do you know how long it took our driver to find it? From three o'clock till eleven. For eight solid hours he searched for it uninterruptedly in that little township, and of those eight hours, we spent six waiting outside in the open air, treated now like friends, now like dangerous criminals.

We began by driving through the town twice, from one end to the other and back again, stopping every now and then while the driver, one must grant him that, conscientiously collected all possible information that might lead to the discovery of the H.Q. He also looked for a stable, but, as was to be expected, he was thrown out of every one into which he tried to go as an unknown stray.

Darkness was already falling when we drove up and stopped outside a cottage. Our soldier disappeared through the door, in front of which a sentry paced up and down. Jumbo got out and sat down on our suitcase in the street, leaned his head in his hands and tried to rest. We forgot how we came to be there; just sought for shelter against the icy wind under the overhanging eaves of the cottage that gave none. The little township was dead, much of it in ruins. Suddenly, as we crouched there, the whole world fell silent, and then the moon sailed up into the darkness and lay there like the pearly inside of a shell on the black velvet of the sky.

I felt hopelessly abandoned and very apprehensive. Mixed up with my fears was another emotion, that I must call grief rather than melancholy, for in such conditions you cannot be melancholy. Melancholy is a luxury which you cannot always allow yourself, and at that time I had not sufficient peace of mind to indulge in even five minutes of it. Simple people are not usually melancholy; they are anxious, troubled, or in a bad temper, but real, genuine melancholy, the true origins of which are unknown, is foreign to them.

The little sentry, stamping his feet because of the cold, walked over to me.

"What did you come here for?" he asked, in a childish voice, his face almost invisible in the darkness.

"I don't know."

"Where did you learn Russian? What's your name? How old are you?"

And so began the usual Russian conversation, to the accompaniment of the incessant stamping of the little sentry's feet. Strange were the things we talked about in that deserted, ruined township as we shivered in the icy wind and frost.

"I," said the little sentry, "am just nineteen. I have been two years in the Army already. I am a volunteer. Before that I went to school and I should have gone to the University."

"What were you studying?"

"Everything. I know everything already."

"What, for example?"

"It's all right for you to ask that, but are you cultured yourself? Have you been educated? I learnt all about literature and music, but perhaps you think I'm lying? Well, we'll soon see what you know." And the little soldier suddenly asked cunningly, "Which is the best opera?"

"I don't know," I answered. "There are so many operas and they are so different that there isn't one that is best. You can only say which one you like best."

"No, no, that's not right. There you are. You don't know. You didn't study that. I know which is the best, *Rigoletto*, and the second best is *Tosca*, and the third, I think, *Carmen*, but I've forgotten that. You see, it's awfully easy to forget at the front. But the third best isn't really important, it's the first two that matter."

"All right," I answered, and in the darkness he couldn't see my smile. "And do you know literature?"

"Which one? You see, I know them all: English, German, French, and of course our own. It's true I haven't read everything, but I know who wrote what. I," the little lad was talking quickly as though afraid I would suddenly disappear and he be left alone again, "I like French best of all, for the French language is the most beautiful. Did you know that?"

"With us, there is no most beautiful language. Each likes his own best."

"Oh, no! That's not right. I don't know French, which is a pity, but I do know that it's the most beautiful. And do you know Russian literature?"

"I do. Both the old and the new."

"I prefer the old. What about you?" And, without waiting for an answer, "What of Leo Tolstoy's do you like best?"

"*Childhood Memories, Youth,* and *War and Peace.*"

"You're wrong. You've given the wrong answer again. *Anna Karenina* is his most beautiful book. You see? You didn't know. You thought it was *War and Peace.* And the best German writers are Schiller and Goethe, and the English, Shakespeare, and the French, Zola, Victor Hugo, and Maupassant. Which do you like best, Leo Tolstoy or Maupassant?"

"Tolstoy," I answered, dumbfounded, "if I have to choose."

"Wrong! wrong!" triumphed the lad. "You don't know. There's another thing you don't know. It's obvious that Maupassant is better, because French is the most beautiful language. You can't ever have been at the University?"

"No," I answered shamefacedly, and to myself I thought: Heavens, what do they teach these poor kids there?

"And do you know French?" I asked. "But you said yourself that you didn't. So how are you sure that it is the most beautiful language?"

"No," answered the childish voice in the darkness with a sigh. "No, I don't know French, but I have learned about it. And the best musicians? Come on, you tell me which were the best musicians. You're supposed to be cultured, educated."

"I am cultured and educated, but for all that I don't know which are the best. There are many best, and of them each chooses the one he likes best."

"There you are! Again you don't know. You're just trying to get out of it. And you said that you were educated! It doesn't say much for your sort of education. The three best musicians are Bach, Beethoven and Moljer."

"Who?" I asked.

"Molière," the childish voice repeated, this time quite distinctly.

I did not correct him. What was the use?

At long last the driver found, not, it is true, the H.Q. but a stable in a half-demolished cottage, where there was a room in which we were allowed to warm ourselves.

We followed him into a dark room where a small iron stove, covered with a perforated tin bowl instead of a lid, belched out smoke. You couldn't see anything but the smoke, and we felt as though we had fallen into a chimney. Half the room was taken up by bunks improvised out of a chest-of-drawers laid on its back, and from there came several snores. A lamp, as usual without a chimney, stood smoking on a table round which sat some soldiers and one officer.

When the driver went and left us alone, we were treated to hostile glances and silence. Suddenly, out of the silence, someone said, "We've caught some German spies." At once I set my "nice pussy" system in motion, gaily relating our own version of how we had got there and praying that the driver would not appear and give the lie to my story. I told them how we had been brought there specially to see the Colonel, for we had important information to give him; how nice and kind the Russians were to us, what wonderful food they had given us, the cigarettes, two packets every day, and the very best quarters. Here, at the front, it was different, of course. We had only come in to warm ourselves, for the Colonel would be sending for us almost at once. This improved the atmosphere somewhat and, as a sign of grace, Jumbo was given some old magazines to look at. I was interrupted once or twice, and told that I was lying and that I was a spy, but gradually the conversation did take on the intimate note of real friendship.

"You, listen! What do you call the medicines for syphilis in this country?"

I gazed in amazement at the Captain. "For syphilis?"

"Well?" said the officer impatiently. "Don't you know what syphilis is? Haven't you ever had it?" And to remove any doubt, he showed me where you get it.

This was a subject that took up a lot of time, and it developed into a discussion of which was the most effective cure. This was generally considered to be vodka, strong vodka, because it burns the blood. All the soldiers took part in the discussion, and when an hour later the driver returned the atmosphere in that dreadful hole was of the very best. "Nice pussy" had come off.

The driver announced that he had met someone who was quite sure that the H.Q. was in the village after all. The soldiers gave him advice how to continue his search, and we listened resignedly while the tears streamed down our faces from eyes that the smoke made sore. We were hungry and sleepy, and already beyond caring whether we were interrogated that day or not.

A wave of icy air swept into the hovel as a little Russian crept in with a billy-can which he gave to our driver. (The men in the hovel would not have fed him for anything in the world.) Enviously we watched the lad cutting up fat pieces of meat. The last time I had eaten had been at six that morn-

ing for I had not even tasted the potatoes brought us during
the afternoon. The driver saw the greedy look in my eyes and,
with a "Here you are!" gave me the remains in the billy-can
to finish. Don't get indignant! That lad undoubtedly took
us for dangerous subversive agents, and, as our driver, it was
no duty of his to feed us. That he gave me a few scraps from
his supper merely shows that he had a good heart. He had,
I think, come to feel sorry for us, but he had no business to
show it, and besides he was afraid of the strange lot sitting
round the table.

We set out on our search once more, this time on foot.
As we made our way through that dead township we could
hear nothing but the thud of our feet and the crunch of invisible sentries' boots in the snow. We walked so quickly
that we did not feel the icy wind. At last we halted in front
of a house and our driver disappeared inside. I squatted in
the snow, my back against a wall, and let my eyelids close.

Jumbo and I had long since stopped talking to each other.
We had always promised ourselves that whatever happened
we would be gay and joke about it, but we already found that
we had not even strength enough for talking, even though
nothing had so far happened to us. The door of the house
kept opening and shutting as officers with despatch-cases under their arms went in and out into the darkness. None of
them even glanced at us. Perhaps this was the place after all?
But no! An hour passed and then our driver came out and
once again we wandered about the empty streets between
lines of ruined houses. Why didn't the dawn come? Suddenly a small, thick-set officer appeared round a corner and
fell into step beside us. This was he, Major Koralchuk, the
man who was to interrogate us, or so we found out later. We
all walked on until we came to a large house on the main
street where we stopped. I had a good look round so as to
be able to recognize the place in daylight should the need
arise.

Jumbo was made to wait outside in the garden, while I

was taken in and shut into a dark and dirty room. At first I thought that I was alone, but then I heard the even breathing of men asleep on the floor. Through the wall came the sound of shouts and curses from the room next door. Out of sheer boredom I listened; they were playing cards. When on earth did these Russians sleep? Or didn't they? A strange soldier came in and summoned me for interrogation. Poor Jumbo was sure to get pneumonia standing there outside.

I walked across a dark hall and suddenly found myself in a brightly lit room. This must have been a high-ranking member of the N.K.W.D., for here for the first time was a proper lamp, clean and with a whole chimney. This room was typical of the provincial, bourgeois home, and at the table sat the same thick-set little Major who had joined us in the street. And so it began all over again, but the man's tone was very polite and quiet, and I breathed a sigh of relief. Why weren't they all like him?

Everything went swimmingly despite my poor Russian, that is until we came to Malta. Once again that thrice-accursed island proved a stumbling-block. Jumbo was sent for and also an interpreter, a wretched, nice peasant lad from a Catholic seminary in the neighbourhood. They began interrogating Jumbo through the interpreter, while I was sent out of the room. When they called me back they were still on Malta.

"How much does a Knight of Malta make?" asked the Major.

"It is an honorary appointment," gloomily answered Jumbo.

Then the Russian wanted to know what were the politics of the Knights of Malta, and patient Jumbo replied that they had none. "None," repeated the interpreter. Jumbo went on to explain that the Knights occasionally assembled for a congress, but that these were outside politics. At the word "congress," the Major pricked up his ears, and all his suspicions came tumbling back. He looked like a weasel on the scent.

The little interpreter took Jumbo's side, and translated everything beautifully, but he could get no sense into the Major's
head. Then I had a brilliant idea.

"Comrade Major," I began, my face very serious, "in the
backward countries of Europe the social institutions are not
so magnificently developed as they are in the Soviet Union.
Private initiative has often to take upon its shoulders things
that in Russia are the concern of the State. These Knights of
Malta have taken upon themselves the duty of building hospitals." And I added, emphatically, "They build hospitals."

I expanded this theme, the young interpreter nodding his
assent to my flow of words. By the time I had finished, I had
made of this snobbish association of idle sons of the aristocracy an organization of benefactors of poor suffering
humanity. The Major listened quietly, then dismissed us,
promising us a further instalment in the morning.

The Major personally conducted us through the dark
streets to an abandoned house where we were to spend the
night. We thanked him politely. We were back on the foot-
ing of guests.

There proved to be no room at all in the house, for soldiers
were sleeping everywhere, so the Major turned the first officer
he found out of his little room and gave us his bed. An
orderly came and helped me to get the stove alight, and then
brought meat and dumplings and hot tea. It was already very
late when we stretched out on the narrow bed and pulled our
sheepskin coats over us. What bliss! When I put out the
lamp, a little orange light from the stove played about the
floor, and the wood crackled in the flames.

In the morning I remembered that this was New Year's
Eve. Jumbo shaved, for which the little soldier brought him
water. The Russians, as you know, have a passion for shaving
and so are very sympathetic towards anyone wanting to remove his bristles. Again we were given tea and some excellent
dumplings. Jumbo began tucking in and asking questions.
Did you thank the Major properly? Did you tell him how

glad we were that the Red Army had come? I calmed his anxiety, as he washed the dumplings down with tea. Yes, of course! of course!

We knew now that the Major was human and rather nice, and that he did not regard us as criminals. Of course, he might still have the worst possible conception of the Order of the Knights of Malta, and suspect its members of being dangerous, because unknown, enemies of the U.S.S.R., but there was hope that I had convinced him. Just as we were saying this, the door opened and in walked the Major himself. After one or two cordial *"Zdrastvujtie's,"* he told us that we were free. We could hardly believe our ears, even though experience had taught us that everything is possible. I felt like hugging the fat major, but didn't as it might have been suspicious to have shown too much delight.

The Major asked how many miles we were from home. "Twelve," we replied.

"Well, you can either start walking now, or wait till to-morrow and I'll send you in my car."

With innocent expressions on our faces, we answered that we thought we ought to go on foot, that we had better go now, at once, because we had children waiting for us at home, and Jumbo asked for a pass.

"There's no need for a pass," said the Major, with a smile. "No one will stop you."

However, Jumbo, the incorrigible European, would not move without some document and insisted on being given a pass. We were given it and proudly set out, I in front munching a piece of Army bread, and Jumbo behind with our suit-case.

That morning the wind was stronger than ever. Though it was hardly light, the place was already swarming with Russians. Only then did we see how dreadfully the township had suffered. We passed the huge manor house of some friends of ours, standing in its lovely park. It was a ruin: its window-frames torn out, the doors wrenched off and half-burned. It

was much more badly damaged than Mora. We would have
to tell Tacitus about that. Perhaps it would comfort him,
poor man. We walked quickly and gaily, I turning round
every other moment to smile at Jumbo, my mouth full of
black bread. Never had I felt so free, so unfettered. On the
very fringe of the houses a soldier suddenly stopped us. There
was an evil glint in his eye.

"Where are you going?"

"Home," I answered and thrust the Major's pass under
his nose.

"What Major? What do I care about your Major? I
don't know this Major of yours. A Major! Huh! Off you go.
Back where you came from!"

They led us back along the same road, back to the house
opposite the Manor. It was swarming with soldiers with green
epaulettes, the Field Security, or Counter-Intelligence, but
that we did not know then. What did they want of us? In
the courtyard was a crowd of ragged figures with sacks on their
backs: obviously poor peasants who had been caught while
trying to make their way home through the front.

Then it began all over again. Where did you learn Russian? How old are you? How did you get here? Why is your
husband older than you? Have you any children? Why not?
The Russians are the most inquisitive people in the world.
Inquisitiveness and a tendency to lie are the two main characteristics of the Russian soldier. After questioning us, they
began writing down, or pretending to write down, the personal particulars of the peasants. Jumbo was to help me act
as interpreter. Perhaps, after that, they would let us go, I
secretly hoped.

When they had inspected the papers of the last of these
tatterdemalions, an order rang out: "Forward! March!"

"And we?" I asked, hoping that now they would let us go.

"You? What are you asking for? Get on, along with the
rest!"

They led us across the yard, through a garden gate, and

lined us up with our backs to a wall: an unpleasant sensation. The peasants were visibly appalled, but none dared say a word.

"But our pass," I called out in despair. "The Major himself wrote it."

But it was no use. We had got into the hands of another command, another lot that just laughed at our major. We all stood there with our backs against the wall, united by our common misfortune and fears. No one dared open his mouth. Then a Russian ordered us to move off one by one. I translated this into French for Jumbo, and he repeated it to the peasants. There was a general sigh of relief, for we had thought that we were going to be shot, and that was what it had looked like with us lined up with our backs to the wall and several Russians standing in front of us with automatic pistols at the ready. Then our turn came, and Jumbo and I were led into a small courtyard. Ye gods, and I had thought that we should spend New Year's Eve at home!

In the courtyard stood a small, pock-marked soldier with a cocked revolver in his hand. His leather harness was grey and uncared for, his eyes evil and colourless like water. Beyond him I could see the bolted door of a sort of stable, a pacing sentry and a young woman in a thin overcoat, weeping. By the door was a window. It was filled with faces, pale, unshaven, exhausted faces.

"To be searched," said the soldier.

This lot evidently had a mania for searching people, for we had been searched twice already: once while they examined the peasants' documents, which none of the Russians had been able to read, and again as we stood lined up against the wall. Now we were to be searched a third time, although the soldiers knew by heart what we had in our suitcase.

"Surrender your watches," was the next order. Jumbo obediently, though rather surprised, handed his watch to the soldier. "You'll get it back after being interrogated," the man assured him.

Why the watch! What could be dangerous about a watch? Well, if they wanted a watch, there it was. Again I tried to explain that we had a pass from the Major, and that they had no right to arrest us as we had been sent home.

"We'll soon check your pass," mocked the soldier, blinking his colourless eyes, "and we don't care about your Major anyway. That's another unit. Who knows what you've been up to since they let you go. A Major! What's a Major to us? Or a General? Get in there and sit quietly."

So we were shoved in through that door at which I had been looking the whole time, and the bolt shot behind us. In that tiny space, half in darkness, stood a crowd of people, standing because there was no room to sit. They were all men, all poor, and all smelt of sweat, garlic and dirt. Jumbo squeezed into one corner, I into another, and we began the first timid attempt to start a conversation. In a little while they began to have confidence in us. We learned that some had been kept there for three days already without food; but why they were there no one knew.

Then a young, pleasant Hungarian, the local interpreter, came in, and Jumbo turned on him his famous eloquence. I did not understand much of that flood of Hungarian, but I was delighted to see that the young man seemed very inclined to help. He kept nodding his head, promised to speak with the Commander, then he went out and we heard the bolt being pushed back into place. Time dragged along as we waited. I had managed to find a spot where I could squat on the floor that was too dirty to sit on, had that even been possible. The crowd of prisoners whispered among themselves, though there were many who remained silent, gazing dully in front of them.

Suddenly the door opened. The sentry called me and I leaped out, Jumbo forcing his way through the crowd with our suitcase. Behind the sentry I could see the smiling face of the nice interpreter, so perhaps he had managed it.

"Well, away home with you. Here's your pass."

"And the watch?" I asked, for I had become infected with Jumbo's European ideas.

"You'd better not ask about anything," said the sixteen-year-old sentry gravely. "Just you hurry home, as fast as your legs will carry you. This is not a healthy place. I'm giving you good advice. Off with you."

I knew that the little sentry was right.

"Couldn't you come with us for a bit, so that we don't get caught again?" I asked.

"I can't. I'm on duty," he replied regretfully. "But they'll all be having their dinner now, so if you hurry perhaps they won't catch you again."

We shook hands with a grip that showed that we understood one another, although we had known each other only thirty seconds.

I had the pass, Jumbo carried the suitcase, and so we hurried away, making for home as fast as our legs would carry us as the young sentry had advised. We passed the unlucky spot where they had caught us before: not a sign of a Russian. Presumably they were still having their dinner. We passed the last of the houses: not a soul about. What a wonderful time for spies!

We did not even talk. We just walked very quickly, afraid to run in case that should look suspicious to anyone who might happen to see us. At last we were out of the town and in open country. We shook hands solemnly, and then, scarcely believing in our freedom, hurried on, hurried for home.

Telephone wires straggled along the road, and in one place there were some soldiers in a ditch, heating up some tins over a fire. A voice shouted after us, "Where are you going?" "Wait," I whispered breathlessly to Jumbo, "don't move. I'll go up and talk to them myself." And I walked towards them slowly and seemingly unworried munching my black bread.

"What do you want, lad?" I asked. "What's that you're

cooking there? Tins? I'm off for my lunch, too. Going home. I've got a pass."

"Well, go then!" they said, not finding me interesting, and turned back to the fire and their tins.

I didn't walk so much as fly back to Jumbo, and we hurried away across fields and meadows, along country lanes full of pot-holes, for a good ten miles and all the time against the wind. We quarrelled about who was to carry the suitcase, rested in ditches beside the road, continually took short cuts along paths known to Jumbo since his childhood, until at last we reached the boundary of the village. Battling with the wind had cost us a lot of time. Jumbo halted, unable to walk any farther. It was growing dark and the whole country was a white wilderness across which the snow danced in clouds, driven by the fierce wind. We felt like Nobile or Captain Scott. I was afraid that we might not find the village in the darkness, and hounded Jumbo on, trying for the hundredth time to relieve him of the suitcase, but he would not let go.

Then we were walking through the village itself. There at our garden gate stood Rudi and Marietta. Rudi had seen us and was running to meet us; then dear Marietta turned and ran in the other direction to announce the great news.

There were no Russians left in Mora. The last had driven away in a lorry that morning, leaving us three car skeletons in the garden.

Mora Boundary

1st–7th January

IN THE morning I ran straight to the cellar. The few days we had spent in it now seemed an eternity, and we had gone through so much in them that I could not tear myself away from it. Tacitus and his family were in the course of moving out, Marietta staggering under a load of rugs and suitcases, while Tacitus himself stood watching her and telling her not to do too much.

"We've lost everything," he groaned, "it's dreadful, dreadful. I'm a beggar."

He repeated this over and over again, so sorry for himself that he forgot to help his wife. At that moment Franzi arrived back from the village with the news that twenty Russians had just arrived with a hundred horses, all of them sick or wounded, and that there was to be a veterinary hospital in Mora. That was a sign that we were now well behind the front, and, as such, good news.

I did not need to work that first day, so I strolled about the garden, still hardly able to believe that I was home. Near the broken fence lay the skeletons of the three cars the Russians had abandoned. All three were of American manufacture. They had painted on them in large red letters: *For the Fatherland. To Berlin. Victory is Near.* They were stuck fast in the frozen mud, and had been stripped of their wheels and engines.

The Russians make excellent drivers, as do the Arabs, for example, and they are also good mechanics, but they are so careless and so extravagant with their machines that this aptitude is not of much benefit to them. They never nurse any bit of machinery and they will always expend three to five times as much ammunition as is necessary. Just as they are appallingly extravagant with Nature's gifts, so they never think of economising with what man has made. This is not due, as many Europeans would think, to a mania for destruction. No, it is just that they have no respect whatever for anyone else's work, nor for the centuries of toil that lie behind our technical achievements. And there is nothing surprising in that. Russia took no part in the research work carried out by the civilized world during the last two or three centuries, though she has benefited by it. Russia received the whole of our civilization ready-made, was given it on a platter, scarcely twenty years ago. It was our ancestors and grandfathers, not the Russians, who gave mankind the magnifying glass and the microscope, who enabled us to hear across the world with the telephone and wireless. They invented the iron horse at a time when in Russia a *troika* was the best conveyance there was; and steamers were puffing up and down the rivers of America and Europe, when in Russia barges were still being hauled to the tune of the "Volga Boatmen." We have learned to respect the machines built by our fathers' toil, as we do our own fingers, our own hands. That is our inheritance, and it has entered into our blood. Our fathers still remember how all these machines took shape, grew and were perfected before their very eyes. We were not given them ready-made: they did not fall down to us from heaven, like manna, as they did in Russia, and that is why we treat them with such great respect. But not so the Russian. All these shiny toys found their way to Russia for the first time a bare twenty years ago, and then, for the first time, the Russians made acquaintance with wireless, motor-cars, typewriters and manufacturing machinery in their present perfected state.

Ever since then they have been playing with those strange toys like children, as though they had just fished them out of their Christmas stockings. They play with steam-engines as with those queer dolls that say "Mama" and "Papa"; they take watches to bits, because for them it's not enough that a watch should go, just as it's not enough for a child that its doll says "Mama"; the best fun of all is to see what is inside, to see how the wheels go round. And they do not mind in the least if after this operation the doll falls silent for ever, or the watch ceases to go. This, too, is the fate of cameras, wireless sets or any other machine. And how the Russians like shooting! After four years of war the Russian soldier had not yet grown tired of firing off his automatic pistol at any time of the day or night, just for the sake of the bang. Russians do not grow up. They remain children. I do not know why that is, but I do know that if you look at the Russian masses from this perspective you will understand many things and pardon many others.

By the evening, Tacitus and his family had moved out of the shelter, leaving only Fifi, Jack and Franzi there. Jumbo had agreed to let me spend one last farewell night with them in the shelter, and to make it as pleasant as possible we invited all three dogs to join us: Isa, Samuel, and Alf.

Isa and Alf you know. Samuel has not as yet been introduced. There is not much to be said about him, for he was a child, a mere four months old, and reminiscent of no special breed. He was small, with pointed ears and a foxy face, in build like a fox terrier. He was never still and gnawed everything. The Russians adored Samuel, for to them he was a toy. He was as indefatigable as they, and gnawed them all day and all night, for they always asked to be allowed to borrow him for the night. These three we invited to our farewell party in the shelter.

With the door shut, we felt like mice when the cat had died. We produced a bottle of old Tokay and stole some sweets that Rudi had carelessly left behind, but only one each, for we still had some morals left. We only gave Franzi half a glass, explaining that his parents did not like it when their son drank alcohol. We petted the dogs, since they were our guests, and I even took Samuel on to my paillasse and patiently let him gnaw me. As we lay there, we talked again of our country, our homes and our families. Latterly, we had been doing this more and more often, a sure sign of bad times.

The second day of the New Year was taken up with moving out of the shelter and domestic bickering, for we had begun to quarrel about the rooms. How we were to heat them we did not know, for there was neither wood nor coal. Tacitus, however, was still in a lord-of-the-manor frame of mind and ordered some old peasant (a young one would not have obeyed) to bring a coke stove from the Manor, and this was brought and installed in the hall. Then he gave orders for coke to be brought, and the coke was brought in sacks and put in the woodshed. Then he gave orders for girls to come and scrub the floor, but here he fell down: the girls refused. Tacitus decided that they must have gone Communist overnight. He was incensed, but did not take it to heart, nor, after that experience, did he cease to give orders which were sometimes carried out and sometimes ignored.

This was a mistake, as orders should only be given when you are absolutely sure that they will be carried out or when you can apply immediate sanctions against the recalcitrant. Otherwise it is always better to ask, and that is why our room never gave any orders: we cleaned our own boots, lit our own stove, fetched our own water.

That day, too, Franzi and Jack went to the stables to work among the Russian horses. Both were horsemen and it was work that suited them well. They had, besides, little choice, for an order had come from the village council that all men must report for work.

There were hardly any men left in the village, for the Russians had sent them with horses away back behind the

front, but by some miracle Jack had managed to get himself
and Franzi out of going with them. Tacitus, Rudi and Jumbo
either were or pretended to be ill, and so did not dare be seen
working, even in the garden. Tacitus would smoke his cigarettes and watch his guests, women all of them, working in
the courtyard. To us it was rather amusing that the men
were not allowed even to help us. With the work we found
a sort of calm: we had the house and each had enough work
to do, food to eat, and cigarettes to smoke. The front had
moved on, and all that we could hear was the sound of gun-
fire from the direction of the capital. The two boys had a
pleasant job and were close at hand. In other words, everything had turned out for the best.

Late the next morning a quartermaster appeared and, as
a result of his visit, Dolly, with many heavy sighs, had to re-
linquish her "indispensable" nursery and the dining-room.
This involved much feverish moving of furniture, carrying of
suitcases, and running about with bundles of bedding.

In the end we finished changing the rooms round, barri-
caded the door to the dining-room with a heavy table, and sat
down to wait for the officers who were supposed to be arriving
in the afternoon. Instead of officers, to our great surprise,
there arrived seventeen drunken soldiers, headed by a middle-
aged Mongol. The next three months, however, convinced us
that to get officers billeted on us was next to impossible, for,
although our rooms were always taken for officers, it was always a horde of soldiers that came. In the end we discovered
the reason: the quartermasters had originally been given orders
not to take billets for the officers in peasants' cottages because
it was thought that the European peasant lived like his Russian counterpart. When it was discovered that the peasants
lived like "Western bourgeois," the officers, who went about
in twos and threes, preferred to have billets in the peasants'
cottages where there were girls and "home comfort," feather
beds, warm stoves, and a stuffiness; where, in other words,

they could feel at home, and our large, "uncomfortable" rooms were left for the men.

Our house was not classed as a good billet. The house was large and there were two or three entrances, so that at least two sentries would be needed, all the rooms opened into each other, there were fifteen people in the house who had a mania for letting in fresh air, the beds were not feather beds, the stoves were seldom lit, and every cigarette end or sunflower seed was picked up as soon as seen. In other words, there was something uncanny about the house and it was better to keep away. And then we ourselves were an uncanny lot: six feet tall, as thin as a lot of consumptives, supposed to be bourgeois and so only fit to be destroyed, yet on closer acquaintance rather nice and cultured, for we knew who Maksim Gorki was and Gogol and Pushkin; some of us even spoke Russian, were Slavs and allies, so they couldn't very well kill us, could they? Yet, taking us all in all, to them we were horribly strange.

I got to know hundreds of ordinary soldiers, and I never found one really bad person among them. I was to hear much of how they stole, looted and raped. They do that when they are drunk, or when their commander is an evil person himself and exercises a bad influence on them. And one must always remember that if the Russian soldier is good and human, it is not due to the discipline that restrains those of other armies but to the inherent good qualities of the Russian nation. In the Red Army what we call discipline just does not exist. The Russian soldier ought by right to have been a dreadful and a dangerous person, for he has neither discipline nor even religion to restrain him, and from childhood has been taught that Europe is inhabited by bloodsuckers whom he ought to destroy. But get to know him properly, which the Government will never allow if it can help it, watch him when he is not drunk, sleep beside him on the same truss of straw, eat with him out of the one dish, share your or his last cigarette with him, and you will see that nowhere are there so many good

people as in Russia. To the outside world it would appear exactly the reverse, and I cannot help it if no one believes me.
I shan't go into the reasons for this phenomenon, but merely
write what I saw and experienced. In trying to keep as close
as possible to the truth it may seem at times that I am con-
tradicting myself, but that is merely proof of my accuracy, for
truth is many-sided like a well-cut diamond.

After appearing one morning in the kitchen, one soldier
called Ignaty came back day after day with unfailing regu-
larity as long as he was in Mora. He came to chat with me
and to play with Samuel, and he would bring me cigarettes
and lay them rather shamefacedly on the kitchen table, saying
each time, "We've got a lot of cigarettes in the lorry. Take
them, Lida, we've got lots left. Smoke away. I don't smoke,
so I need none."

Then he would sit down, pleased and smiling, crack his
fingers, which many of the others also did, and wait for
Samuel. The pup would be summoned and the game begin.
Samuel would attack Ignaty, Ignaty would laugh and pretend
to defend himself, and so on *ad infinitum*. Ignaty felt quite
at home. He never spoke much, and, as he played with the
dog, would slowly sip the tea that Matilda would set down
beside him.

It was on the morning that Ignaty first appeared that I
also became acquainted with Nicolas, a sergeant and my great
friend. I shall never forget him. Ignaty had just taken his
departure, well gnawed by Samuel and happy at having
exchanged a few sentences in Russian, when I heard the quavering voices of the Hungarians calling, "Lida! Lida!" Whenever the Hungarians called, "Lida! Lida!" like that, I knew
that there were Russians in sight and tore as fast as I could
to the kitchen. That morning it was Nicolas who came in.
His tunic was dirty, his forage-cap pulled over his eyes, his
face dusky and serious. He was tall, looked thirty-eight, and
was twenty-eight. He greeted me, sat down when I asked

him to, and I opposite him; and that was the beginning of our friendship.

Nicolas did not want to know how old I was nor why I had no children. Nor was he interested in the reason why I had left Poland, nor whether the Hungarians ill-treated me as all Europeans did the Slavs. Nicolas just wanted to talk about himself and was delighted to have found someone who could understand him and whom in a few days he would lose sight of forever.

Nicolas had never had a home (I think he must have been the son of a Kulak) and he had no friends and no acquaintances. Without even knowing that such a word existed, he was a philosopher, and his head was stuffed with unexpressed thoughts, for he was well used to keeping his mouth shut. That first morning, we just sniffed each other over like two strange dogs, but before very long Nicolas was talking with absolute trust, which I still don't know what I did to deserve.

"I come from the Ukraine, but when I was twelve, or something like that, I was sent off to Siberia to prison, and I don't really have a country, for I got out just before the war and was sent straight to the front. I was just a common soldier, for I had been in prison, but now after four years I am already a sergeant," and he proudly repeated, "a sergeant."

"Are you married?" I stupidly asked.

"How could I be? I'm twenty-eight now. When I went into the Army I was twenty-four or twenty-five, there was no time to get married. They put me away when I was a child."

"What for?"

"I don't know," answered Nicolas, with the greatest indifference. "With us there were millions who spent years in prison not knowing why they were there. Then the war came and freed them. They were all sent to the front."

"But how can they imprison children and keep them shut up for years? It's horrible! Why do they do it?"

"Why?" repeated Nicolas, with a smile. "Why? What

a strange question. People are always asking why, here. I'll tell you something: suppose some drunks come to your house, break it up, kill your husband, rape you, and not content with that, smash your windows before they leave. Then you sit there weeping and wondering why. Why did they do it? And they who did it go back home, sleep it off, and when they wake up remember something vaguely and think to themselves: now why did we do that? Why? And no one knows why it happened, so much unhappiness, so much damage, and no one got anything out of it."

"That's all very well, Nicolas, but those are private matters between individuals that the law punishes. But the State cannot be judged by those standards. The State isn't a drunkard, nor a defenceless woman."

"The State? It's just the same. The State is people, too, only they are allowed more scope. Now, listen," said Nicolas patiently and seriously, as though trying to explain something very simple to a stupid child, "there are States that are rich, and they have lived peacefully and could have gone on living peacefully, or perhaps even better, but, no, they want war, so they let the people who will help them in it come to power and they bring a war upon the country. And the other States, their neighbours, they too have to elect the same sort of people to defend themselves properly. And hundreds of thousands of people are killed, maimed, cottages burned, cattle slaughtered, and for what? Why? And yet, it has always been like that. Look at the world now! Will anyone get anything out of this? Will even one person benefit by it? And yet millions and millions are gladly taking part. And, why? Come, Lida, tell me why?"

"I don't know, Nicolas."

"There you are! And yet, you ask why they shut me up when I was a small boy, and why they kept me in prison for years, and hundreds of thousands like me. What is my wasted youth in comparison with what is happening now? I'm not in the least bit interested why I was in prison."

And I did not know what to answer. I tried to explain that Hitler was guilty of it all, but Nicolas, with a grave shake of his head, refused to accept that.

"No, Lida," he said. "Hitler to-day, but to-morrow it will be somebody else. And always because people want it that way."

"Mankind is evil," I said.

"Oh, no!" and Nicolas waved his hand, as though brushing away an old, worn-out lie, "people aren't bad, just people. Neither good, nor bad. And what do you expect of them, poor fools? They can't be different. They are as they are. Just people," and Nicolas spread out his hands in a hopeless gesture, seeing that I did not understand. "Their lives are too short, that's what's wrong. You see, if they could live longer, for two hundred years or so, they might be able to see what things were worthwhile and what were not, in this world. But what can you do; before a man has time to look round properly, it's all over and time to die."

For a while neither of us spoke, then Nicolas changed the subject.

"I'm a sergeant now. I've gained that much promotion. Perhaps I shan't be killed, and then I'll go back to Russia. I have no family and no home, but perhaps I'll find a girl who hasn't a home or a family either, and then a new home and a new family will arise from us two homeless orphans." And a smile flitted across his face.

"And do you want to live, Nicolas, and to have children?"

"Indeed I do! I haven't lived at all yet. I learned everything in the Camp. When I saw that it is possible to have a family and children and a woman of your own in your home, I at once thought that I, too, would like to live like that. Why?" and he gave me a cunning little smile. "Well, Lida, why?"

"Nicolas," I asked, pretending not to have heard the question, "why did you come to see me? How did you get here?"

"They told me in the village that there was one of ours

in this house. A woman who spoke Russian. And I looked in for a chat."

"Hm, so I'm 'one of ours,'" I thought, and then added aloud, "I'm very glad you came. Come again; every day if you like."

"As long as I'm in the village I'll come every day."

Then Nicolas stood up, gave me his hand, pulled his cap even lower over his eyes, and walked out, and I went back to my work.

When I looked at the notes which are the basis of this book to see what else happened that day after Nicolas' visit, I found the rather mysterious sentence, "the usual domestic intrigues," and then I remembered everything. We used to quarrel almost the whole time in those days. Quarrel, perhaps, is not the right word, for it was quarrelling that never broke out, but just seethed below the surface like lava in a volcano. Each bore some grudge against the other, each complained of the other but never outright to the person concerned but behind his back. We intrigued one against the other, which made me more expert at it than I had even had to be before.

I, for example, had a permanent complaint that Marietta, Elsie and Dolly either did too little or no work at all. It incensed me to see them going about normally dressed, washing their hands five times a day in water that I had carried from the well, which was a long way away, powdering and painting their faces. This wasn't just the jealousy of a dirty woman in rags, but because their clothes and hair made my work with the Russians more difficult. It was difficult to pretend that we were paupers and that we did not know where the bourgeois, who had lived there before the Russians came to Mora, had gone, when Dolly was liable at any moment to trip into the kitchen on her high heels, dressed in a faultless English coat and skirt and playing with a string of pearls lying on top of an Angora sweater. She looked like something out of a fashion book: slim, tall (5 feet 7 inches) and very pretty.

Of course, her beauty was not a thing to attract the Russians. It was quite beyond their comprehension; they hadn't developed far enough to appreciate it, nor yet her English coat and skirt which to their minds was a very ugly garment for a woman.

Usually they would hardly have stopped gaping at Dolly when Marietta would come into the kitchen, too. She was thinner and still taller, and, like Dolly, she too wore a sports costume of home-spun, an Angora sweater, and a string of wonderful pearls. The two of them at once was too much for the Russians. They could understand one such monster being born, but that there were two of them meant some sort of race. They would at once ask who they were, and their whole attitude was one of uneasiness, even apprehension. They did not know in what category to place these two strange figures who moved about the kitchen like a couple of greyhounds, sticking their noses into the pots and giving the old servants orders in muffled voices. You see, every Russian automatically took Lina and Matilda to be the mistresses of the house, for the simple reason that they saw that they were supreme in the kitchen, cooking, washing, and cleaning boots. Then, suddenly, two supernatural beings would appear and begin giving them orders, so, of course, there was a flood of questions: were Lina and Matilda the mistresses? Was Lina my mother? Who were those women and why did they interfere in the kitchen? Why didn't Lina and Matilda turn them out? Was the old man cutting wood outside (Tacitus) Lina's husband? No! Well, the other's, then? Not her's, either? Why didn't he help Matilda and Lina to get rid of those two? And what about you? Are you the thin one's servant? It's obvious she doesn't give you enough to eat, that's why you've got as skinny as she, the mean bitch. Starves herself, and won't let others eat. Or perhaps she's a bourgeois? Are you the servant of a bourgeois? Admit it. You don't want to say so because you're afraid that if we do anything to them they'll take it out of you. You're a fool. You look like a stick, what did you take such a service for?

So you see it wasn't only feminine jealousy that made me so furious with them. Elsie was more modestly dressed, didn't wear pearls, and was, besides, more normal in her measurements, so that she didn't attract attention. I was pleased with her.

The Russians have no conception of what breeding means. They have no idea of the significance of a slender leg, a narrow hand, a delicate oval face, or good masculine features. The strange thing is, that, as these are things that just don't exist in Russia, they ought to notice them all the more. To them any cook wearing a hat with a drooping veil and a fur coat of imitation rabbit, is a bourgeois, absolutely bound to be, yet a woman like the Austrian Empress Elizabeth would pass unnoticed among them as long as she had dirty nails and a scarf around her head.

The Russians often asked me sympathetically whether I wasn't consumptive, and twice I was asked whether I hadn't had an operation, for they just could not understand how I could be so thin if I ate normally, and could only attribute it to an operation. I was often asked, too, whether Honono was Muki's mother, and I always said that she was, begging Dolly not to admit to her own child, as long as she did not deign to look after it.

Then, too, I had a grudge against Tacitus. He did chop wood, but very seldom, and though he did have only one kidney and dared not show himself outside in case they took him off to forced labour, it always annoyed me that he waited for everything to be done for him. It took a long time before he finally understood that no one was going to do his work for him, and set about chopping his own wood with many groans and sighs.

I was angry, too, with Matilda. Ever since the Russians appeared, she had stopped treating me as one of the gentry.

The fact that I drank and joked with the soldiers, that I went about dirty and in rags, degraded me completely in her eyes. As she once told me, she liked real ladies!

Then Marietta. Marietta never did any work on the grounds that she had had such a bad time when she gave birth to Franzi, eighteen years before, that Tacitus had forbidden her to do anything but look after him.

Elsie was capricious and preferred abusing Tacitus to working, while Dolly had her knife into her because she never seemed to do any work except when it meant being alone with Dolly's husband, Rudi.

Jumbo was the only one whose state of mind was still normal, and so he acted as confidant for us all, a post that required a great deal of tact and diplomacy.

Now you understand what I meant by "usual domestic intrigues."

Rudi and Muki

8th-14th
January

ACH morning I got up at six to light the stove. Kindling a fire is one of the oldest of the human arts and, in my opinion, there is something wrong with those who do not know it. I do not trust such people. Fire is like a living being, and the kindling of it a thing you ought to have in your blood. Each morning at daybreak, I would, like Prometheus, call my fire to life and feed it on fir-cones, twigs and the love-letters of my niece, of which I had found a boxful in the attic.

First, I would light the candle, then quietly, so as not to wake the others, steal across the room to the stove, open it and remove the ashes. Then I would build an ingenious little pyramid of sticks, surmount it with two well-dried fir-cones and some fir bark, selecting my material as a chef does the ingredients of a sauce; then I would light one of the love letters at the candle and slowly and carefully, so as not to knock the fragile pyramid down, push it in under the sticks. That done I would quickly close the little iron door so as not to scare the infant flames, and in a moment or two, a warm, orange glow would appear in the ash-tray, and the newborn fire would crackle merrily in delight at my gift of life, and the glow from it would leap on to the floor in a quivering patch of warm light. I would crouch there beside the stove and all around me would be silence and dark night. The fire would crackle away for a while, then I would open the little iron door again and carefully lay a log on the dancing flames. The fir-cones without changing shape had now changed colour, becoming red, and the heat in them would pulsate like blood in a vein, and the whole stove would be filled with gleams of light and dancing, leaping shadows. Then I, witness of one of the oldest miracles, would shut the little door again and crouch there motionless, watching the patch of light on the floor expanding and contracting, and listening to the fire seizing upon the log and roaring in the chimney as it devoured it. It was as though I had been a magician, and the fire I had created raged in the confines of the stove, mastered and tamed. Is it any wonder that fire used to be a powerful god in the old days when it came to life of itself and consumed what it liked and as much as it liked?

The room would slowly grow warmer and warmer, and I would remain crouching there, spellbound by the fire panting in the stove. I would light a cigarette. That was the nicest moment in my day.

Then I would go for water. The Russians had broken practically all the pumps, and the old well by the river, with its tall crane, was one of the few places left where water could be drawn.

Nicolas came in the morning. We sat down facing each other across the kitchen table and again we talked of the world and of how queer people are.

"You know," said Nicolas, "I was in Yugoslavia not long ago. I lived with a very rich old peasant. He had two hundred sheep, many pigs, one wife and no children, no grandchildren, nor even relations. He and his wife both went about barefoot, in sheepskin coats, and they lived in a miserable little cottage. I asked him why he didn't give his sheep away to the poor seeing that he lived like a pauper and had nothing from them, but that just made him angry: why should he give his good sheep away? Then I asked why he didn't sell one or two and buy boots for himself and his wife in their old age, and new sheepskin coats. Why should I, he asked, we're not cold. It would be a waste of money. Better to buy another young pig in the spring. Look, Lida, that's how people are; instead of giving things away to the poor and just leaving themselves enough for their needs, when they could afford to, they scrape every penny together, sweat and toil all their lives, seize hold of whatever they can, get every penny out of everything, as though there were no such thing as death, as though they would live for ever. If he wanted to go about barefoot, he could have done so just as well with twenty sheep. But no! the sheep were his. That's how it was. Now, you tell me, what is a sheep?"

"A sheep? How do you mean? A sheep is, well, a domesticated animal. What are you getting at?"

"Repeat after me," said Nicolas, "a sheep is an animal: meat, fat and wool. Meat, fat and wool. Repeat that."

"Meat, fat and wool," I said, smiling.

"But once they are yours, they become your life's blood. The moment you get them, they are no longer meat, nor wool, but the very blood in your veins. Why? Don't they see that a sheep is only a sheep and will never be anything else? Never anything but a sheep. No matter to whom it belongs. Why does a sheep turn into life's blood, the moment it belongs to someone?"

And Nicolas, his brow puckered in the effort of thinking, gazed at me without seeing me.

"And you would think that one sheep was worth a thousand times as much to a man who had only five of them as to a man with two hundred. And yet both are equally attached to it, find it equally hard to part with it. And that old peasant, for example, though I spoke to him about it every day, he never gave even one away, and when I left he still had two hundred. Isn't that queer? And what will he get out of it?" asked Nicolas, and then, added with that twisted, shy smile of his, "Why?"

"If only he had given a few away," Nicolas went on, "it would have given so much pleasure and he would have had something out of life. Such a lot of pleasure, and he himself would have had less bother, less work. But people love the bother that goes with wealth, they prefer it to giving a poor man a present. They even prefer it to their own lives. That's mankind for you!"

Nicolas spoke the words "That's mankind for you!" as though he did not include himself in that category, as though there existed other, higher beings on our planet, of whom he considered himself one and who to him were straightforward and comprehensible, in contrast to mankind which was unenlightened, with no knowledge of life and unable to learn how to live it. How badly I wanted that Nicolas should come every day and give me the illusion that there were such beings on our earth!

He sat on for a while without speaking, lost in thought, then he shoved his cap right back on to the crown of his head, a sign of amazed puzzlement, stood up, gave me his hand to shake, and walked out without a word. He came just once more, and only to say good-bye.

The door had scarcely closed behind him, when I heard the usual cries of "Lida! Lida!" and into the kitchen crept Ignaty, a shy smile on his face, and three dirty, crumpled cigarettes in his outstretched hand.

"Hullo, Lida!" he said, and his childish smile was as grave and lovely as if he had been some herald angel. "Here you are. I've brought you a few cigarettes."

He put the cigarettes on the table and remained standing there, like the angel, a little embarrassed, but at the same time happy and feeling honoured.

Ignaty was followed by his friend, a fat, elderly, conceited soldier, who looked inquisitively all about him. I was just on the point of summoning Samuel to come and play with Ignaty, but then I saw from the look on the friend's face that there were to be no games that day.

When you are continually on your guard, continually afraid, and continually on the watch, your perspicacity develops amazingly. In time, I grew so good that I was able to place a Russian into one of several categories the moment I saw him, and so treat him accordingly. This friend that the unfortunate Ignaty had brought with him belonged to one of the worst categories: that of the thick-headed, self-appointed agitator who is blind to everything he doesn't want to see, the type of person that can wander all over Europe and learn nothing from it. Such was the friend poor Ignaty had brought with him, and, as though this were not enough, they were followed by a young Hungarian, the joiner in Mora, who now went about wearing a red armlet. Young Ignaty was greatly impressed by these two, and evidently wanted to show off in front of them: how clever he was to have discovered such a house as ours; for to Ignaty our house was like something out of the Arabian Nights. But to his friends it was anything but a fairy-tale. The young joiner had come as an interpreter, and and we were in for a real interrogation, which Ignaty's elderly friend conducted.

Having been told everything about me including, of course, that I had no children and why, he began a tirade against the bourgeois. He told us straight out that we were bourgeois, pointed at Matilda and roared that we were sucking her blood, even though she was old and scarcely able to stand. And as he roared, the row of medals on his chest waggled quickly from side to side. I explained that Matilda was a friend of the lady of the house and that she didn't work at all hard, which was true. Matilda, seeing that we were talking about her and proud of it, ruffled her invisible feathers, and flapping her arms like a vulture defending its carrion, launched an attack.

"Yes," shouted Matilda, understanding nothing of what was going on, and so quite off the point, "twenty years I have been serving the master and mistress, faithfully serving. Twenty years I've been in the family. The old mistress, I won't say she was bad, but the amount she tormented you, may she rest in peace, that's beyond description, and yet I stood it all for I loved her." Here her voice gave a pathetic sob and tears appeared in her eyes and began twisting down her old face that was grey with dirt.

I did not know what she was driving at, nobody did, not even the cunning little joiner.

"And what have I gained by it?" Matilda was well away now. "Nothing, thanks to this cursed war. Why can't you stop fighting? Kill whom you have to, and go home! What am I to do, poor orphan that I am? Twenty years and my good mistress is dead, my dear one, only one, and her son, the very spit of her, just as choosey, won't leave me in peace either. Only the best is good enough for him!"

Matilda's harangue, though quite pointless, was listened to carefully by all present.

"A bourgeois?" asked Ignaty's friend, pointing at me.

"Yes, yes," replied that nice, intelligent woman, "great bourgeois, proper, genuine bourgeois, gentry: one's a minister, the mistress a countess in her own right, the sister-in-law, too: a great family, very rich, there's another estate beside this one," she went on, undeterred by my poisonous glances.

It was as though Matilda wanted them to know that though she might be only a cook, she was cook to no mean family.

"What horses they had here," she went on, "and so many cows, more than anyone else in the whole parish." (Which was not true.)

The young Hungarian, who understood every word, gave a slight smile. Matilda punctuated her harangue with wild gestures and peppered it with Slovak and Russian phrases lest the Russians should not properly realize how splendid was the house and family in which she had had the honour to spend twenty years.

I spent the next half-hour dodging the word "bourgeois."

"How can you call him a bourgeois?" I said (we were

speaking of Tacitus). "Compared to the director of a *Kolchoz* we live here like pigs. The director of a *Kolchoz* also lives in a fine house, and in a prettier one than this, and he has a wireless, a gramophone and a car, and yet no one in Russia accuses him of being a bourgeois.

"Do you mean to tell me," I went on, "that a house like this is anything unusual to you? If we seem bourgeois to you, how dreadfully you must live at home. And one of your Majors told me that he had a ten-room flat in Moscow, and he only a Major. What do you say to that?" The Russian had nothing to say to that.

Here I must mention that I had meanwhile invented a mythical Major whom I always produced at critical moments. He let me in for a lot of teasing and chaff from Fifi and Jack, but in the end even they realized that he was a very useful person. He exercised great authority over the Russians. From him they learned, through me, what a paradise Russia was, for my Major lived like a prince. As well as a ten-room flat, he had a car, a five-valve wireless, and a gramophone, he ate nothing but the tastiest of food, and all his information about the Soviet Union and the Red Army was such that no one dared give him the lie.

On this occasion my Major again proved invincible. Unable to counter my arguments, Ignaty's friend pulled his cap down over his nose, stood up and took his leave, remarking as he went that we ought to buy a cock for our canary, for, as everybody knew, it was a dreadful life for a hen-canary without a cock.

The last to go was poor Ignaty. He was thoroughly miserable and discouraged. Political discussions were not in his line. And he hadn't even seen Samuel.

During the day the peasants brought us back some of our silver, which was the first indication we had had that they had been looting, too.

In the evening it began to snow—slow, silent, gentle flakes. The world would be white in the morning.

We were discussing what could be done about the constant stream of Russians of all kinds that came and pestered us in the house. Franzi said that the Major who was head of the veterinary hospital was a very nice, quiet man. Perhaps we might invite him? If it got about in the village that the Major was always coming to see us and was in and out of the house, it might perhaps bring us a little peace. So it was decided to invite him that very day, and, immediately after lunch, I was sent to the stables with a formal invitation.

The Hungarians were highly delighted. In their imaginations a Major of whatever army was always a Major, that is to say, a serious, cultured man of the world, talking the same language as themselves. Were we to make friends with a Major, they thought, and particularly with one who would be for some time in the village, we ought at last to be left in peace. We might, perhaps, invite him to take up his quarters with us, might even feed him, if only he would come to live in the house. These were the arguments they hammered into my head. Then I was told to go and do my hair, wash my hands properly, and go down to the stables, where the Major lived in the bailiff's house. Rudi was to go with me in support.

When we reached the stables it turned out that the Major did not live with the bailiff at all, but in a wretched room in one of the cottages. This made us feel sure that he would be all the more glad to come to us. Rudi remained outside while I went in. At my entrance a little middle-aged man in an unbuttoned uniform stood up. His hair was ruffled, his face covered with soap, and in his hand he held a cut-throat razor which he brandished dangerously in the air as he invited me in. I introduced myself and explained my errand to the queer creature. He smiled nicely and replied that he would come in an hour, for he, it appeared, was the Major himself. I had a strong suspicion that he stank of vodka, but put the thought from me.

Rudi and I returned home in triumph. There was great excitement among the Hungarians; the Major was coming and at last we should be able to have friendly, social relations with a staff officer, and not just one passing through the village on his way to the Front, but a veterinary surgeon, a well-educated person who had studied medicine. The tone in which the Hungarians pronounced the words "veterinary surgeon" was that in which a month before they would have spoken of a prince of the Royal blood.

And he came. He came, and was not even late, nor was he alone. There were three of them: first, the little Major, now with his uniform buttoned up, and his hair brushed, and after him two young Captains, each carrying a bottle of champagne. We had only one bottle of Tokay for them, for Rudi had no intention of sacrificing the last of his wine for so trifling an occasion. And they had brought champagne! We were touched and rather ashamed.

We all sat down in the little drawing-room and began drinking and chatting. Tacitus and Marietta were all that a host and hostess should be, and Fifi and I laboured indefatigably as translators. One of the young Captains, fat, rosy-cheeked, with a kindly face, was called Kolka; the other, thin, and with sly brown eyes, Sashka. Our Tokay disappeared like lightning, the Russians swallowing it with an effort as though it were bad gin. Then we began on the champagne. I saw at once that the officers had already had a good many drinks before they came, and presumed that the champagne was merely the remains of their after-lunch refreshment. The Major soon grew bored of talking with Fifi and looking at an album of photographs of Rome and Lucerne, and announced that he would like to play chess or dominoes. As we had neither game the Major and Sashka went off to fetch them, leaving Kolka in pawn with us.

Time passed. Kolka began to get bored and so did we, but still there was no sign of the Major. Night began to fall and we lit the lamp, but still the Major had not come back. Finally, we heard sounds of furniture being overturned, and there was the Major, back at last, and drunk. Then we began playing chess, the Major and I. I know how the pieces move, but have not the faintest idea of how the game should be played; nevertheless I won the first game. (I must admit that Kolka was heart and soul on my side and made several moves for me.) The Major got very angry when the others who were watching shouted, "Mate," which I myself had not noticed, and he immediately demanded his revenge. This time he forbade Kolka to help me, speaking to him as his superior officer, and quickly "mated" me, as I had been praying he would. At once his good humour returned. I now suggested that we should play a four at dominoes, which meant that Rudi had to join us. At this point, as was always happening, into the room walked two N.C.Os. shouting that they wanted billets. Our guests just raised their heads from the dominoes and informed them politely that there were none as the whole house was occupied. The lie came out as pat as you could wish and without any prompting from us. Their game of dominoes was obviously much more important to them than that two of their fellows should have somewhere to spend the night. Grateful as we felt to the Major we were surprised and amused by this lack of solidarity that you could have found in no other Army. The two N.C.Os. gave a deep sigh and went away.

There being no organization in the Russian Army, such things were everyday occurrences. It was very rare to find a Town Major or a Quartermaster in a village, though sometimes, but very seldom, there would be several. When this happened, they never worked together but behaved more like competing firms. Naturally, when there are no authorities in the village, both officers and men find their own quarters, knowing that otherwise no one will allot any to them. Our village was crammed with men, but there was nobody to worry where and how they lived. It was surprising that one careless word from the Major had sufficed to turn the two N.C.Os. out on to the street, and that without any reason.

Surprising, too, that the Russians who are accustomed from childhood to lying should still believe each other. It took me just three days to stop believing a word any of them said, and yet always they seem to manage to take each other in.

It is difficult to cheat at dominoes and yet the little Major managed to do so. We were playing for love, so that it could only have been desire to win that made him cheat like a spoilt child. Major Sergiej was a child like most Russians, and for him the pleasure of a game consisted only in winning it. The noble doctrine of the sporting spirit was a thing he had never heard of. He cheated naively and as often as he could. Honest Kolka watched him with a smile and pretended not to see what he was doing. Each time he won, the Major bounced on his chair with delight.

Once again the door opened, this time to admit an old Cossack with a large moustache. This was the Major's orderly who, having grown tired of sitting in the kitchen, had come to see what sort of time his Major was having. He stood and gazed round the room, and the movement of his cap seemed to say that his Major had struck lucky. Not knowing who he was, we were about to throw him out, but Kolka just nodded to us to show that there was no need, that he was one of theirs.

Ye gods, we thought, how boring it would be to have to play dominoes night after night, and yet what a good thing it would be if Major Sergiej would come and live with us, for then we would have his orderly in the kitchen to drive strange soldiers away. At the price of a few lost games of dominoes we should be left in peace; it was almost worth while.

Having won every game, Major Sergiej stood up and announced that it was time to go home. I tried to make him stop for supper, but the Major politely said that he had a better one waiting for him at home, in face of which I, too, got up intending to see him home.

As we made our way out in the dark, the Major barging

into the furniture as we went, he said, "Lida, you're a grand
one, Lida. One can talk with you. And there you are, you
read Russian and know our literature."

"Indeed I do," I answered, and, thinking that it might
charm the Major as I had been told to do, I began declaim-
ing my star piece, the beginning of *Ruslan and Ludmilla.*

But the Major did not even listen. "Ah, you're a grand
fellow, Lida, indeed you know our literature! Ah, my dear,
just to meet that here in a foreign country!" and swaying on
his drunken feet, Major Sergiej tried to clasp me to him.

Thinking I could turn this flood of cordiality to good account, I suggested that he should take up his quarters with
us, but the mere thought that he might have to live with us
almost sobered the little Major.

"No, no," he said, "far too far from the horses." And
then, stroking my arm, "How glad I am, my dear, my golden
one, that I made your acquaintance."

All right, all right, I thought, call me dear and golden and
stroke my arm if you like, if only you would come and stay
here. With some difficulty I got the old drunkard to the door
of the kitchen where his orderly was waiting for him, and
went back to the others. The Hungarians were enchanted
with the Major, all except Rudi who had so strangely lost
every game of dominoes. I had no desire to disillusion them.
The Hungarians were so civilized that they had not even
noticed that the Major was tight. Fifi and I exchanged
glances:

"Wash out," whispered Fifi. "I prefer the ordinary soldier to their Majors; they have more style about them."

The twelfth day of January was so lovely that I shall never
forget it. Nothing happened on it and there were no visitors.
No one knows, no one can even imagine, what it meant to
me for one whole day not to hear the Hungarians call "Lida!
Lida!" That cry to me was a trumpet call, a tocsin, an ac-
cursed call to arms that jerked me to my feet, whether by day

or by night, and sent me plunging and snorting, like an old cavalry charger, to the kitchen. But the 12th January was a day of blissful peace. Having done my chores I wandered about from room to room, looked out of the window, played patience, and at times felt even bored. And I enjoyed that sense of boredom as though it were a new, unknown experience. I patted Alf, scratched Isa behind the ear, and went visiting from room to room, to Rudi's and to Tacitus'. None but Fifi knew how tired I was, or what a lovely day I was having. And nothing happened. At dusk I went out and stood in front of the house. The day was dying and there was a scent of frost in the air. Across the dark sky raced still darker clouds that the wind tore into strips. There must have been a strong wind up there, but down below it was calm. When I went to bed I told Fifi that that must have been the nicest day I had ever spent. In my diary it was described in five words: An ideal day. Peace. Bridge.

The next day was peaceful, too, until eleven o'clock, when some soldiers arrived; but they kept to the kitchen. Then an old veteran turned up wanting to buy onions. When I told him we had none, he was quite offended. "What do you mean, none? Not even one? But I'm willing to pay!" And at that he pulled out some crumpled bank-notes. Everybody else was stealing and looting and here he, poor old chap, wanted to buy one onion! There were many such contradictions. Another was Fifi's admirer, Hrycko, a Don Cossack.

Hrycko was obsessed by Fifi, and whenever she appeared outside he would attach himself to her and never leave her alone. Some of the soldiers, our friends, found out about this and were highly indignant. They assured us that in the Red Army the punishment for rape was death, or at least being buried up to the neck in the ground for twenty-four hours. Opinions were divided about the punishment: some that it was death and only death; others that you were only buried. The question, however, was an academic one, for, as they said, the penalty could never be applied, as though many

women were raped it was never possible to find out who had
done it. Nevertheless, they volunteered to bury Hrycko up
to his neck for as long as we liked if anything should happen
to Fifi. Others promised to shoot him, and asked Fifi if she
had been raped by him yet. I am sure that these same soldiers
had themselves raped women when they were drunk and forgotten all about it the next day, as they forgot their head-
aches.

That morning we had an exceptional number of Russians
asking to be shown the "landlord," for, as they told us, all
the other bourgeois had fled the district and we were the first
they had been able to see. They came to look at us without
resentment, just out of sheer curiosity. This made us feel
rather like a race of animals that was dying out. We learned
from the men that all the manors and big houses round about
were deserted. We were alone, a unique museum piece, the
only ancient monument in the whole district, and thousands
of those young Russians came to look at us.

The usual alarm, "Lida! Lida!" had sent me scurrying to
the kitchen, where I found only Lina and Matilda. They
were horribly pale and, without saying a word, just pointed to
the door. Gazing outside I saw some Russians in jerkins, automatic pistols in their hands, trying to drag Tacitus out of
the woodshed. Poor Tacitus' eyes were wide open with
amazement. The scene to me was like an anti-Communist
poster; a gentleman, for Tacitus was every inch a gentleman,
with a speckled beard, dressed in rather worn shooting clothes,
stood with his back to the woodshed door, his well-shaped
legs wide apart, an expression of boundless surprise on his
face, his chest heaving, while two soldiers in dirty jerkins
waved automatic pistols under his nose, clawed his shoulders,
and shouted at him, "Bourgeois! Lousy bloodsucker! We'll
teach you! Don't you know why the Red Army has come?
To free the people and make a quick end of you and your

kind. And that's what we'll do, all over the world. Just you wait, damn you!"

I walked up then and asked in Russian what this was all about. At that one of them slipped past me through the open door and disappeared into the house, while the other went on shaking poor Tacitus without even looking round. He was tubby with a fat, impertinent face and angry, piggy eyes. "To the garden," he roared, "we'll talk there!" Poor Tacitus just opened his hazel eyes still wider and dug his feet into the step, looking from me to the muzzle of the pistol, and understanding no more than that something was wrong and that he might be shot at any moment, but why he had no idea. He looked just like a dog about to be punished for something it had not done. The hands with which Tacitus distastefully removed the Russian's paws as they clutched at his jacket, were thin, dry and nervous; the soldier's paws red, heavy and thick at the wrist. The legs of the one thin and well-shaped, those of the other like young tree trunks. And their faces, too, were as different as though they did not even belong to the same white race. Tacitus, tall, slender and nervous, looked like a thoroughbred; the Russian like a Siberian pony. It was a sight worth seeing.

"Leave him alone. What do you want with an old man? It's not nice to shout like that," said I, touching the soldier's arm.

He turned to look at me, and he gazed at me for some time, for I was rather a strange figure.

"Go away!" he said, but much more politely now. "You're not wanted here. I'll settle his business in the garden; not here, for I'm afraid to. You come on now!" he shouted at Tacitus, pointing his pistol at his stomach.

"Don't move!" I whispered in French, and then, with a smile, and in Russian, to the soldier, "How can you shout at an old man like that? He's old enough to be your father. Supposing the Germans shouted at your father like that?

Why are you frightening him? Don't you see how frightened
he is? It's not nice to frighten civilians. That's what the Germans did; but you're a decent chap, so you'll leave him alone,
won't you? You're cultured."

I stroked that fat face once, and again. It smiled.

"Come along inside," I said. "What's the point of freezing out here? Leave the old man and come inside. We'll
have a chat. Your friend's there already."

I talked to him as I would have to a child, all the while
stroking now his arm, now his face. We went into the
kitchen, leaving Tacitus outside in the same position and as
amazed as ever. There heroic Fifi was doing wonders dealing
with the second hooligan. She knew now what they wanted:
loot. Jumbo had already had to give up the only pair of high
boots he possessed. My hooligan now started dragging me
towards the bathroom. "Come," he shouted, "don't be afraid.
I want to show you something; just show you something."

I went. The soldier shut the door and stood in front of it,
cutting off my retreat. Without letting go of his automatic he
began taking down his trousers. "So that's what you want to
show me!" I said, as disdainfully as I could, but all the same
the blood froze in my veins. This is the end, I thought. This
is me finished. The soldier, seemingly paying no attention to
me whatever, with a theatrical wave of his hand, pointed to
his drawers that were black with dirt and began to take them
off too. Instinctively I glanced at the window, though I knew
it to be barred. What a fool you are, why did you come in
here. You ought to have fought him in the kitchen. Now
it's too late.

The soldier finished disengaging the shreds of his drawers
and held them out. "There, look!" he said, in a tone of re-
proach, "look what I've got to go about in! Swarming with
lice. Look. I'm sure you don't believe me. Look! And that's
what I've got to go about in, because it's all I've got."

I swallowed quickly. "I'll try and get you a new pair at

once. I believe you've got lice. I can see them from here. Indeed I can," I assured him.

"And now, tell me," went on the soldier, quickly putting his drawers and trousers on again, "tell me, what king was it lived here in that large house at the end of the village?"

"King?" I asked, and began quickly racking my brains to discover at what he might be getting.

"Don't pretend," said the soldier angrily, "I saw his portrait. He is sitting on a white horse, and he's got a feather on his head. His daughter lives here with you. I've found it all out. I want to meet his daughter. Understand? Don't pretend that she's not here. I want you just to show me, which is she."

"Wait. I'll see, find out. Perhaps there's some mistake. Come with me, we'll ask," so I enticed him, and we went out.

The first hooligan was just beginning plundering Rudi and his family. Rudi, with a pistol in his stomach, was being forced into the kitchen and then outside.

"No," I shouted, running after them. "That's not allowed. You must tell me what you want with him. You'll get everything you want if you ask nicely, but not that way. Put your automatic away."

In between sentences I would turn my head round and shout in Polish to Fifi, "Keep an eye on the other one. Don't leave him for a moment. Tell him a general is just about to arrive. That he took billets here yesterday," and I also found breath to give Rudi directions in French, "Smile and don't stop smiling. Give him everything he asks for. I'll stay here. I'll translate. Give him everything gaily, without hesitation, as though it were a joke."

Then we began quarrelling. The hooligan wanted to take Rudi to the garden, as before with Tacitus, while I insisted that no one was allowed to be marched about with a pistol pointed at his back, as this was very uncultured. Rudi was amazing. He just smiled and looked on interestedly. Nor was I afraid for him. I felt that not even Russians negotiate for a pair of drawers from someone they are going to shoot. But I was afraid that the hooligan might stumble on the uneven path in the garden and his automatic go off. Finally I got out of him what he wanted: Rudi's leather jacket. Without lowering his pistol, the hooligan watched greedily while tall, slender Rudi with a quick, graceful movement took off the jacket. Then, with the charming smile of a man-of-the-world and a low, ironical bow, Rudi handed it to him. He at once put it on, holding his automatic between his knees.

"Please tell him that it suits him excellently; that he looks very nice in it," said Rudi in French.

I repeated this in Russian. The hooligan was fearfully proud, and at once became pleasantness itself. He threw up his head, devoutly smoothed the leather and, taking Rudi's subservience seriously, felt slightly ashamed of himself:

"Now, you give us some wine and we'll have a drink," he said to Rudi, as though nothing had passed between them.

"We have none," we answered.

"Then we'll go and find some," the hooligan answered, and waved us back to the kitchen with his inevitable automatic.

In the kitchen sat hooligan No. 2 guarding Lina and Matilda who stood, pale and silent, by the wall. The thought passed through my mind that perhaps they would shoot us after all. What made me feel so sure that nothing would happen?

"Can I offer you anything to eat?" I asked them, as though they might have been dear, long-expected friends. In Hungarian I told Matilda to give them something to eat quickly, and the two old dears threw themselves with a sigh of relief on their pots and pans, filling the kitchen with their clatter.

"We want wine," insisted the hooligans. "Afterwards, perhaps, we'll eat."

At that moment the door opened and, oblivious to what was going on, in walked Franzi. Then he stopped in his tracks, and looked now at me, now at the pistols pointing at him.

"Ah!" I said, pointing to him, "here's one who knows where you can get wine. You go with him: he'll show you. Very good wine. We drank some ourselves last night. It's not far from here."

Then I quickly explained to Franzi in German that he was to take the two to the stables, choosing a way where there would be the least other soldiers about, give them the slip there and tell the Major what was happening to us. Trembling, poor Franzi promised to do this, and disappeared followed by the little hooligan, his pistol pointing at Franzi's behind, for Franzi's back was on a level with the Russian's forehead.

We, meanwhile, were driven by hooligan No. 2 to Marietta's room for this was next on the list for looting. Marietta was sitting beside the window, peacefully looking out of it every now and again just as though nothing were going on in the house. When the Russian ordered her to open her suitcase, she did so with a smile. There was no need for me to ask Marietta to smile. She did everything with the expression of a bored queen, with a smile that seemed to say: how boring all these revolutions are! The hooligan began choosing the things out of the suitcase that appealed to him, while Marietta stood in the middle of the room holding the sock she had been darning. She never asked me to explain what was happening, just smiled gently and pityingly.

"Listen!" I whispered to the hooligan, "that's the daughter of the man with the feather on his head. Stop rummaging in those cases and listen. That's her."

The Russian almost leapt out of his skin. "Kiss me, beautiful one!" he said, and stood there waiting for me to translate.

"Ought I kiss him?" Marietta asked in French, as though afraid of offending against some new etiquette.

"Better," I advised.

Then tall Marietta stooped, and still smiling, kissed the pale, dirty cheek of that soldier. The Queen and the Swineherd. The Russian raised himself on his tip-toes and touched her face with his fingers as though it were a flower, then, like a child, he kissed the corner of her mouth. After that he turned and, without touching a thing more, left the room.

The next to be looted was Dolly. The hooligan took everything she had and gave it to me as a present. What was happening with the rest of the family I did not know, for I never left my hooligan for a moment. He was called Victor and his friend, who had gone for wine, Wolodja.

"Here you are," he said, throwing the things he had taken from Dolly on to my bed, "here you are. Here's a coat. You haven't one of your own so take this. And this other one, too."

In this way I became the owner of Dolly's coat, her shawl, my husband's sheepskin which was hanging up in her cupboard, and even of my own shawl.

"That's mine," I said. "You don't need to give me that."

"You're lying, Lida. You're just saying that because you're afraid of the bourgeois. But I'll come back to-morrow, and if you've given any of these things back again, they'll remember me here. I'll take every damned thing they've got. I'll shoot them."

But I was not nearly so afraid of Victor as of his friend Wolodja; he did not brandish his automatic so violently and you could joke with him.

Suddenly a shot rang out in the next room. I dashed in and there saw Fifi standing calmly in the door to our former dining-room, now emptied and ready for the General. Beside her was Wolodja. How had he got back? Where was Franzi? Where was the Major? And who had been shot?

"Pretty. Very pretty!" Fifi was saying in the hurt voice of a chiding governess, "and what will the General say now? When he complains of the wind blowing in through a hole in the window, I shall tell him that soldiers came and fired

off their pistols when I told them that this was a General's
room. Yes, yes! I'll tell him that they came and fired off
pistols in the rooms. Is that good behaviour? Shame on you!
Shame on you!"

"I didn't fire at the pane. I aimed specially so as not to
hit the pane," answered Wolodja.

"That makes no difference," said Fifi. "People don't fire
off pistols in other people's rooms. Who ever heard of such
a thing?"

"Oh, come on!" said Victor, tired of all this talk and eager
to be off with the pair of women's slippers he had stolen from
Dolly firmly grasped under his arm.

But what had Wolodja done with Franzi?

So anxious were we to get rid of our guests as quickly as
possible that our leave-taking in the kitchen was almost gushing.

"Good-bye!" cried Wolodja.

"Good-bye!" I answered from the threshold, hoping to
God that I would never see them again.

"Wait! Wait!" said the two hooligans, suddenly remembering something. "Call the master of the house. We won't
do him any harm. Call him! What are you waiting for?"

Poor, tormented Tacitus was summoned.

"Chickens! Hand over some chickens!" roared Wolodja.

"We haven't any," I answered for Tacitus.

Then Victor slouched back into the kitchen, and I followed, leaving Tacitus alone with Wolodja outside. Victor
settled himself comfortably on a stool.

"Perhaps you don't believe that I'm a soloist?" he asked.
"But of course I do!"

"Wait! I see that you don't really believe it. Look!"

Then he seized the skin above his Adam's apple between
two fingers, gave it a gentle shake, cleared his throat, flung his
head back like a hen drinking water, and let out a tremendous
bellow, *Toreador*, that shook the walls and made Matilda and
Lina almost jump out of their skins with fright.

Victor was well launched into the Carmen aria, when the kitchen door opened to let in a wave of icy air and a frightened child, the little daughter of Teresa, our neighbour.

"Please Ma'am, please Ma'am, a Bolshy's stealing our hens."

"I'll come," I said and dived out through the door. Running across to Teresa's little yard, I found Tacitus standing there unconcernedly watching Wolodja seizing two of her last four hens from a shrieking, tearful Teresa.

"Put them down!" I roared. "Aren't you ashamed to take a poor woman's hens? Give them back at once! Who brought you here?"

Wolodja obediently gave Teresa her hens, and then, pointing to Tacitus, said, "He brought me here."

"I suppose you would like me to give him our turkeys," hissed Tacitus.

I was very angry with my brother-in-law. Wait, I thought, I'll teach you not to bring hooligans down on poor people's heads.

"Come," said I to Wolodja, and led him to the wooden hut in which Rudi's last two turkeys were shut.

"We have no hens or chickens," I said, gazing wrathfully at Wolodja, "but the one whom you stripped of his leather jacket has two turkeys. So now you've got new drawers, two pairs of shoes and two turkeys. Take them and never try to rob poor people again. Weren't you ashamed to take a poor woman's last hens?"

Wolodja dexterously caught the two turkeys and lifted them up by their legs. Then Victor emerged smiling from the kitchen.

"The boots are for a fellow in the unit who's going about barefoot, word of honour, and the lady's shoes, they're for a poor girl in the village. What does one woman want with ten pairs, when another has only long boots? And the drawers are for me, and the leather jacket for Wolodja's friend, and the turkeys for all of us. Now, let's get going!"

"A fine friend you've got," I shouted after him, "tries to rob the poorest woman in the village and fires off his pistol in the General's quarters."

"To hell with your General," said Wolodja conciliatingly, and quickly disappeared round the corner after Victor.

The Hungarians fell into a mood of resignation: so the Russians did steal and loot after all! Then they went to the other extreme and began wondering whether the Germans' anti-Russian propaganda might not have been accurate all along. How were we to protect ourselves from the next lot of robbers that came? Perhaps that first Russian soldier we had encountered had been right when he told us to bury all our valuables (which we had done). What were we to do? At any rate we must tell the Major. The Major? But where in Heaven's name was Franzi? Then we all began running about calling him.

We found him, faint with fear. He had been hiding near the house ever since getting back with Wolodja. They had never even got to the stables. Half-way there Wolodja had put him against a wall and pretended to aim his pistol at him, making him put his hands up. What happened after that we were unable to find out, but they never reached the stables, and both returned to the house without wine and, what is worse, without the Major.

Franzi was now sent back to the stables. As he knew only three words of Russian and those highly indecent, he was to explain what had happened in gestures and we made him repeat, "Soldier, papa, bang, bang. Soldier, bang, bang, automatic, hooligan, no good," until he could say it convincingly. And off he went.

We had hardly managed to snatch something to eat when good honest Kolka appeared puffing and panting, and behind him an officer we did not know, in a long stiff cape and a soldier's cap. Despite the cap we could see at once that he was an officer, for he was the sort of person who could only have been one. He had delicate features, stubborn, narrow lips,

and a gloomy face. Behind him came Franzi, but he got no
farther than the middle of the hall. Here he broke down and
that gigantic child, who overtopped the two Russians by a
head, suddenly broke into loud sobs and threw himself into
the arms of the first available person, who thankfully passed
the trembling and excessively heavy boy over to his parents.
The Russians watched the scene in amazement.

"What's happening?" asked Kolka.

Then, and for the first time, Franzi faithfully repeated his
lesson, "Soldier, papa, bang bang."

Kolka was still as amazed and as much in the dark as
ever. "What sort of bang? Your papa's alive."

But Franzi continued stubbornly and unnecessarily, "Soldier, papa, bang, bang."

I then explained the whole story of the two hooligans.
Franzi, it appeared, had been convinced that the two had
watched him running to the stables and had been afraid to
repeat his lesson, thinking that if he complained thus he
would find us all dead when he got back home, and so he
had dragged the two officers away without even telling them
what it was all about.

The two officers sat down and wagged their heads over the
affair. The stranger, it turned out, was a Major on his way
through the village.

"I'll stay the night here," he announced suddenly, in a
cold, lisping voice.

Then Kolka stood up and went to tell Major Sergiej the
whole story and to invite him in our name to supper. The
gloomy, strange Major remained alone with us. I wanted him
to take off his cloak, for it was very hot in the room, but he
just grunted "No need!" and waved me rudely aside. Nor
would he take off his cap. We began talking, an artificial
conversation that was almost impossible to keep alive. I told
him that I had a nephew in the Red Army. How nice that
was. What a good school for the boy, but the Major did not

even listen and just sat there never even saying a word. Finally I stopped and there was an uneasy silence.

"What class do you belong to?" he suddenly asked, looking round the room.

Fifi did not understand the question and asked what he meant.

"Come now," said the Major sharply, "are you gentry or aristocrats?"

Poor Fifi almost shrivelled up. We had only just got rid of two hooligans and here were we landed with a political Commissioner or Heaven knows what.

"Well," insisted the Major impatiently, "you must belong to one class or another. What are you? Countesses? Is that it? Aristocrats, eh?"

"No," I answered swiftly, "we are middle-class," and I pointed to Fifi and myself.

It was no use trying to lie, for perhaps the damned peasants had already told him that Rudi was a count. So far no Russian had shown any interest in titles, except the hooligan who had wanted to know whether Marietta's father on the way to the coronation wasn't a king, so we were not prepared for this kind of interrogation. The Major shook his head rudely and disbelievingly, then he suddenly stood up.

"Are you sure you're middle-class?" he asked ironically.

"Where are you going? But you're invited to supper! Please don't go away!"

But the Major just mumbled something and stalked out, to the great indignation of the Hungarians.

It was dark outside. The General, of course, had not come and so, as usual, we had got the rooms ready unnecessarily. It was an almost daily occurrence for the room to be taken as billets for someone who never arrived, making the thirteen of us sleep in three rooms one of which had no stove.

Heavy footsteps in the corridor and cries of "Lida! Lida!" from the Hungarians announced the return of the Tall Major. He was followed into the room by Major Sergiej and a village girl in peasant dress, with tall boots and a carefully made-up face framed in a kerchief draped round her head; a strange combination of modern cosmetics and exaggerated peasant costume. The two officers took off their things. Sergiej was dressed normally and at first sight it was difficult to see that he was a Major, but the other was wearing huge golden epaulettes, a spotless, newly-pressed tunic, and all his medals.

Major Sergiej begged our pardon for bringing another guest with him.

"The marauders are plundering everybody," he explained, "and she" (pointing to the girl sitting beside him) "is afraid. I'm even going to them after supper to sleep. Poor girl!"

The "poor girl" nodded her head in assent, seeing that we were talking about her. She felt uncomfortable with us and we could see how she was torn by conflicting emotions: as a daughter of one of Tacitus' outdoor servants, she was proud of being taken to supper with the gentry, but on the other hand she did not know how to behave with us, and so was inclined to panic. Her conception of Communism, as with most women of the proletariat, was confined to hating the upper classes, and the programme of this simplified form was in her eyes a very simple one: her father would be given the blood-sucker's land and she his wife's dresses, and in that way justice would be done and a new order established in the world.

The Tall Major, as usual, said nothing, but Major Sergiej talked enough for two. He was so taken up with his village girl that he never looked at me; but she kept looking round at us disdainfully. Ha! she was surely thinking, see how times have changed! Here am I invited to sup at the Manor with my Major lover! We saw now that it was hopeless to think of getting Major Sergiej to take up his quarters with us, for we could offer him no one for his bed. So, we must do our best to charm the Tall Major. It appeared that neither he nor the Captain Sashka, who had drunk champagne with us the night before, belonged to the veterinary hospital; but, whether they were merely birds of passage or not, that we could not learn.

The Russians were exaggeratedly discreet about information of that kind. Everything, literally everything, was a military secret to them. Yet you had only to sit down with them and get talking to learn many things of greater interest than the name of their General. You could learn, as I did from Grigory, that after defeating the Fascists the Soviet Union would set about fighting the capitalists. Grigory foretold a second, even bloodier war in the West as soon as the Germans were defeated. I don't know whether Comrade Stalin confided his plan to Lieutenant Grigory, but I'm sure he would not have approved of his talkativeness. But for Russian talkativeness there is no cure, I can assure the Soviet leaders of that. You can train the Russian soldier not to betray the division or regiment to which he belongs, or to pretend that he does not know the name of his Colonel, but you cannot prevent him from talking about such natural and self-evident things as, for example, that Alaska must be taken from the Americans because they made the Tsar drunk before getting him to sign it away; or that after the defeat of Japan, Russia was to get the whole of Manchuria, that after the defeat of the Fascists, *i.e.*, the Germans, it would be necessary to destroy the capitalists in Europe, *i.e.*, the English, and to take Switzerland as they went along because it was harbouring all the Nazi leaders. These things were so self-evident that they must be obvious to everyone; they lay in the natural course of justice, so what could be the harm in talking about them.

To return to the Tall Major: we had to try and charm him, for we knew this much, that he hadn't a mistress in the village and so might possibly agree to billet with us. I showed him the two rooms we had vacated for the mythical General: the former nursery that contained the only bed in the house, and our old bedroom now littered with paillasses for the General's suite and guard, which we had been told would be numerous. The Major chose the paillasses and gave the bed to his orderly. "Phew, a diehard Communist!" I said, in a whisper to Fifi. "He won't be easy game." Then supper was announced.

As a valued interpreter I sat between the two Majors. We had chicken, now the height of luxury. Marietta took the platter to the Major's girl, who stared round at us in wide-eyed amazement. Never, at home or anywhere else, had she yet helped herself first, and it never even crossed her mind that, as the only woman guest, she took precedence over the two Majors by whom she was so impressed. "Guests are served first," I said to her in Hungarian, seeing her confusion. But she had already begun helping herself, a little triumphant smile on her lips. She understood: this was the first sign of the old order crashing. The gentry were so afraid of her that they served her first. With the confidence of this newly gained power, she took a drumstick in two fingers and began calmly gnawing at it, so that the fat ran down her chin and dripped into her sleeve.

Major Sergiej, being a Bolshevik, had a different ambition. He was out to show how elegantly he could eat; so he speared a piece of chicken on his fork and tried to bite pieces off it like that. This caused him a deal of trouble, as did his little finger that he stuck out at such an angle that he was in danger of poking out his own eye with it.

The Tall Major was the only one perfectly at ease. He used his knife, fork and napkin normally, and politely poured out water for the ladies and handed them whatever they might need. This was the first Russian we had yet seen with normal European table manners. Where did he fit in?

After supper Major Sergiej tucked his captive's arm under his and, with a casual farewell, went off for the night to his promising new quarters, leaving us alone with the Tall Major. I shall always call him the Tall Major, for we never even learned his name. We sat on a pile of mattresses in the hall. The Major's golden epaulettes glinting in the light of the paraffin lamp. He looked as though he were fifty, and yet was only just over forty. The Russians grow old quickly, as quickly as people in tropical climates.

Now that Major Sergiej had gone, the Tall Major smiled at us for the first time. Then we began talking, feeling our way very carefully. First we talked about the hooligans. The Major was incensed at them, not just frightened by what they might do as Kolka had been. "Stupid bandits," the Major exclaimed, "please let me know if anything like that happens again. I'll soon deal with them!" Then I began telling him about myself, how I painted. The Major looking round the room saw two rows of prints on the wall.

"You must always tell the idiots that those are all your work," he said, pointing to the pictures, "that will always help and they'll believe anything. And, also, tell them that your husband is a doctor and that he works in the Red Cross."

"And if someone comes to him for treatment?"

"Then he's a surgeon; has left his instruments in the capital and can only operate with his own," answered the Major calmly.

Then we got on to the subject of politics. After giving me that advice I was beginning to trust him, but when he began talking politics my new-born confidence in him fled.

"The Germans are still very strong," he said. "It is a great mistake to suppose now in January, nineteen forty-five, that the war will be over in a few days. It will drag on a while yet. And here, just here between the capital and the hills, the Germans are very strong and will be stronger still. It's a dangerous spot.

We laughed at this, for we felt quite safe behind the Russian lines and for us the Third Reich was a thing of the past. The Major, however, stubbornly shook his head.

"This is a dangerous spot. Haven't you any friends or relations on the other side of the river, somewhere about seventy miles behind the front? That's where you ought to go."

"How? On foot, with children and invalids? What for?"

And at this Fifi whispered to me that we ought to be careful with him. Perhaps he was sounding us and our attitude. I would have liked to have changed the subject, but then Isa came and did it for me.

"O-oh!" exclaimed the Major, as though he had just caught sight of a friend he had not seen for a long time. He made us call the pointer over to him, looked her over, patted her, and looked into her eyes like a vet. He was the first Russian I ever saw who handled dogs as though he knew about them. I don't know what it was like in the old days, but from what I saw the modern Russians have no feelings for dogs. A puppy is treated as a toy, a grown-up dog as an unclean animal. But our Major was a connoisseur of dogs, though that does not mean a dog-lover, and his specialty was sporting dogs. He inspected Isa all over, asked if we had any hounds and what game we used Isa for. And I wondered how a Russian Major could be a hunter, for he was neither from the Caucasus, nor from Siberia, so where did he hunt or shoot? I know that there must be game all over Russia, but I don't imagine that every Tom, Dick and Harry can get a gun-licence and wander about the collective farms in search of a hare. And there are certainly no more packs of hounds kept there, so how on earth did our Tall Major know all the secrets and the vocabulary of the hunter and sportsman.

The Major began describing wolf-hunts with hounds. He became fired with his subject, and his description was so graphic that we could see the racing hounds and the fleeting shadow of the wolf. It reminded me of the description of the wolf-hunt at old Rostow's in *War and Peace,* and old aristocratic Russia suddenly came to life again in Mora. Yes, hunting was obviously his passion.

"I adore hunting, you see," he explained, a little bashfully.

There's no need to tell us that, we thought. And who doesn't? Then I asked him what he hunted in Russia.

"I? Now, in Russia?" he repeated, as though flabbergasted. "I used to hunt with my father, when I was a boy."

We didn't ask any more. Fifi and I were dumbfounded

and a little frightened by our new guest. He did not fit into
any category of Russian we knew. When talking of hunting
and describing how he used to hunt wolves with hounds, he
had used the beautiful old Russian of former days. It had
been like reading a short story by Turgenev and we had not
found it easy to understand. Yet, when he had talked of the
Germans' war potentialities, Turgenev had vanished and with
it that lovely, melodious accent. He had used the new, un-
lovely Bolshevik Russian and we had been afraid lest he
should prove an *agent provacateur*.

Getting up, the Major took his leave of us and went off
to his paillasse in that icy room where one of the window-
panes had a hole in it made by the bullet Wolodja had fired
that morning. On the way the Tall Major looked into the
kitchen where sat his orderly, a charming old man with a
huge moustache, draped in a long, grey cloak with the hem
of which he never stopped rubbing his automatic. Those who
have never made friends with one of those old Russian soldiers have missed a lot. They are entrancing people with the
heart of a dove and that purely Russian charm that you can
find nowhere in Europe.

The old orderly went to his room, looked round it and
announced that it would be difficult to find a better billet.
I asked the Major to excuse the fact that he would have to
wash in his orderly's room that night, but that that was the
only wash-basin we had and the water and towels prepared
for the mythical General were all there.

"I don't need anything," growled the Tall Major rudely,
and stalked off to his own room, followed by the gaze of his
orderly who was now lolling in the General's feather-bed.

It was ten o'clock and the Tall Major had still not
emerged. The whole house was in a state of anxiety. According to Moscow time it was already midday, and there he
was still asleep. Or, perhaps, he had died? Perhaps he was a
German spy and hadn't slept in the house at all, but had

slipped out during the night? We listened at the door, but could hear nothing. Then Fifi and I went to the dining-room, trying to make up our minds whether to break in the Major's door or go on waiting, and at that moment the door was flung open and the Major, with a hardly audible "good morning," swept like a hurricane through the three rooms towards the front door. I followed him at a gallop, shouting, "How did you sleep?" but he was already outside. He barked, "Well," and that was all I saw of him.

Franzi

15th-17th

January

SUMMONED to the kitchen by the usual shouts, I found there two of the child-soldiers of whom there were many in the Red Army. One was fourteen, the other fifteen, and they had come in search of pickled cucumbers. These child-soldiers were given a uniform and full equipment, and the older men looked after them as tenderly as mothers. We once invited one of thirteen into the shelter and wanted to give him jam. His name was Nicholas, but everybody called him "Gieroy," the hero. The Hero politcly refused the offer of jam, saying, with a charming smile, that he wouldn't eat it, for he had heard that we were poisoning Russians that way. I told him not to be afraid, that we would eat out of the same jar, but the child merely shook his head, smiling, and said, "Better not. I don't want any. One has to be careful." He was quite convinced that we had enticed him into the cellar to poison him.

The kids who were asking for cucumbers hastened to tell us that their families had been massacred to a man by the Germans in the Ukraine. Then we told them that ours had too, only in Poland, and they took their leave, for we had no cucumbers. They were nice, quiet children, but they knew life better than many grown-ups.

For the first time in three days we are able to have lunch. After lunch Tacitus decided to pay visits on Major Sergiej and on the Tall Major, and to invite the latter to supper. There was a long consultation whether it would be best for Tacitus to go alone, or with his wife, and which would make the better impression on the Russians. They could not understand that these were details no Russian would ever notice. In the end they went together, and returned fascinated by their reception, for they had been given champagne. The Tall Major had promised to come at seven o'clock; Major Sergiej, included in the invitation at the last moment, had excused himself on the grounds of having to rescue distressed maidens in the village; in other words, we bored him beyond measure.

Seven o'clock came, and there was no sign of the Major. At eight o'clock when he had still not come, Tacitus decided to wait no longer and ordered supper to be served. We two Poles were appalled at this lack of tact, but the Hungarians, being more European than we, are very sensitive about punctuality, and so we had supper without the Tall Major.

"So that's the end of him," said Tacitus disdainfully. "What's wrong with them all? They're so nice at first and then suddenly, for no reason at all, they drop the friends they have only just made."

"I suppose he's just had enough of us," remarked Rudi, "but he might have sent his orderly to tell us."

Thus the Hungarians; but Fifi and I in our heart of hearts still believed in the Tall Major. And we were right, for he came dashing in about nine o'clock, his cape flapping, and out of breath. And he did not even have an orderly with him, which no other high Russian officer had yet done. He begged our pardon for being late, and said that he had already eaten, a polite lie that the Hungarians accepted, but Fifi and I knew that it was not true, but not being in our own house we could not offer him anything. Tacitus, however, gladly agreed to open a bottle of our Tokay.

We settled ourselves comfortably in the hall with our glasses. Ahead of us lay a quiet evening, like a fertile cool plain at dusk after a day of heat. We felt safe and comfortable with our Major there, and he was in an excellent mood. He had just begun telling us about something, when Jack, who had been released from his forced duties with the Russians for a couple of days, came in, and the words died at the Major's lips and his face assumed its usual graven expression.

"It's only my nephew whom I've told you about," I said quickly, seeing the change that had come over him. "He's just back from two weeks at the front with the Counter-Intelligence."

At the word "Counter-Intelligence," the Tall Major instinctively glanced round the room. That look delivered him into our hands.

"There's nothing to be afraid of," I said.

But the Major remained uneasy and stubbornly silent. No *agent provocateur* could have pretended fear as cleverly as that. I, too, had reason to know the N.K.W.D., and in all I was to have dealings with it on eight occasions, but I saw then that the Major was more afraid of it even than I.

"Please, there really is nothing to be afraid of," Fifi and I assured him, smiling.

"Aha! So this is the famous Ogpu man," exclaimed the Major. Then he pulled himself together and, with a smile, gave Jack his hand.

The uneasy silence lasted for a while yet, but the incident gave us courage to ask the Major who his father was. He had been, it appeared, the manager of an estate belonging to one of the Naryszkins. So that was how our Major knew the joys of hunting and could remember better times.

Growing more confident, the Major then admitted that ever since he had heard that there was "a family like yours" (he didn't use the word "bourgeois") living in the village, he had been wanting to see us and to get to know us. "I saw at once what sort of people you are," he said, with a sort of charming, naive pride. "Ye-es," said the Major, slowly and sadly, and relapsed into silence.

We could see how he was struggling with himself, wanting to tell us something, but holding himself back as though thinking he had already said too much. Then Jack got up and went off to bed, but the Major still remained silent.

"Do please talk," I hazarded. "No one understands Russian here except my friend and I."

I could hardly believe that I could have had the courage to say such a thing, for you must remember that just as the Major was afraid of the N.K.W.D. so for years I had been trained to fear the Gestapo. We were like two of Pawlow's dogs, experimental dogs with the same reflex actions to fear. We had grown accustomed to living under terror and no free person can possibly understand us, for he cannot know what it means to live in fear for years on end. We both had the same reactions and this we quickly recognized, perhaps just because we belonged to the hunted and not to the hunters. Anyway, the Major needed no further encouragement, but began at once to talk. He talked eagerly, but kept breaking off every now and again, as though still afraid of saying too much, and at the same time, of not being able to say it all. Then Muki's nurse, Honono, came into the room, and the Major stopped at once, with a reproachful look at me.

"A servant," I said. "She doesn't understand a word."

"You never can know," replied the Major gravely, "and besides, a servant, one of the people. How can you know that she's not spying: that she doesn't hate you?"

"But she adores us," I replied. "She gets on wonderfully with the family."

How were servants treated in the old Russia, I wondered. What is the present-day Russian's conception of the bourgeois of to-day? Do they judge them by those they used to have? What ideas have been put into their heads during these last thirty years, if such a nice, friendly creature as the Tall Major could imagine that our servants might hate us? Does he believe the Soviet propaganda, or is he going on his own experiences from the old days?

"She's very fond of us," I repeated, "and besides, she

doesn't understand a word of Russian. Anyway, she's gone to bed now."

Perhaps the Tall Major was incapable of conceiving that Honono could sleep on the ground beside Dolly, or of believing that till those mythical Soviet Generals appeared on the horizon, she had slept in the same bed with Dolly, the only bed in the whole house other than Matilda's and Lina's? How could Honono hate us or spy on us? What for? She thought worse of the Red Army than we. Even the peasants and the down-and-outs of the poor quarters despised the Russians more heartily than we, though they counted on the Russians bringing a new order with them.

"We aren't bloodsuckers," I assured the Major with a smile, "though I admit that in our system there can be and are such people who prosper very nicely and will do so until the State takes over that role from them."

The Major calmed down then and went back to his story; but again he was interrupted by a noise from the kitchen. It was strange to see this man, so stern and gruff, looking anxiously round the room.

"That's just the two old women in the kitchen," I said to calm him.

"More servants?"

"Of course," I answered. "But they've each been twenty years with us and are as attached to the family as if we were their own children. In fact, if there are any dyed-in-the-wool Conservatives in this house, they're to be found in the kitchen. The kitchen's the very home of reaction."

The Major found it difficult to believe in this love of servants for their masters. He was like a nervous horse, that, having been frightened by something, requires much patting of its neck and talking to, before it will quiet down. In the end, however, another glass of Tokay made him himself again, and he began talking once more.

It is difficult for me to repeat what he said. Even that evening it was difficult to translate and I did so badly and

only in part, for I was afraid none would understand his mood
and that they might ask stupid questions and spoil it. Besides,
the Major never waited for me to translate, but talked on
nervously and quickly, and really for himself alone.

In his talk were fragments from the early days of the revolution, bits about the awful terror and about a faithful friend,
Feidja. They were alone and defenceless in that strange
world, mere children really. There were thousands of such
children all over Russia, said the Major bitterly, and almost
all of them became bandits. But he and Feidja were sheltered
children and they did have a little money, so they hid. The
Major had a tiny little room and Feidja would come and
knock three times according to a complicated system they had
agreed on, then they would sit together on the bed, and Feidja
would begin to sing, but softly, so as not to attract attention.
And Feidja's voice was so lovely that anyone who heard him
sing forgot even the worst of his cares. He had a wonderful,
angelic voice, said the Major, as though he were telling us a
fairy-tale, a voice that could not help but charm everyone who
heard it. So the two kids would sit there enchanted by this
fragment of music, the only beautiful thing left them in that
strange world in which they lived like two hunted animals.
To us it was like vodka, a sort of narcotic, said the Major.

Then he told us how times had gradually improved, how
there were periods when life was quite tolerable, till a new
wave of terror came and cast a shadow over the whole country. Time passed and the Major had married. They were
happy together. (Of course, we never learned where they
lived or what his wife was called.) Things were best in 1938
and 1939, when life seemed to be completely stabilized. Then
suddenly war broke out. The Major's wife joined up and was
a Major, too, on the Ruthenian front. They had not seen
each other for four years.

At that the Tall Major stopped and there was a long
pause.

"Aah! How I would like to go hunting with you after the war; or duck shooting at dusk when they're fighting," said I to break the silence. And at once the Tall Major forgot about the war and the Ruthenian front, forgot what he had been talking about, so that there was only one thought in his head, hunting and shooting.

Suddenly, Tacitus asked him if he would not come to him after the war and look after his other estate in the south with its forests and fish ponds; provided, of course, added Tacitus, that God preserves us from agricultural reform. Tacitus liked the Major, whose passion for hunting had drawn them together and prompted the offer. But the Major's face only clouded; it was as though the shadow of a cloud had fallen on a sunlit piece of water.

"No," he said, "everyone should live in his own country, whatever it is like. And he should die in his own country, too. Russia will always remain Russia, my Russia, whoever should govern her, for no government can ever change the character of a nation for good. No." Then he paused for a moment, before going on. "However good and wonderful life may be elsewhere, you can only live among your own people, at home, there where you came into the world, where you were taught its language. But you, you must go now to those forests in the south. I have to go to my H.Q. to-morrow, and I'll find out how far the front has advanced in those parts. If it's well past them, then you go to those forests of yours. For this is going to be a bad spot, a very bad spot to stay in."

"Why?" we asked, "why is it going to be so specially dangerous just here?"

"Because the Germans are going to concentrate a big force here."

"But how can we go two or three hundred miles on foot? We haven't even a cart. Nor if we had, have we so much as an ox to pull it."

"All right," said the Major, "I'll see what I can do about that for you."

At that moment Lina came from the kitchen to tell us that the Major's orderly was waiting for him, so he got up, said good-bye stiffly and coldly, and walked quickly away.

Another day like all the others: slight frost, clouds everywhere, and the snow on the ground turning grey. A dull countryside, and a dull life. Not dull through lack of things happening, but because the same things happened day after day for weeks. Every day each did his share of the housework, of preparing quarters for officers that never came, and then, there were the Russians to amuse.

I have never met anybody so dreadfully and so continually bored as are the Russians. Most of them can play cards and chess; they can all sleep endlessly like a dog or a cat, and yet nothing can cure them of their boredom. One of their greatest amusements is talking, so that the moment they heard that there were people living in the village who knew Russian they at once came running to us, and then we would have to talk and talk for hours on end.

One of these Russians came to the house for firewood, saying that he was a cook. He had a look round the kitchen, saw the canary in the cage hanging from the ceiling, and we had him with us for more than an hour. Fancy talking about a canary for a whole hour! If you are expecting your country to be occupied by the Russians, don't keep a canary. Our wretched bird had visitors every day. They came singly and in groups, and all these canary-fanciers were unanimous in condemning our cruelty in keeping it without a mate. "Why don't you find him a mate?" "It must be lonely for him by himself." "He must have a mate." We also learned many things we did not know about the life and habits of canaries. Ornithologists, I am sure, will be interested to know that they are indigenous to the Ukraine. They fly about freely there both in summer and winter, and no one tortures them by keeping them in cages. Good gracious, no! We asked whether they didn't freeze to death in winter; but evidently not. Not Ukrainian canaries.

I asked one of these fanciers why they all came to look at our canary when every tree at home was full of them. The answer was that it was nice to see a bird they knew. Those Russians could not bear the thought that we had something that they had never seen in Russia. We also learned that our canary was a hen and not a cock at all, and that it sang out of sheer longing for a mate. Yes, we learned a lot about canaries in general and our own Mandim in particular.

The cook had only just gone, when an inexpressibly ragged man from the village appeared in the kitchen door. He was wearing a red armlet. He was quite young, but walked with a stick, and wisps of tangled black hair stuck out from under his cap. He had the restless, uneasy eyes of a thief. He asked to speak with Tacitus. As it turned out he was the son of one of the four village communists who had been arrested and taken away before the Russians came. He had come from the southern part of the country, but why he had been there and when he went, we did not know. Tacitus summoned him to him, for the Tall Major had fired us all with his talk of making for the south, and Tacitus wanted to find out what was happening there.

"Well, Stefan," said Tacitus, "tell us about it."

Russian occupation or no Russian occupation, Tacitus still used the same old lordly tone to the peasants; he never received them in his room, never gave them his hand. He just went on as though nothing in our lives had changed and as though he were still the Lord of the Manor, though he no longer lived in it and himself slept on straw.

Standing in the kitchen door, Stefan told us what he knew; it would be almost impossible to make our way to the south, only perhaps if we went on foot and dressed as beggars. But even beggars were stopped and made to dig trenches or to pull Russian ammunition lorries out of the mud, or load

the ammunition into another lorry. Anyone with a horse and
cart or carriage would have it taken from him, whether rich
or poor. There were none of the gentry to be seen. The
manor houses were all empty, all in ruins. In the south itself
things were better. The front had moved on more quickly
there; food was still to be had in plenty, and there were fewer
Russians.

"Good," said Tacitus, and then, turning to me, "in view
of what we've just heard, kindly tell your Major to let us have
two vehicles and a Russian escort for each. We'll need two
horses a-piece, for one won't last the journey. Then we can
get going."

"All right," I managed to say.

What on earth did he expect?

The Hungarians were very fond of black coffee and we
had very little left, which is probably why they thought that
their wretched coffee would be a great attraction to a Russian
officer. They thought that if they sent me to invite the Tall
Major to coffee he would leap to his feet and come the instant
he heard the magic words: black coffee. I came back with his
acceptance and the important news that Sashka was now living with the new headman.

This was another of Tacitus' trials. The village had gone
behind his back and itself elected a new headman, an old
peasant who somehow or other had picked up a little Slo-
vakian so that he could make himself more or less understood
with the Russians. He had once worked for Tacitus on the
home farm, but had been dismissed under a cloud. He also
had a pretty daughter (the one who had stolen Dolly's blouse
from under her nose while cleaning the Dower House after
the first wave of Russians had passed). In other words they
were a bad lot. There is always one such family in every village. Tacitus was counting on the man not daring to oppose
him openly, because of his bad conscience, as though the Russians would have believed him rather than a peasant. Anyway
Tacitus sent for him to make him give up Sashka, for the

Hungarians had got it into their heads that if they could not get the Tall Major or one of the veterinary officers to take up his quarters with us they might manage to get Sashka, who, we learned, was commander of the men guarding the mill, and was obviously going to remain some time in the village.

The headman came and was received in the dining-room. Tacitus even shook hands with him, so badly did he want Sashka. The old peasant was not very pleasant and most unwilling to give a straight answer, but in the end he agreed to give up Sashka, which was rather remarkable. In those days Russians were at a premium among the peasants. To have a permanent one in the house meant safety from ruffians and the nocturnal visits of drunken soldiers which usually ended in rape. I could hardly believe that the old peasant would keep his promise and, anyway, Sashka, whose opinion none had yet asked, would have been mad to consider it. With the headman he had a warm, fuggy room, three pillows and a feather bed and under the feathers his host's pretty daughter; while with us he would have a well-aired room, only one pillow on his bed and the most he could expect in it would be Samuel. And yet Tacitus still believed that none would dare dispute his will!

When the Tall Major arrived the Countesses rushed to the kitchen to see how the sacred black coffee was progressing. The moment he was comfortably seated we gave him a map and he began explaining the position of the front. Unfortunately, either he did not want to tell us everything or the local H.Q., which he had visited the day before, was not very well informed. Tacitus kept pestering me to ask him about the horses and vehicles. In the end I did so.

"I can't give you any horses," said the Tall Major, which I translated with a sort of spiteful delight.

Consternation among the Hungarians! "Why?" "But he promised!" "What does he mean?"

"For the simple reason that I haven't any horses at my disposal to let you have," explained the Major.

After this blow Tacitus wanted to know whether it would at least be possible to get a cart to bring up coke and potatoes from the Manor. Yes, that would be possible, and the Major began explaining how we were to set about it. Tacitus, it appeared, had no right to his own coke, nor to his potatoes. It all belonged now to the Red Army. However, Jack and Franzi were entitled to ask for some potatoes and coke for themselves and their families because they worked for the Army in the Veterinary hospital. They were not entitled to have the use of a cart, but that could be arranged with Kolka and Major Sergiej, who, being our friends, would certainly do that much for us.

The Tall Major was now thoroughly at home with us. It began to grow dark and he still sat on. We were talking once more about dogs, horses and hunting, everything else forgotten. Marietta came to ask him to stay to supper and he gladly accepted. He was always telling us now how much he liked being with us, how delightful a surprise it had been to him to discover us. He was afraid of us no longer.

It was that evening that the Tall Major began telling us about his grandfather who had studied in Germany and spoke the language like a German. He had been greatly impressed by this grandfather of his, and it was from him that he had learned about Europe and to esteem and love what it stood for. This grandfather had outlived the Major's father, who was killed during the revolution, and had been the young lad's only moral support, the only eye through which he could look out into the world. The old grandfather had told him about a different, better life that he had once lived across the frontier, as might he have spoken of life on some strange, exotic planet where everything was different, and his every word had stuck in the head of the young lad who listened so attentively.

Those tales of the olden days became the Major's gospel, the legend on which he based his whole life and that enabled him to bear it in the worst and darkest times, the legend that somewhere there was another, better and juster world, and that not far away were people who lived in good and proper houses, who grew rich and were content, not because they knew nothing, but because they knew so much. It was difficult to make the Major see that it was no great achievement merely to live better than in Russia, and that that did not by itself mean that people were happy, nor yet that they had achieved that state of bliss about which he was always speaking.

I see now that it was thoughtless of me to shatter his illusions. We were the first people from that other world that he had met, and that was why we were so interesting to him. Yet, all the same, with true Russian distrustfulness he would not believe us when we shattered his illusions, would not let us spoil for him the wonderful fairy-tale he had been told in his childhood, nor destroy the foundations of the splendid edifice that he had built out of it. When I shook my head at some exaggerated praise of our Western European culture, it was like laughing at an ardent believer when he tries to explain that Jesus' mother was a virgin. The Major could not understand that if something were not black it need not necessarily be white. Like many Russians he was inclined to be categorical, and could only see the world in those two colours. He did not even harbour a grudge against his country's government, for he considered that the fault went much deeper, that it was due to something in the Russians themselves, who were a nation worth nothing and which he yet must love more than life itself, even though the doors of Paradise in the shape of Europe were now opened to him.

After supper the Tall Major asked Jack and I if we would see him back to his billet. He said that he had never expected to stay so long and so had not told his orderly to come for him, and he did not like going back alone in the dark: who knew whether someone might not shoot at a solitary Russian officer? We, however, knew that the Tall Major did not always bring his orderly with him, because he did not want to have to admit to the others how frequent a guest of ours he

was. We put on our sheepskin coats and set out with the
Major. As we walked along we spoke of the theatre in Moscow and Leningrad. Passing the house where the Counter-
Intelligence had its quarters, Jack referred to his connection
with it and at once the Tall Major's expression changed. He
stopped, gripped Jack so hard by the arm that it hurt, and,
with a motion of his head, bade him be silent. There was
no thought of the Moscow theatre in the Major's head now,
only fear. What a fearful life he and so many others in Russia must have had! Yet it seems possible to grow accustomed
even to that, for otherwise every rabbit among them would
have committed suicide long ago. Is that all they have in the
Soviet Union, I thought, good theatres and good Counter-
Intelligence? I shall never forget the contrast of that moment
on that dark country road where the only light was that of the
stars: one moment we were laughing and gay; the next, the
laughter had died at our lips and we were looking in pity at
our terrified friend. Poor, unhappy people! said the look Jack
quickly turned from the Major to me. When we reached
Kolka's house, the Major said good-night abruptly and coldly.
He was back in the Russian Army again.

The following day began badly and looked as though it
would continue thus, if only because Tacitus went about like
a thundercloud. Poor Tacitus!

Some Russians accompanied by ragged Stefan, son of a
Communist the Germans had arrested, appeared in the yard.
They first asked after the master of the house, and then, inevitably, whether we had a wireless or arms. This was followed
by the usual search. They looked everywhere with the greatest enthusiasm, despite our assurance that their compatriots
had, on several occasions done exactly the same, and had
found nothing. We suggested that they should make en-
quiries of the local Counter-Intelligence, but they did not
even listen. At the end of the search they all assembled in
Tacitus' room: the officer, a Captain in a black cap with a

green peak; Sashka, the N.C.O., with his common, broad face; the interpreter, who spoke not a word of Russian but only Ruthenian; and Stefan. They had found nothing. Then the N.C.O. Sashka, first glancing at his officer, stood up, and walking across to Tacitus, roared at him, almost in his face, "Get dressed! You're coming with us!"

Sashka's was a dreadful face, and a dreadful voice. He was the complete opposite of his officer, a quiet, placid individual who was looking at some of my sketches they had found in my suitcase. He was a Ukrainian, and he had a good face, nice features and must have had a good ancestry. He never spoke, except to exchange a few words in Ukrainian with the interpreter. He seemed to be thoroughly ashamed of the whole proceedings and in a hurry to be gone.

I happened to be standing beside Stefan when I heard the interpreter's voice whispering in Hungarian, "Too late now. Too late. He's already arrested. You shouldn't have informed against him." I looked round steathily. Stefan's face was deathly pale, his hands quivering, although he kept his fingers clasped so tight that the knuckles showed white. Judas!

Tacitus quickly kissed his wife and was led out. He had not even time to say good-bye to us.

Child-soldier on a Pony

I GOT up before dawn to go with Marietta to the new headman. We made a small parcel of bread and ham and set out in the grey twilight. The door was opened by the headman's pretty, light-fingered daughter, but shut again in our faces the moment she saw us. Then we heard her announcing our presence, calling us just by our names without any "Mrs." or title, and we stood patiently waiting in the freezing cold until at last the headman himself poked out his head. Yes, he was going to the next village. No, he could do nothing at all about my brother-in-law. The bread and ham he could take, but he could not interfere with the course of Soviet justice. Then the door was slammed in our faces again.

The battle had now begun: a battle between the headman's family and that of the Lord of the Manor. It was to be a long affair, in comparison with which the feud of the Montagues and Capulets was nothing. You see, the headman's great-grandfather had once tried to shoot Jumbo's and Tacitus' great-grandfather, but he had missed and been thrashed for it. Perhaps, had that worthy old aristocrat given the peasant a rood or two of land for shooting so badly instead of thrashing him, the feud between the two families would never have broken out a hundred years afterwards. But that was how it was.

About eleven o'clock a Russian cart drove up to the Manor with yet another search-party. Wireless and arms again! Down from the cart jumped that revolting Sashka, a tall, fair-haired man with European features whom we had not seen before, another officer, and a soldier. The driver stayed with his horses.

"But you searched yesterday and there was nothing," I said to Sashka, aggrieved at such a display of cynicism. "You searched the place yourself and know better than anyone that we are innocent." But it was no use.

The tall, fair-haired man was a Czech detective. He spoke every known language and was a cynical opportunist who cared not a jot for the Russians or their ideology, but merely wanted to make a fortune out of the changed situation in which Slavs were "brothers" and no longer "swine." In the hall he pulled a letter out of his pocket, a mere scrap of paper, and thrust it under Marietta's nose.

"Is that your husband's writing?" he asked.

"Yes," said poor Marietta.

"Please read it."

Meanwhile, the other Russians had scattered about the house. Not being able to believe that the Counter-Intelligence was stupid enough really to suspect us of having arms hidden, I could only suppose that they had come to steal. Sashka must have told them that there was an untouched bourgeois home and they had come to help themselves. So now we all chased after the Russians who were dispersing about the rooms, for though we could not stop them looting, petty theft we would not allow.

Marietta calmly read the letter. She was fearfully pale. "My husband writes," she said suddenly, raising her voice, "that I am to hand over at once," and here she read out a list of arms enough to fill an arsenal. Poor Tacitus had included almost everything: revolvers, shotguns, rifles, pistols, and ammunition as well. Without thinking, we all burst out laughing: all except Marietta. She was wondering what they had done to force her husband to write such a letter. And how, we wondered, could Tacitus expose his wife to such danger. He knew perfectly well that we did not possess even one firearm. Why had he admitted to something of which he knew himself innocent? It was most disquieting. Jumbo examined the letter, and then Rudi. There was no doubt that it was in Tacitus' handwriting. The Czech smiled triumphantly, while with heavy hearts we watched the soldiers plundering us, feeling impotent to stop them.

"So, you are not going to hand over the arms," the Czech asked viciously, and the politeness of his tone was offensive after the vulgar shouting of the Russians.

"I don't possess them; so I can't hand them over," answered Marietta.

"In that case your husband was deliberately deceiving us by writing such a precise list of hidden firearms."

"I don't understand why he wrote such a letter," replied Marietta, in the same calm, even voice. "He best of all knows that there are no arms in the house. It is his house." And Marietta gave a sad smile.

Jumbo had all the while been watching the Czech closely, and seemed to have come to the conclusion that this was the right moment to start negotiations, and here Jumbo was very much at home. The Czech also seemed to think that the time had come to get down to business; he called Jumbo over and suggested in the polite tone of a man unwilling to force his presence on the ladies that they might go somewhere else to talk things over together. The two of them then disappeared into Jack's room. I ran after them, but Jumbo would not let me into the room. "Leave us alone. I know what I am doing," he whispered in French, so I ran off back to Tacitus' room where the Russians were already at Marietta's suitcases.

As usual it was the toilet-paper that aroused the greatest interest. No Russian could think what we wanted it for, unless for rolling cigarettes. After Marietta's they began on my cases. At that moment Jumbo came looking for me. He and the Czech had come to terms. It appeared that the Czech was in need of a civilian suit, boots and overcoat, because he was being sent to Vienna as a plain clothes detective. A civilian outfit, indeed! Many Germans had also found it suddenly necessary to have civilian clothes, so we were no more surprised by the Czech's demand than we had been by theirs.

Meanwhile Sashka was in our room, losing no time. Poor Marietta had to stand there impotently while two gold bracelets disappeared from Jumbo's bedside table, not daring to say a word. Later, when I angrily reproached her, she admitted that she had purposely not called me, that she had even tactfully turned her eyes away. "What could I have done?" she asked. "I couldn't very well tell him not to steal, and to have watched him do it would have been disgusting."

Those petty thefts made me furious. I could stand being plundered. After all, the Russian soldiers had conquered the country, and that they should rape the women and loot everything worth having was at least in accordance with age-old tradition. But to steal? That a soldier should steal things while searching a house on duty, looking round stealthily in case anyone was watching, that, I can assure you, is a far more disgusting sight than that of outright plunder, when a pistol is thrust into your tummy and no bones made about it. What was sadder still, we noticed that the Russians stole most expertly, and their idea of where best to look for grenades and firearms was in ladies' handbags and small suitcases, where there was scarcely room for them, but in all probability a watch, cigarette-case, rings or money. Practically all of them were expert pickpockets, as I know, for I often saw them at work, both officers and men.

To get the Czech what he needed took a long time and necessitated much running from room to room, for no one wanted to give up his last remaining garments. While we searched and collected, the Czech had strayed into Rudi's room and began looking to see if there was anything there that might take his fancy, for they had all long since forgotten that they had come to search for wireless sets and arms. In a cupboard the Czech found a camera. "Oh! You're not allowed to have this at the front," he exclaimed happily, and slung the camera over his shoulder. Then he discovered Elsie's famous silk dressing-gown in which she usually appeared in the morning and again in the evening, for she had not yet got over the mania of dressing for dinner, despite the fact that it was long since she had even possessed an evening dress.

"Here's a bourgeois thing," the Czech exclaimed, waving the dressing-gown about. "You won't find this in Russia. Real silk, by Jove!"

I knew by the tone of his voice and the impertinent look on his face, that he was trying to frighten us in order to make us give him a better suit and overcoat, so I replied in Russian, which the soldiers would also be able to understand:

"What are you talking about? We had some Russian women quartered here, and they all, every one of them, went about in silk like that. Are you trying to tell us that Russia is so poor that the women can't afford to buy a piece of silk for a dressing-gown?"

The Czech didn't even turn a hair. He just narrowed his cunning little eyes and looked at me as much as to say: don't try to be so clever. I'm not a fool, either. Will you try and tell me about Russia?

"They didn't wear silk in Russia," he said in Hungarian, in a low voice, "if they have anything decent, they got it here. In Russia they never even saw anything like this," and, throwing the dressing-gown over a chair, he gave a laugh and smiled confidentially at us.

Elsie ran across and seized her unfortunate, crumpled dressing-gown, clutching it to her breast as though it were her child she had just rescued from a burning house; then she bore it off to a safe place, all that remained of her huge fortune, and as she walked away she hissed like a snake.

"Hi! Lida!" roared Sashka. "Show us the attics and the cellars now. Don't think we won't find your arms. Don't fool yourself, my dear. Come! Come! We're not idiots."

I went to the attic where there was nothing. Sashka, and the soldiers with him, knew that as well as I and so they did not even bother to clamber up the steep stairs. When I reached the top, I heard them shouting from below, "Come down! Come down! What did you go up there for? Come, show us the cellars now." But, before I came down, I made a discovery. In a corner of the attic was a hen-coop. After the affair with the turkeys, the Hungarians had evidently thought it necessary to hide their remaining poultry from me, and I must admit that they were right. I could well understand their fears.

We then went to the cellars. As before, the Russians sent me down alone while they remained at the top of the stairs. "Well what's there?" they asked, as though I were their orderly and not the sister-in-law of the chief accused. "Potatoes," I answered politely, and clambered back up the steep stairs.

When I emerged into the daylight, I noticed that Sashka was gazing intently at me.

"How is it you're so thin? What have you done with your stomach and breasts?" he asked. "Are you ill? Have you had an operation, or what? What's wrong with you? Have you all got the same disease in this house?"

I did not realize then why Sashka was taking such an interest in my health, so I replied:

"We're made that way."

"Well, if you're not ill come and show me the stables. And you," he added, turning to the soldier with him, "you stay here and see that no one leaves the house. Take damned good care that not a soul comes out."

So I took Sashka to the stables, assuring him as we went along that there were no arms there either. As we stepped into the warm darkness that smelt of manure, I said:

"There you are, there isn't even a loft, so where could we hide any arms?"

But Sashka was not even listening. There was a piercing look in his eyes, as he stared at me, and then, suddenly, he smiled, a nauseating, sugary-sweet smile.

"Listen, Lida dear. You would like your brother-in-law to come back home to-day, wouldn't you?"

"I would," I replied enthusiastically.

"All right. You just stay with me in this stable for ten minutes. No one will come in now. You're a Pole and I'm your brother Slav. Do you understand?" And he stroked my face with his huge, dirty paw. "And I'll promise you in return that your brother-in-law will get back home to-day unharmed."

"My brother-in-law will come back anyway, because he is innocent," I said, edging carefully towards the door and trying to smile as charmingly as I knew how.

Sashka, however, anticipated my manoeuvre and barred the way.

"Lida, we are good fellows, no one will ever know anything about it, and your brother-in-law will get home to-day. I've only to say a word to the Captain. The Captain respects me, and what I say goes. Look, we haven't even stolen a thing from you because we're decent chaps."

"I know that you are awfully decent and that's why you're going to let my brother-in-law go, too. You haven't found any arms. Someone was making a fool of you, telling you that we had hidden arms," I said, and made another attempt to reach the door. The only result was that Sashka's revolting smile disappeared and his face clouded.

"Listen, you! I'll find arms hidden here if I want to. You wouldn't make all this song and dance if it were your husband who had been arrested; but your brother-in-law, he's nothing, you don't mind about him. You be careful, Lida! You realize you're killing a man?"

Where was my quickness of wit? Where all the cunning about which I so often boasted? I just stood there like an idiot, unable to gather my wits, my eyes searching for a way out of the stable and that nasty situation, like any cornered animal.

"Lida," began Sashka again, "I'm a soldier. Do you know what sort of life I've had? For four dreadful years I haven't seen my family, and here are you making an appalling fuss, as though I were asking you to do, I don't know what." Then, as an afterthought he said, "I promise, I'll never forget you," as though he considered that the best reward he could give me and the best thing I could receive. "Do you hear?" he went on, taking the amusement in my face for agreement. "*Nikogda, nikogda,* never will I forget you. I shall always remember you."

That would be a real comfort, I thought, and then said, "Let me go, Sashka. I'm very fond of my husband and I can't betray him."

That made Sashka really angry, and he seized me by the shoulders and began shaking me like an apple-tree, shouting into my very face,

"Don't you talk to me about your husband. No one will ever find out. Aren't you sorry for your brother-in-law? Don't you want to save a man when you can? No arms, what? I'll soon find some, and what will happen then do you think?"

This, I thought, is the end. Where was Jack? Where were the others? Why did no one ever guess anything, never sense what was happening? Here was I on the point of being raped and no one came to save me, although they were only a few yards away. Just let someone mention the word telepathy, and I will soon tell him what I think about it. You mustn't be afraid, I thought, don't be afraid; just keep on smiling.

"All right," I said, "but wait."

"What for?" asked Sashka, very reasonably, and he was so surprised that he let go of me.

"Sashka!" came a voice from outside. "Sashka! Where have you got to? The Comrade Lieutenant's calling you."

Just like an American film, I thought with the remnants

of my wits. Life imitating art. Then I dived out of the stable, followed by glowering Sashka, pulling up his trousers. The Czech detective had ordered lunch and wine and was inviting his subordinates.

My virtue cost the Hungarians a pound of bacon, seven inches of sausage, a loaf of bread, and two bottles of red wine, but as they never knew about it they did not even have that comfort. I was so ashamed of my own stupidity that I never told them.

As far as Sashka was concerned, it was not my fault that he had been summoned, and he remained horribly polite. The Hungarians struck up a friendship with the Czech and talked normally with him, so that the Russians understood nothing of what was said. Stefan appeared in the dining-room, but no one offered him as much as a cigarette.

Having eaten and drunk and smoked cigarettes, the Russians finally took their leave. We parted the best of friends. Sashka gave my hand a very hard squeeze, and even smiled at me from the cart. As I was ardently hoping that this was the last time I should ever see him, I smiled back as nicely as I could, to the huge delight of Fifi who already knew the whole story.

We were sitting after our lunch discussing Tacitus' letter when the door opened and two Russians came in and asked, without any of the usual preliminaries, "Seen anything of a sheep-dog?" And they looked round the room, as though there might be one hanging among the pictures.

"There hasn't been one here," I said.

"And where did you learn Russian?" asked the elder of the two.

"I'm Polish. There are three of us Poles here."

"Well, then, I've got news for you. Our army has taken Cracow without a fight."

That launched us into the usual interminable chat, and the dog was forgotten, for, of course, it had never existed. They had, it is true, described it minutely, as they would with their Russian imagination. They had just come to look at us as they might have gone to a museum or a Fun Fair. To come and see us and our house and pictures was a great attraction, and no self-respecting Russian ever omitted to pay us a visit; but, as the Russians are an Eastern people, they never said so straight out.

Later that afternoon little Alec came rushing breathlessly into the room, shouting, "Uncle's come back! Uncle's come back!"

"What a banal ending to a very original day," I said to Elsie, and we made for the door and through the kitchen into the courtyard from where we could see poor Tacitus, obviously exhausted, ploughing his way up the hill. Having got him inside into the hall, we surrounded him and showered him with questions: "Did they beat you?" "Why did you write that stupid letter?" "Did you see the headman?" "Did you get our bread and bacon?" We all wanted to know everything at once.

In the end Tacitus was allowed to speak. They had treated him well. He had been locked up with two peasants from the village, who were struck twice on the face, but he was never touched. They had fed him, once, with bread and soup. The Captain had forced him to write the letter at the point of his revolver, but otherwise he was a decent chap. They had let him go that day after lunch without giving any reason, but the two peasants had been kept. They had never interrogated him; just gave him back everything they had taken from his pockets the day before, and let him go. The Captain was nice rather than otherwise. He did not know who the informer was, but supposed it was Stefan. So, at least, the two peasants had said.

I did not get up the next morning. I was so tired that I made Fifi and Jack do my chores for me; then I undressed, a thing I was never able to do at night, and lay there just enjoying bed.

To make it a real holiday and to try and forget what was going on, I got one of my late mother-in-law's books, a volume of Maupassant's stories, and, pouring myself out a large glass of vodka, settled down to read about a former world in which sex seemed to have played the chief part. Ye gods, what sort of stories would Maupassant have written had he been living now!

Through the window I could see the dull, cloudy, wintry sky and a couple of naked branches gazing in at me. It looked as though we were not going to see the Tall Major again, as though he, too, were afraid of us, as were the peasants. Jumbo sat beside the window in his grandmother's chair, reading his Richelieu. I could hear Tacitus and Rudi chopping wood in the woodshed, and from the hall came the sound of Elsie's voice reading a fairy-tale to Alec, who had a temperature. How good it was to lie in bed, undressed. What a tiny, every-day pleasure, and yet how marvellous now.

I heard the door between the hall and the dining-room creak; Lina coming to put on more coke, I thought. But it wasn't, for immediately afterwards, I heard Elsie say, "*Zdrast-vujtie*" with her English accent, and I could tell from her tone that she was smiling. Then our door opened and there was the Tall Major, a smile on his face. "May I?" he said.

The Tall Major sat down beside Jumbo, laid an army paper on the floor, looked round the room, gave a deep sigh, and clapped his hands down on widespread knees. "I'm going away," he said. "My orders have come."

It was only then that I realized how attached to the Tall Major I had become. At first we would not believe him, but it was only too true. He promised to drop in for a moment in the evening to say good-bye; now, however, he had some good news to comfort us. He picked up his paper and began reading slowly in his even voice, glancing up at us every now and again. "Warsaw, Zyrardy, Radom and Czestochowa occupied by the Red Army," and the Tall Major smiled with pleasure at being able to give us such good news. He then advised us how best to protect ourselves from the Army in which he served. "Lie, lie brazenly," he said, "and look them straight in the eyes, for the Russians have a superstition that a liar never looks you in the face. So lie and keep on lying. Tell them that you are doctors, artists, and try to believe it yourselves, but always stick to the same lie." We laughed and thanked him. Then he stood up. "I'll look in again this evening," he said.

"Please come to supper."

"All right."

Then he crushed our three hands and went.

It was the grey hour of dusk. In life there are occasions when time stands still and those are the moments you remember, such grey hours that last but thirty minutes and yet are remembered as though they had occupied a whole day. This was one of them. We seldom lit the lamps those days, so as to save paraffin, and it was now too dark to read. "Tell us about something," I said to Jumbo, and he chose something as far removed as possible from the life we were living, Egypt, the Egypt of the rich. As he talked we could see the luxury hotels (we did not want to hear about the others), we were served by swarms of obsequious servants, and huge, shining cars stood waiting our pleasure in the hot Egyptian sun. In the streets we were surrounded by beggars to whom we graciously gave alms. Palms stood motionless on the fringe of a desert whose sand was sometimes lilac, at others rose-red. But what interested us most were the menus, for our food was beginning to run out. As Jumbo told us about Arabian dancers, cute little page-boys, greedy guides and the cataracts of the Nile, I looked out of the window, beyond which I could just make out the two naked branches and the shadowy figure of a soldier slipping past on his way, perhaps, to the kitchen. Then it was supper time. I had mine in bed, alone except for the mendicant Alf, who had to keep licking his chops the whole time, and even so he dribbled on to the blanket.

The Tall Major arrived after supper. He sat down beside my bed and we began talking about literature and Russian humour. We laughed so much that we all forgot that the Major would be gone the next day, until Lina shuffled in in her slippers to say that some peasants had arrived with a Russian soldier looking for the Major. Evidently hooligans from the front had got into their house and were trying to carry off the women, and would the Major help, for he was now renowned in the village.

"I'll be back immediately. I'll just settle this and come back," said the Tall Major, righting his belt and heavy pistol, as he ran for the door.

We waited an hour for him to come back, then another; but he never came.

We were at breakfast, the whole family except for Jumbo who was ill and still asleep, and we were eating the last of our potatoes, washing them down with the last of our tea. Heavy steps sounded in the corridor; the door opened, and, yes, it was the Tall Major.

"I'm just off. I haven't time to take my coat off. Well, perhaps I will." And he removed his cap and overcoat. "I have come to say good-bye." Then he turned to me and whispered diffidently, "If there's a little wine, I would like to drink with you."

I fetched a bottle of Tokay and poured out a glass for each of us; then the Tall Major stood up and said,

"I've grown very fond of your family. I like you all very much. Now, I am going away and, perhaps, I shall never see you again."

He had spoken in Russian, but very slowly and using only the simplest words, yet I still had to translate what he had said. Language is a cage. It was only Fifi, I, and the Tall Major who were moved. While Fifi and I saw a man in the grip of a boundless sorrow, choosing the simplest words in the hope that we would thus better understand him and his sorrow at parting, all that the Hungarians saw was the ridiculous sight of a giant in Russian uniform standing with a glass in his hand and tears in his eyes.

Then the Tall Major bowed slightly to Tacitus, touched his glass with his, and, bending lower still, kissed him on the cheek. He did the same with us all, going up to each in turn, clinking glasses, and kissing us on the cheek. The Hungarians were taken aback and a little scandalized, but being people of the world they had enough manners to keep their giggles to themselves. The Tall Major's face was intolerably sad and deadly serious, as though he were performing a religious rite, and there were tears in his eyes. He was neither ashamed nor proud of his tears, but cried because the tears were there, as Odysseus had cried when he felt like it, as men and gods did in the days of Homer when men were so undoubtedly men that tears could not stain their fame.

When he came to Fifi, she stood on tip-toe and flung her arms round his neck. Then it was my turn. I put my arms round his broad shoulders and gave him a hearty kiss, the kiss a Pole will give a relative or a good friend.

Then the Major looked round anxiously, like a sheep-dog in charge of a flock. He had missed Jumbo, and wished to bid him good-bye. I took him to our room.

"I'm sorry that I couldn't get back last night," he said, "but I had no sooner restored order in the one cottage than I was called to a second, and then to a third, and it took all night."

But Jumbo did not hear. He was asleep. I shook him and he woke up and raised his head, blinking in surprise. Then the Major bent down, his face hard and as though carved out of wood, placed a farewell kiss on Jumbo's sleepy face, seized his hand, gave it a hard squeeze, and hurried from the room.

Jack helped him on with his overcoat and handed him his cap. I felt dreadfully ashamed that so much friendship and emotion had found no response and, running after the Tall Major, I caught him in my arms again and hugged him. There were still tears in his eyes, and now in mine as well. And so the Tall Major hurried away, escaping from his own emotion, back into the routine of the twentieth century, the war and the whole business of daily life; and I went back to the dining-room, the tears still quivering on my lashes.

"A nice chap!" said the Hungarians, their mouths full of potato.

N.K.W.D.

21st-23rd January

THE early morning was peaceful, and life seemed at last to have settled down. No new units had come, and the two boys had not been taken for work at the front and were still in the Veterinary Hospital. The planks from the fence had all been collected and cunningly hidden in the attic, and we had got a sack of potatoes from the bailiff and another of coke. In other words, we were well supplied and the outlook was less hazy. For the time being we had only one worry: the occupation of the capital. We knew that when Budapest was taken the war would move on quickly away from us and then things might have a chance to change for the better.

It was close on midday when a pleasant young soldier came to request billets for himself and his Lieutenant. His name was Nicholas and he was as sure of himself as are most young Russians. The most cocksure of all are those between the ages of fourteen and twenty-one, the age when youth does not think, not just in the Soviet Union but all over the world. By that I mean that they think a lot but that nothing sensible comes out of it, for they do not think as they should. That is why dictators are always so eager to get hold of their country's youth. I have always been repelled by the juvenile, and the present fashion of gushing over it disgusts me. The conceit and impertinence of those young Russian lads was just as intolerable as that of their European contemporaries in Fascist countries. Is its youth a nation's flower? Not a bit of it. It's a dangerous charge of dynamite that ought to be kept under lock and key.

We promised to take Nicholas in, and even wanted to put a second paillasse in Jack's room for his Lieutenant. Nicholas gravely told us that for four years of warfare they had slept in the one bed and they would not change their habits now. Then he went off to get his things and his officer.

Lunch passed off peacefully, then Nicholas arrived with his beloved Lieutenant. He, too, was quite young, but more intelligent than his orderly and so less sure of himself. Having inspected the bed we had prepared, he asked why we had put one pillow at either end, instead of both together. He wanted to know whether in Europe we made up the bed for a man and a woman so that one slept with the other's feet under his nose. Fifi and I, in some embarrassment, assured him that for married couples we put the two pillows together at the one end. Well, make the bed like that for us, too, said Nicholas enthusiastically, and he and his Lieutenant even helped us remake the bed. That done, the two Russians sat down and we began the usual conversation with its inevitable personal questions without which no one's acquaintance is ever made.

Meanwhile troops were pouring into the village, and we heard vague rumours that every house was now occupied, that there were troops everywhere. Jack came back with a Lieutenant, whom we received with open arms because we were afraid that, with the village being so full, we might have a fresh horde of soldiers descend upon us. It is always like that with the Russians: if you know them personally they won't touch a hair of your head, though you were the "king bourgeois" himself; but those you don't know are always incalculable and full of possibilities that I advise no one to try to plumb. By evening, however, the overflow was already coming to us in search of billets, and one lot even turned out Nicholas and his beloved Lieutenant for they were numerically stronger. The two departed quietly, without any of the usual fuss and cursing, which confirmed our suspicions.

From the main road came a continual roar of heavy lorries grinding their way up hill. Where were they going? A strange cook came and installed himself in the kitchen, and, as evening fell, the artillery started up.

Some strange officers came and requisitioned the hall and the dining-room. Jack's room was rapidly filling up with Russians, of whom there were already seven on the bed intended for the unfortunate Nicholas, lying in every possible direction. We were kept running with blankets, pillows and mattresses.

It was a young Captain who moved into the hall, the first Hero of the Soviet Union we had seen. We had heard this and that about these "heroes," and now for the first time we saw the little star of pure gold, hanging at his chest, which, as the owner proudly assured us, meant that he was such a Hero. The strange cook had meanwhile occupied the entire kitchen and there was no question of Matilda being able to cook supper for us. We had had little to eat for several days and the rapturous smells of meat and cabbage that reached us were torment.

A new figure suddenly appeared in the hall, a tall, dark-haired man, neatly dressed in a clean uniform, Captain Fedia. He was followed by others in a continual stream until it was almost impossible to make your way through them. These officers, though, were different, silent and deathly tired, and they fell asleep the moment they sat down. This made me instinctively anxious, but I could not voice my anxiety for there was no real reason why this should have been a retreat.

By dawn the men had all left Jack's room and, as the cook was not preparing breakfast, perhaps the Hero and his lot would also be leaving soon.

The officers were all awake now, and it was possible to have a look at them by daylight. There was one young one

with a nice-looking, intelligent face. Had he been a Pole, I
would have said that he was a smart suburban counter-jumper,
but as a Russian, he looked among his companions like an
aristocrat. There was a European look in his eye and his gaze
was sharp and concentrated. Anyone who has had to spend
any length of time with the Red Army will confirm how difficult it is to find there a European-looking face. I don't mean
European in respect of racial features, but in expression, and
how to describe that expression I do not know, nor yet of
what it consists.

We only see Europeans with such faces in old portraits
where the genius of the great painters has preserved them for
us. For example, Charlemagne, who although he could not
read or write was nevertheless a great Emperor, must have
looked like a modern Russian. To-day you could search
Europe in vain for a face like his because apart from features,
shape of the skull and racial characteristics, it must be remembered that *the expression* of the average European has
changed beyond recognition. Not so in Russia. If you look
at the old portraits of the Middle Ages up to the XVIIth
century, not those of the clergy or the learned who constituted
the most cultured class, but those of the various kings and
aristocrats, you will see that although their features are often
magnificent, the faces are those of peasants; a type of face
which survives largely in Russia to-day. It is this facial expression that digs the gulf between Russia and Europe because it points to one simple fact: they look as we looked a
few hundred years ago. That means that they are several centuries younger than we are.

It takes months to convince a European parliament that
its army budget must be increased, and much talk of demo-
cratic ideals, European achievements, culture, civilization, of
hard-won freedom that must be defended in the name of the
whole of mankind before the European masses will take to
arms and march away reluctantly, bidding their families a
tearful farewell, to sacrifice themselves. But the Russian sol-

diers will give their lives for a watch with a second hand. They have freedom and ideals of the revolution talked at them, but only because that is the thing to do. They do not sacrifice themselves as our men do. For them war is what it used to be for our ancestors: an integral part of a gentleman's life; the greatest of all sports. They fight for booty.

It is not easy to live long in the same house with Russian officers, for you cannot stop them coming into every room, looking into every drawer and suitcase, or asking politely whether there are any women in the house who would like to spend the night with them. None of those Russians could ever have had a room to himself, so had acquired an entirely different technique of living from ours. They could not even begin to realize that it is essential to have a place of your own and a private life. And this is not just the result of their collective upbringing, but brought about by their wretched poverty. We can see the same thing here on a much smaller scale; people of the working classes as a rule do not appreciate what we call privacy because they have never had it, having been brought up to live under conditions that exclude the very possibility of it. A Russian on sentry duty is ready to howl with boredom, and later I came across several cases of two soldiers who had to patrol a deserted village, where no danger threatened, preferring to do so together for the full eight hours rather than separately for four hours each. Anything so as not to be alone. He will go into a cottage, sit himself down beside the stove and stay there for hours on end, just peeping out every now and again to make sure that the enemy is not being too active in his area. Perhaps you can now imagine what it must be like to live together with such people in a small house. It is like sharing quarters with a flock of monkeys, which not only have to pick up everything and open every drawer but with which you also have to talk uninterruptedly.

Fedia and the Hero sat down to a game of cards and a jug of wine almost as soon as they were awake. A wireless was installed in Jack's room and the door locked. How that day passed we did not know, we did not even remember when it began to grow dark. Fedia suggested that I spend the night with him, but he seemed to do so mostly out of politeness to his hostess, for when I said, "No, thanks," in the tone of one refusing a cigarette, he did not insist.

Breathless officers were continually rushing in with reports and messages. Fedia and the Hero would lay their cards down on the table, listen, scratch their heads, and then go back to their game. Otherwise, nothing happened.

I did, however, notice that the name of the nearest town was often mentioned. Had the Russians started an offensive, or could it possibly be the other way round? That was a thought we stubbornly refused to entertain, for even to imagine such a possibility seemed like treason. As dusk fell the Hero mounted a lorry and drove off, as he said, to the front. The others stayed behind, but then a Hero has to be a hero. The Hero was back again in no time, and we heard Fedia and the others swearing with him about conditions at the front. That was most disquieting.

The cook began packing up in the kitchen. The men in Jack's room dismantled their wireless and rolled up their telephone wires. Then, without so much as a word to us, they all disappeared as suddenly as they had come. All we heard was the grumble of the lorries in the misty twilight as the garden emptied. Then, as one man, we rushed into the rooms to open the windows and tidy them. By dark everything was ready and the furniture back in its place.

The door, as it was always doing, opened and in walked not the usual Russian but a whole horde of them. They were all officers. I had to get out of bed and fetch pillows and cushions for them, for they, too, were exhausted and almost asleep on their feet, and again they spoke only in whispers and the name of our town still cropped up in what they said. Almost everything with the Russians is a "war secret," I know, but there was something about all this whispering that I did not like, for usually they spoke in Neanderthal tones.

It was still dark when the whole house suddenly became the scene of feverish activity. The officers who had woken us had already left, and the kitchen was now occupied by a Mongolian cook who had arrived some time during the night, and he was now preparing breakfast, it seemed, for a whole division. A field-kitchen had appeared in the courtyard, the first we had seen, for the Russians like to feed in private houses or cottages, and each larger pack had its own cook. Did the appearance of a field-kitchen mean that the front would soon reach Mora, too? The garden was alive with grey figures carrying bundles and boxes of ammunition. All had automatic pistols slung round their necks. Then, as it grew light, they began making their way to the kitchen for breakfast.

I was intrigued to find a girl-soldier in the kitchen, lapping her soup with the rest at the table. She looked like a feather bolster tied in the middle with string, and so did all the others I was to see. Any normal-looking Russian girl in the Red Army went about in civilian clothes. Was it because the uniform did not appeal to them, or to give them a better chance of getting a rich lover which, for all their Communism, meant a higher-ranking officer, or an especially clever thief? And where did they get the money to buy those civilian clothes? That girl lapping her breakfast soup, however, was typical of the Russian girl-soldier. She had almost no nose, deep-set slit eyes of blue, and thick, flat lips. Her companion, a twisted little cripple, suddenly took off his jerkin and began dancing in the hot, steamy kitchen.

The soldiers quickly formed an interested circle about him. The dwarf contorted himself without moving from the spot where he stood. He was rather like a dog shaking itself after a bath, but those were convulsions that had been studied, redolent of Eastern tradition. The ammunition was forgotten and all came running to watch. Someone began playing on

a mouth-organ, others clapped their hands rhythmically and
the little monster danced more and more furiously, now approaching, now withdrawing from the girl, and making his
stomach move as though it had a separate existence and life
of its own. From time to time the girl would lift her face
from her plate and give a shrill quavering laugh, or giggle,
covering her mouth, full of black bread, with her hand. The
voices of Russian women are the exact opposite of those of
the men: high-pitched, squeaky and quavering. Pinch a Russian girl and you will hear top C reached with the utmost ease.

Despite her hump and sixty-two years of spinsterhood,
Matilda liked a little fun with young people, but this cook was
a Mongol. Does a young Mongol count as a young person?
Not to Matilda! To her every Russian soldier whose appearance was silghtly exotic was a Chink, and that was the end of
it. To Matilda the poor Chinese are a kind of monkey, well
trained and clever, but monkeys for all that, and so, of course,
not fit for social intercourse however playful. The end of the
world had come to the kitchen, or so Matilda thought.

Leaving the kitchen to go and clear up after the Russians,
I found the Hungarians already at work and the windows
opened, though they could not be left like that long as those
who cut and chop their own firewood will readily understand.
At length we restored the hall to order and sat down in it,
like true bourgeois, pretending that everything was all right.

To some, our mania for immediately airing and cleaning
up the rooms may seem strange. And it was in a way senseless, like the work of ants repairing their ant-hill that man is
destroying, unable to understand that the spade is more
powerful than their will. The world was falling about our
ears and we just aired our rooms! And Tacitus would still
keep looking at his watch (which miraculously had not yet
been taken from him), so as not to be late in taking his gruel,
despite the fact that a Mongolian ballet was being staged in
the kitchen.

No one now called "Lida! Lida!" for the Russians were

beginning to filter into the hall themselves. One such was a short girl with black hair, a merry expression, and an automatic pistol slung round her neck. Another feather bolster! She gazed interestedly round the wall, then, as though to remove our doubts as much as hers, she said, "Pictures, aren't they? Pictures?" She was so pleased to find that she could speak Russian with us that she at once sat down and made herself comfortable. This is my meat, I thought; I'll soon find out from her where this flood of Russians has come from. And I was right, for Mariusya did not have the mania for "war secrets" nearly as badly as the others. Where had they come from? From the nearest town, of course. Why all the commotion? That she did not know; but she cheerfully supposed that, perhaps, they were retreating. The order had come and they had had to hurry like anything. And whose was the artillery that we had been hearing all the last two days? That, said Mariusya, nobody knew. Usually both sides fired at the same time, that was the whole point of war. Mariusya had been fighting for four years now and she knew, knew that both sides always had to fire. So there was a German offensive, we asked. But Mariusya was not in the least interested in anything but the pictures. "We, too, have a picture in our house in Odessa," she said proudly. "We have Marx hung up, a very pretty picture; Marx, such an old man with a beard. It's very pretty." "Ooh! Marx, indeed!" and we nodded our heads in respectful admiration. "Now you show me whom you've got hanging here," said Mariusya, and we showed her Tolstoy, whom we did have hanging in the corner. "And there's Pushkin," I added, pointing as usual to Schubert. Mariusya gazed intently at Schubert's curly head and Biedermeyer coat, "Yes, indeed, Pushkin," she agreed admiringly, and after that she was most reluctant to leave such cultured people.

My mother-in-law had had a collection of engravings of famous people. These used to hang in a row high up under the ceiling, but we had taken Tolstoy down from his rusty

nail so as to have him at hand, and he had rendered us priceless service ever since. We showed him to everyone that came,
and most of them actually knew him. They would come to
ask whether there were any women in the house who would
spend the night with them, and our reply was to show them
Tolstoy. Schubert I turned into Pushkin in the very early
days, and I even had a Lermontov too, though I had no idea
how he looked. Luckily, neither had most Russians. Once it
was Melanchthon, on other occasions Berlioz, that I chose for
him, and each time speaking with great assurance as the Tall
Major had advised, I said, "There, look! Lermontov!" and
the Russians would nod their heads in admiring approval of
our high state of culture, and ask whether elsewhere in Europe
people had portraits of Lermontov and knew that Russian
writers were the greatest in the world. And I would assure
him that undoubtedly Lermontov, and certainly at least Pushkin, would be found hanging everywhere.

Comfortably settled, Mariusya embarked on a rapid account of her life's history, for to have made friends and not
tell us all about herself would have been bad manners. She
had been soldiering for four years, having volunteered and
gone to the front at the age of sixteen. Her father was fighting in Poland on the Ruthenian front. He was a full Lieutenant. What other father would have let his daughter, little
more than a child, go off soldiering by herself? He would
have done everything to have her with him, even as his orderly.
Yet the ties and sentiments of parenthood and family seem
considerably weaker in Russia than in the civilized world. As
the soldiers often said, "Women are everywhere, and you can
make as many children as you want, whenever you like."

When Mariusya at last went, we returned to our tidying.
We thought now that we would concentrate all our worldly
goods in three rooms, for we felt that something was brewing.
There were too many soldiers wandering about the rooms and
gardens for our liking, and the Mongol cook was feeding a
succession of new arrivals. Our trouble was useless, however,

for shortly after we started an elderly Cossack came in and announced that we must vacate the house at once. This news was greeted with deathly silence. Behind the first came a second Cossack, as like him as two pins, and told us that we could stay where we were. Then we began trying to find an officer who could tell us which was right. We never found one, but instead came an elderly, very dirty, ragged sergeant who with as many regrets as though it were his personal doing, told us that we must all get out of the house at once and take our things with us, for which he promised us a cart.

This bolt from the blue brought a spurt of questions: "Where to?" "Why?" "Was the village being evacuated?" "Who was turning us out?" The answers were far from clear, for once again we were up against the mysteries of "war secrets." Where were we to go? Were we to camp in the fields? "You will be told all in good time," was the only comfort they could give us as they urged us to get on with our packing.

I now officially told the Hungarians that we were to get out. They were most indignant that I had not found out why, nor where we were to go, refusing to believe that it was a "war secret" and that they would not tell us. Anyway, it was nicer and easier for the Hungarians to vent their anger on me, than on some invisible Russian officer whom they could not curse to his face. In the end, after much persuasion, the old sergeant, who was up to the eyes in work, went outside with me.

"You will live there," he said, pointing at the village lying in the hollow.

"Where? In which house?"

"In the yellow one," replied the sergeant, still pointing at the village, where forty per cent. of the houses were painted yellow.

"In the one on the right, or the one on the left? In that big one, or in the small one there?"

"In that one there!" said the sergeant, still pointing vaguely at the village, as though that were enough.

"But why?"

"Because," and that was all I could get out of him.

We turned back into the house, and he patted my shoulder and said comfortingly, "We'll give you a cart."

The Hungarians were already feverishly at work packing, the only thought in their heads to save what they could and take it with them. It was not till I saw a group of shackled figures with spades in front of the house that any of us thought that things might be getting dangerous. Spades, however, meant digging, and digging meant that danger was expected, and to us, the possible return of the Germans and death. The thought sent shivers down my back and I went outside again to have a better look at those creatures with the spades. There were a dozen of them, Bashkirs, who called to each other in an exotic, throaty tongue. They had begun digging a hole in front of the terrace. I asked them in Russian what it was, why they were digging it, but none of them understood a word that I said. They were gloomy and tired, and worked dully like animals. The hole deepened, slowly, for the ground was well frozen. From time to time a Russian would come over and curse the wretched Bashkirs as a matter of routine.

The whole garden was swarming with soldiers, the yard was full of carts, and the firing sounded progressively closer. Then my conscience began to prick me, for not helping them pack, and I went back to the house. What a scene! Lina and Matilda were packing in their room, making periodic heroic dives back into the kitchen to snatch some other saucepan from under the Mongol cook's nose. They were so scandalized at our being turned out of the house that they were unable to speak. They would just raise their eyes to heaven and shake both fists at the Russians' backs. Then their fists would unfold and their hands go together in the attitude of prayer.

Nothing about this strange race of conquerors had ever

appealed to Lina, but Matilda, as has been already mentioned, had a weakness for the young, and especially those who gave her wine, sugar, or kissed her. At this moment, however, she hated the Russians and, as she assured me several times, regretting her inability to do it herself, would have liked to summon a battalion of Vikings to murder the lot. Yet it only needed a drunken young soldier to kiss her hand or cheek, or give her a pair of stolen stockings for Matilda to become an ardent Communist again. And it is such as she who make up "the people."

A nice old Ukrainian soldier stopped fitting up the telephone he was supposed to be installing, and came over to help us pack.

"You're from the Ukraine, I from Poland, so we're neighbours," I told him, and he blushed with pleasure and bowed low to me. He spoke the old, pure, melodious Ukrainian as you seldom hear it, that condemned language, among the soldiers of the Red Army. I am afraid that Ukrainian is doomed, not so much by the present regime as from long ago. The average young Ukrainian nowadays forgets his language in a year once he has joined up, for the simple reason that it is so similar to Russian.

The sergeant came to tell us that our cart had arrived. We wanted to cover the bottom of it with our carpets, but these we were forbidden to touch. They were all to be left, and none of us knew why. Even then we still did not realize that a rug or carpet, product of the East, was the only article of luxury whose purpose and usefulness the Russians understood. We could have taken away as many mattresses, rubber pillows, thermos flasks, hot-water bottles, coat-hangers or shoe-trees, as we liked; but the rugs and carpets were sacred and not to be touched. Then there was the question of Muki's cot. That piece of furniture the sergeant regarded with deep suspicion, and refused to let us take it. In the end, we had to put Muki into it to prove that it was just a child's bed and not an infernal machine. Once he saw and understood what it was for, the sergeant let it be loaded on to the cart. We piled everything on, surprised that we still possessed so much.

There were now two officers in the kitchen, one older who had spent the night in the house, and a younger one. I told them that they were only giving us one cart. The young officer at once ran outside, shouted something and came back, wiping his spectacles that the steam in the kitchen had misted. He promised that the cart would make as many trips as necessary. At that the first party set out: Tacitus, Marietta and the two boys, walking behind the cart that was loaded with as much as it would take and driven by a silent, glum Mongol.

We had now discovered, not without difficulty, where we were to live. Our new home was on the hill, called by us Half-wit Hill, near the mill, and we were most curious to see which house they had allotted to us. When the melancholy cart had disappeared from sight, I went to have another quick look at the Bashkirs. They were digging a zig-zag anti-aircraft trench. So that was what was brewing. And we had been thinking that the German Air Force had ceased to exist! Perhaps, perhaps, the Tall Major had been right.

The remains of our treasures were all lying in the rooms packed in great, unwieldy bundles. Elsie remembered the valuables we had buried in the shelter. Was it worth unearthing them? Probably not! Who was going to occupy the house? Presumably at least a General, and a General's suite ought not to be thieves. Perhaps Tolbuchin himself was coming to Mora, from there to make his entry into Budapest when it was liberated. And presumably neither Tolbuchin nor his people would steal our things. Besides, to go digging about in the shelter now would just attract the attention of the soldiers, and they might throw us out and dig our things up for themselves. Better leave them alone. The old Ukrainian kept fiddling with the bundles, tightening the straps with a kindly, embarrassed smile. I went back to the kitchen. The elderly officer was still sitting at the table and, with a hospitable gesture, he motioned me to sit down beside him.

"We Slavs," he began, while I watched his exaggerated gestures, "we Slavs have big hearts, and the Russians especially so. Our hearts are very big. Please sit and eat with us, Soviet officers." Then he turned to the cook and ordered, "Soup for the lady of the house!"

The Mongol handed me an overflowing plate of steaming soup. In it swam bits of cabbage and chunks of fat meat, onions and bacon: an excellent soup.

On going back to our rooms I was hardly able to recognize them. The Russians had got to work like Snow White's dwarfs. They had scrubbed the floors, washed the window-frames, polished the panes, swept out every corner, and were now removing the furniture.

"For once they are clearing up after us," I remarked bitterly to Fifi.

They were carrying the furniture outside through the great, broken front door.

"Don't be afraid," said our old Ukrainian, leaning on his broom. "You've got too much furniture here. We're putting it in the garden. Nobody will steal it, and when we go away you can bring it in again and put it back in your rooms."

Fifi and I looked at each other: so we were going to lose that, too, even though it wasn't going to be stolen.

"And now, you get out of here," said our Ukrainian, "or the sergeant will be angry. Take all your beds but one, the best, and everything that goes with it. Somebody's going to sleep here. Somebody important," he added in a whisper.

We now felt sure that some general was intending to honour our house. We collected the rest of the paillasses, which the Russians grandiloquently called beds, picked up a rug as we went, and struggled with our burdens against the current through the kitchen and outside. On the very thresh-old the sergeant saw us and the rug! Slowly and without a word he pulled it from under my arm. To save face, I pre-tended not to notice. In the courtyard was Jumbo, looking more than ever like a bourgeois in his proletarian clothes, guarding the potatoes that we had with such difficulty got from the bailiff. To be on the safe side he kept one foot on the sack, like a big-game hunter with his trophy. Oh, my dear European husband, that conqueror's gesture was hardly suitable to us! I gave him a kiss, and led him inside to see what the Russians had made of our rooms.

The furniture had all gone, except for a table and a few chairs set against the walls. The clean floors were covered with our rugs, carpets and whatever else they had been able to lay hands on. It was like being in a mosque. The floors were still wet and there was a smell of cleanliness in the rooms into which clean, frosty air flowed from outside through the broken door on to the terrace. The little doors of all the stoves had been opened wide, and flames were crackling merrily in each of them. What a pity Tacitus could not see it; and what a good thing we had cut so much wood latterly! The rooms now all looked like audience chambers, except that in Jack's there was the bed covered with curtains torn from the windows and a large number of pillows, like in a rich peasant's cottage.

"Pretty, now, isn't it? We know how to arrange a house," said the soldiers proudly, leaning for once not on automatic pistols but on brooms. "Now you see that we know what culture is. The Russians know and can show it, when they like." And they smiled happily, like children, as they accompanied us through the rooms, looking round carefully to make sure that the sergeant wasn't anywhere about.

I walked out into the courtyard. Two soldiers were cleaning a carpet near the terrace, picking off the pieces of dirt and scratching out the dust with their finger-nails. Every now and then they would seize the great heavy carpet and give it an angry shake in the air, and then a cloud of dust would descend over the silent Bashkirs where they were still digging. The Bashkirs would just look round disdainfully, gaze glumly at the laughing Russians and go on with their digging. I went and fetched two carpet-beaters.

"Here you are. This is what you use to beat and clean a carpet."

But the Russians wouldn't believe me. Having inspected the carpet-beaters, they shrugged their shoulders and remarked, "Nails are better."

I told them to hold the carpet tight, then showed them how to beat it, using both carpet-beaters at the same time. A colossal cloud of dust rose from the carpet and hung in the still air for a considerable time, before it slowly settled on the heads of the Bashkirs. The soldiers, of course, now understood the use of carpet-beaters, but pretended that they did not so as to get me to go on working for them. Unfortunately for them, the average Russian's cunning is sufficient to take in another average Russian, but not me.

"No, my children," I said, "if you haven't grasped it yet I'll take my carpet-beaters away."

At that they laughed and took them, and I went back to the kitchen door to await the return of the cart.

When it came back for the last time, we loaded on to it our sacks of flour and potatoes; a young officer came up and asked if we knew already where our quarters were and assured me that in a few days we would be able to move back. I took poor, ill Jumbo's arm, whistled to Alf, and the cart moved off with much creaking. With a last quick look at the house, Jumbo, Alf and I set off across the fields for Half-wit Hill and the new life we were to lead there.

B EFORE the river, Jumbo went on ahead with Alf up the hill, while I continued down to the bridge where I met Franzi.

"Why aren't you crossing by the bridge?" I asked him suspiciously, for there was a black crowd of people beside it.

"Because it has just this moment collapsed under a Russian lorry," explained Franzi, scratching the back of his head in true peasant style.

I looked round: crowds of soldiers everywhere, carts all over the place, and the road blocked with lorries facing in either direction.

"Hi! What are you standing there for, you——! Help, don't gape! Can't you see that the bridge has collapsed," roared a red-haired, pockmarked soldier, and gave Franzi and me a shove in the direction of the bridge.

The crowd thinned slightly, as the peasants and one or two of the Russians scattered in search of wood to repair the bridge, and I could see the lorry, its back wheels in the water, the front ones still supported by the broken planks. Round about stood the Russian driver and some of his passengers cursing monotonously and without stopping; while others chivvied onlookers and passers-by to go and help. There were several other Russian lorries at the bridge and many soldiers, but it never even occurred to one of them to go and help.

The collapse of the bridge and the possible loss of a new American lorry seemed to be the private concern of the lorry's driver and passengers. From time to time someone would stop out of pure curiosity, nod sympathetically, or wave his hand as much as to say that the lorry was gone and that was that, then he would walk away with the heavy, elastic, lumbering walk of the Russian.

Franzi and I began carrying stones from a nearby cottage. These were stones that belonged to the parish, deposited there with the intention of repairing the road. The Russians chivvied us as though we had been slaves, making us fetch more and more stones to fill up the stream. They were in a great state of excitement and in an obvious hurry, from which I concluded that grave things were happening. Then they ordered us to bring wood. "Where from?" we asked naively. "Where from?" roared the soldier. "There!" and he pointed to the nearest cottage which belonged to a poor peasant with five daughters and one cow, who went by the name of "Uncle Joe." So, we and some of the peasants began taking all the wood from the pile beside Uncle Joe's cottage, while his angry, frightened daughters watched us through the window. We collected all the logs and planks there were, and then, with as much shouting and uproar as must have accompanied the building of the Pyramids, they began levering up the lorry.

After one or two vain attempts it occurred to one of the Russians that, instead of trying to build up heaps of slippery stones from the river-bed, it would be better to use the concrete cover on Uncle Joe's well as a support for the levers. The peasants refused to move, so the Russians went themselves to get it. They prised it up and, with great enthusiasm and energy, began rolling the heavy cement ring towards the river. Of course, they were quite unable to stop it when it reached the river, and amid general laughter it plunged with a huge splash into the water. No one could be bothered to pull it out of there, so they looked round to see what else they could use as a base for their levers. Their gaze

lighted on poor Uncle Joe's outdoor oven in which he baked
his bread, and irritated by the jeers of their compatriots from
other units, they set about dismantling it with redoubled
energy.

The N.C.O. in charge, who stood waiting by the lorry, was
growing bored, and, being bored, he gave the cement ring
lying in shallow water a push with his foot, and slowly it
rolled on and quietly disappeared into the river. Then he
looked around in triumph at the crowd of spectators. In less
than half an hour Uncle Joe was bereft of his firewood, his
fence, his oven, and the cover of his well, but the lorry had
got out of its unfortunate predicament and was on the other
side of the river, so there was still hope that the war might be
won.

The Russians drove away without attempting to patch up
the bridge for the others. It was several days before anyone
could even be bothered to put up a notice to say that the
bridge was down, and all day long carts, cars, lorries and other
vehicles would drive down the precipitous road to the river
only to have to turn back again. The horses slipped and fell
on the steep, icy slope, and the lorries roared helplessly in first
gear, their wheels spinning for a long time before they could
surmount that slippery hill. Although scores, even hundreds,
of people had had to turn round, not one of them thought of
putting up a notice to inform others that there was no way
across.

I clambered up Half-wit Hill, eager to see what our new
home looked like. The road to it led through a close huddle
of cottages. That the peasants should have built their cottages in that steep, horrible spot proved that the hill was
rightly named. In front of every cottage lay only small piles
of manure and straw, for it was long since there had been any
need for bedding. In their little stables now stood none but
small, wounded ponies given them by the Russians. In two
of the pigsties, though—oh, wonder of wonders!—squealed
real pigs.

At the very top of the hill stood the cottage assigned to us; painted pink—not yellow. It comprised a kitchen, a tiny entrance-hall with glass doors, and one room without a stove. In that one room the Hungarians had inserted themselves. Jumbo, wishing for a little peace, had chosen the entrance-hall as a lair for himself and the three Poles. Matilda and Lina had installed themselves in the kitchen. Although they had all been hard at it since morning arranging our things, the confusion was still indescribable. But then it is difficult to accommodate fifteen people, three dogs and a canary, in one tiny cottage. And Matilda was not helping.

During the move Matilda had been robbed of her hand-bag with all her savings and documents, and she was plunged in the depths of despair. Lina had long since lost all her possessions, stolen from the Manor, and she was as free of worldly goods as Buddha Gautama himself. This had happened in the very early days. When the Russians turned her out of her room, they had assured her that there was no need to take anything with her. "We leave poor people alone. You won't lose anything. You'll see, when you come back to-morrow." And the next day she had been able to confirm that she was poor indeed, for they had robbed her of absolutely everything. Matilda, however, still had the wooden box of huge dimensions that contained her treasures, and on this she now sat alternately snivelling, groaning and cursing, all because she had had her handbag stolen.

Some soldiers, presumably from the same lot that had turned us out of our house, came and installed an iron stove, which as we found out later, they had calmly stolen from our neighbours. The owner of the cottage, Tacitus' and Marietta's old cook, Julie, kept poking in her head and gazed in horror at what was happening to her home. But what could she do about it? That morning every house in the village had been counted and had a number painted on it in green. In this way every house had passed without their noticing it from the hands of the owners into those of the Red Army, which did with them as it liked.

The Russians went from house to house, taking from one what they needed in another, and whenever we poked our heads out of the door we would see a swarm of soldiers, like ants, bustling about with stoves, mattresses and tables, and the silent stony-faced figures of the peasants watching their antics.

By evening we had settled in properly, and we all had supper in the kitchen. Our house was ready and we were very proud of it. It's true that you couldn't move in it because the entire floor-space was covered by our paillasses, but nevertheless it was ours and they our beds. The quarrelling about mattresses, pillows and blankets finally died down, and, exhausted though we were, we even began to laugh and joke. In a day or two, we hoped, we would be back in the Dower House.

We slept peacefully that night, and, thanks to our exhaustion, excellently. Slowly we all got up, fetched water from the river down below, washed perfunctorily, and ate breakfast all together in the kitchen. There was no doubt about it, either the Russian guns were sited just beside us or the Germans were firing at us. We sat there the whole morning frightening each other. If this was a German offensive, then we ought to try and get away; but where to? The Capital had not yet fallen and all our side of the river was still in German hands. Fighting was going on in the nearest town, so that we could go neither to the north, nor south. What wouldn't we have given for the door to open and admit the Tall Major! How right he had been. He would have been able to tell us what to do, and, as we did not know ourselves, we decided that this must be a Russian offensive and that we would wait till the morning. If the situation had not improved, we would ask the Russians for a cart or a lorry to get us away.

Looking down into the village you could see in every open patch of ground, in every alley-way, lorries, carts, cars or horses. The streets were swarming with soldiers. The village was just not able to house all that horde. Peasants with bundles on their backs were wandering from cottage to cottage in search of a roof for the night. What a good thing that we had a house. We had the last of our hens hidden in the loft, along with two of Rudi's ducks, dying of starvation and dirt, all that was left of his once huge fortune; we had flour, we had bacon, and we had a cook. If only the Germans did not come! And, if they come, will they kill us? But who will give us away? The whole village! And first and foremost the so-called Communists, those who to-day are running about with red armlets, people like Stefan.

The Hungarians insisted that I should go to the Dower House and get a certificate to say that we had been evicted from our house and were entitled to Cottage No. 72 as our rightful quarters, from which we were not to be turned out. I made my approach from the front, but, though I pleaded hard, the sentry turned me back. I then walked round to the back of the hill on which the Dower House stood and clambered up the steep little path that led to Teresa's cottage. I reached the top and saw Teresa's poor sticks of furniture standing in company with our Louis XVI under the eaves that had no gutter. An excellent place for furniture in winter! There was no sentry on that side, but when I got into the courtyard the soldiers began casting wolfish glances at me. I vainly searched the sea of heads for a face I knew, then cautiously walked round to the front. The main doors, off their hinges, stood wide open. I reached the terrace and on the threshold bumped into the thin, red-haired little officer.

"May I?" I asked, pretending to be fearfully shy.

"But, of course!" he answered, and, with a courtly gesture, invited me inside. The large bedroom was brightly lit by a large paraffin lamp. In the middle of the room was a huge table covered with maps. The doors of the stove were open and an indescribable heat came from it. The room was obviously arranged as a council-chamber, and I could imagine a general, colonel or major sitting on each of the empty chairs, while in the big armchair would be a marshal. Obviously that was why the sentry had not let me pass, but the officer with true Russian inconsistency invited me in, as though wanting to show off his work.

"How beautifully you've arranged it!" I whispered with feigned admiration, for I felt that that was required of me. The soldier standing at the door near the stove, gave a satisfied smile that stretched from ear to ear, and the officer coughed slightly as much as to say: of course, I'm accustomed to preparing quarters for the staff. I know how it should be done.

He agreed at once to my request for a certificate, and while he sat down to write it some soldiers came in with wood for the stove. I remembered every knot-hole in that wood for I had cut it all myself. The soldiers tried to walk on tip-toe so as not to dirty the rugs on the floor, and that made their gait more bear-like than ever. They lifted their feet just a shade too high and kept them up a fraction of a second too long, so that they began to overbalance and had quickly to change feet. This strange gait was a gesture of respect for the place in which they were.

This was the first time I had seen Russian soldiers intimidated and obviously feeling humbly servile. Though the only people then in the room were a Lieutenant and a woman civilian, it was shortly to be honoured by some great hero, general, or marshal, and so was already a holy place. There was something Eastern in the men's servility, and in their quiet, awkward gait and in their whispers. Where's your famous democracy, I thought, if you can so easily and quickly change your attitude? You have the Mongol's humility before his leader in your blood. This was not the cheerful, almost child-like embarrassment of the Anglo-Saxon soldier when confronted by a high officer, but the servility of the East towards the padishah.

The Lieutenant finished his writing, I took the certificate, thanked him and went back to Half-wit Hill, to delight the Hungarians with my useless piece of paper.

The morning was one of great activity. A strange lot of soldiers came to warm themselves in the kitchen, so that there wasn't an inch of room in the cottage. We could not get rid of them, and when we produced our certificate they went off into peals of derisive laughter. They took all the wood we had so laboriously collected. I begged them to bring us some in exchange, and a quarter of an hour later one of them appeared and, with a gallant gesture, threw down at my feet a large, heavy gate, complete with hinges, that he had just torn out of the fence surrounding one of the neighbouring cottages.

"There you are! See, we're men of our word. There's your wood, and better, because it's dry. Chop it up and you'll see."

I thanked him as politely as I knew how for keeping his promise so quickly and honorably, and set to work.

Again, as yesterday morning, one of the local militia wearing a red armlet, came with a Russian soldier to round up the peasants and take them off to work on the road. It was freezing, and again there was a biting wind. Poor peasants!

The door had hardly closed behind the men we had had in the cottage overnight, when a fresh horde appeared. One group occupied the cottage's one room, the other the kitchen. Of the former I remember a tall, fair-haired Ukrainian, Alosha; of the latter I can recall them all, for they were to haunt us for a considerable time. They had a Lieutenant with them, a Kalmuk whose favourite food, as we later discovered, was bones, but the person really in charge was Misha, the driver. Then there was a second driver, Alexy; and the sergeant, an arrogant, quiet, dull-witted man with fair hair, whose name I have forgotten. This, too, was the day when Kuzma, the Tartar, paid us his first visit, of which, unfortunately, there were to be many. Misha threw a duck on to the

kitchen table. "Pluck it and roast it for us by the evening.
And here's a bag with our flour. We'll be having fritters
later." With that he rushed out again.

The house emptied for a moment and I went outside to
gather a little kindling; then I carried the iron stove and a
basin out to the front of the cottage, helped by the refugees
living with Teresa who, having been driven out of her own
cottage, was again our neighbour. There were seven of these
refugee children, as black as gypsies and so ragged that they
looked almost theatrical. One of them, a young boy, was
wearing a pair of women's shoes, short pants and a man's long
jacket: nothing else. Another had on galoshes bound round
with sacking, flannel trousers tied up with string, and a shirt
in tatters on his back. The third little lad went barefoot, and
his little behind was quite naked, for he only had a large handkerchief tied across his chest.

I fetched some water and kindled a fire under the basin,
in preparation for plucking the duck. As I squatted on my
heels beside the stove and blew on the slender flames that I
encouraged with leaves and maize stalks, the snow melted
round me. Beside me lay the white duck, shot through the
breast. The clouds, like grey tatters, scuttled before the wind
across a leaden sky.

I plucked the duck. Isa and Alf came to lick up the blood
from the snow and gnaw at the damp feathers. We had lunch
in the room, for once without Russians. Then we cleared up
after the horde that had spent the previous night there. We
hardly had time to draw breath when a fresh lot descended
upon us and, despite our assurances that the quarters were
already taken, they piled themselves and their kit into our one
room. One of them had his face horribly disfigured with
scars. His lips were contorted and one corner of his mouth,
that had been badly stitched, hung down limply. There was
another called Victor. He was fair-haired, impertinent, cocksure and smooth-spoken; then a third soldier and a young
intimidated Lieutenant. The real leader of this lot, however,

was the scarred one, whom we christened "Squint Face." They had only just settled themselves on their straw among the Hungarians, when Misha came for his duck. Matilda handed it to him from the kitchen. Misha tore off one leg, ate it, and shoved the rest aside. "There you are, Lida, eat it. That's for you." I flung myself on the meat, like a starving tigress, bore it away to the darkest corner of the hall, and there crouching over it, like a vulture over its carrion, I tore the soft flesh off the bones with my teeth in huge mouthfuls. Those who are really fond of meat will know what it is like to go without it for a long time, as we had.

It was after Misha left that Kuzma made his first appearance. He was a Tartar from Siberia and belonged to a small unit commanded by a bespectacled Lieutenant whose job it was to keep the roads serviceable. His men were all elderly and comprised the weirdest mixture of nationalities. Among them was Mahomet, the Georgian who will appear later, and a Ruthenian driver. Kuzma was over fifty. He had slanting blue eyes that were always bloodshot and watery, a red nose that was half-aquiline and half-Mongolian, a strange combination, and his lips were thick, damp and pendulous.

The moment Kuzma got himself inside, he stretched out on the bed beside Jumbo, shook hands with everybody, and introduced himself: that is to say, he stuttered, "Kuzma! Kuzma!" several times in a drunken voice, and then fell fast asleep. We woke him up and tried to turn him out, but it couldn't be done. Knowing that the kitchen and room were occupied by soldiers, Kuzma had no intention of trying to get into them but had decided that our part should be his residence and we his victims.

"Come over here," he stuttered. "I've got something important to tell you. Something secret. Come closer. I must whisper it."

"You can say it aloud," I replied. "No one will understand anyway."

"Listen," began Kuzma, dragging me towards him by the

arm and breathing sour wine fumes into my face. "I've got a request to make. You must help me. I must have a woman. I shall have a nice present for her. A splendid present: a whole two pounds of sugar. There are so many of you in the cottage. Don't you think one of them would like to? It's different with you. You've got a husband. But there are all sorts of others here. Ask some of them."

From that time on, Kuzma was to visit us several times a day, on each occasion with a different requirement for which he would exchange his hapless two pounds of sugar: one day it was a woman, the next a watch, then a woman again, then a watch or something else, and so it went on for three whole weeks. It took him so long to make up his mind that in the end he was left with his sugar and had neither watch nor woman, nor anything else.

When Misha, the sergeant and the Kalmuk, their officer, came back, they brought with them wine in petrol tins. As they poured it out, circles of iridescence formed on the surface of the thin new wine. They settled themselves comfortably in the kitchen to await their fritters. The door from the kitchen into the room was ajar, and through it came the sound of the other Russians' voices. We rubbed our hands in glee: perhaps, there would be a quarrel. If only each group would try to turn the other out we might get rid of both.

Misha, as head of his group, went to have it out with Squint Face. He explained that they had taken the quarters early that morning, but neither Squint Face, nor Victor, had any intention of giving way, nor did the officers in the least want a quarrel, which, in the Russian Army, can easily leave one or other of the protagonists a corpse or a cripple. Not that that is how most quarrels ended. On the contrary, the great majority went no further than curses and appalling abuse, but there is always the possibility that shots will be fired and that is why the Russians are rather inclined to avoid quarrelling, and, when two do get down to it, crowds of others come running up to mediate, soothe them, or drag them apart. On this occasion there was not even the usual abuse, for Misha was not backed up by his officer. He withdrew to the kitchen and then they began drinking. Alexy, the second chauffeur, brought a pile of bones from the kitchen for his officer, the Kalmuk, as a sort of *hors d'oeuvre*. Matilda made the fritters according to a recipe supplied by Misha, turning them out in a seemingly endless stream. It was growing dark outside and the peasants were returning, frozen to the marrow, from their work on the road.

Now at last we shall be able to get to sleep, we thought, but it was not long before the door opened and revealed a patch of starry sky speckled with clouds. The wind gave a whistle and sent in a gust of penetrating cold, and in walked the black figures of five or six soldiers.

"All right. Come and try," I called ironically from where I lay under my sheepskin. "It's all occupied to right and left."

"Shut the door!" roared Jack.

We were tired, sleepy, and by now quite indifferent to everything. The Russians began moving about in the cottage and, having convinced themselves that both rooms were in fact occupied, they just settled themselves in the overcrowded entrance-hall. Alf gave a growl and withdrew into a corner, worming himself on to Jack's paillasse. The porch was so full that there was not even room for the Russians to sit on the floor. So, standing their automatic pistols in a corner, they calmly lay down on top of us.

Although I never closed my eyes that night, I never discovered exactly how many of them there were. Jumbo did not want to light the lamp, so that the Russians should not see that they were lying on women. They must have been exhausted, for without a word they curled up like dogs, and for a while we thought that they were asleep. But only for a while. Three of them, at least, became very active in their attempts to discover on what they were lying. The one on Jumbo soon disposed of any doubts he may have had. The huge size of Jumbo's boots was enough for that. Fifi's Russian by pinching her up to her thigh, discovered at once that she was a woman, and Fifi had to beat a retreat to her pillow that lay on top of her suitcase, and she spent the night crouching there like a mouse in a trap. This deprived the Russian of any possibility of flirting, but it gave him the paillasse to himself, which was in itself a feat, and probably what he wanted most. I, however, was not going to give up my bed and resisted, with the result that I was pawed, pinched and scratched the whole night. I think they took it in turns to test whether I was a man or a woman, and could never make up their minds. My legs were as thin and tough as those of an old cock, and then my trousers; but having discovered that there were no flies, they would try to proceed further. At first, I thought I might grow accustomed to this "massage" and get to sleep, but it was no use. At fairly regular intervals I would kick as hard as I could, and each time differently, so that my opponents should not get used to my tactics. I would give a long kick that started at the hip; then a series of quick ones with both feet at once, and so on, always varying the type of direction. In the end it did begin to grow light. I had slept, perhaps, an hour, my tormentors at the most two. What healthy brutes the Russians must be if they could afford to waste a whole night pinching my miserable thighs.

A faint silvery light began to filter through the little window in the door. The four misted panes appeared and the black outline of the frame between them. It was still quite dark in the hall. I was as exhausted as though I had been riding a bicycle all night. The third lot of Russians began getting ready to go. I could distinctly see a Mongol's profile silhouetted against the window; a fine profile with pure lines, high cheek-bones, flat nose and thick lips, round shaven head and pill-box cap. Then the Mongol turned to open the door and the vision disappeared. They had gone, and we breathed a sigh of relief, but it was already morning and time to get up.

I told Misha, with whom I was now great friends, that we would cook for him if he would supply the wood. I had hardly made the offer before a wooden outdoor lavatory stolen from our neighbours was lying at my feet. "Is that enough?" he asked politely. To us that piece of wood, the last unburned lavatory on Half-wit Hill, would have been worth its weight in gold. But what could we do? It had already been hacked a bit, and we had no other wood. We burned it.

That day our door never closed. The Hungarians had Squint Face and his lot in their room; the drivers were in the kitchen, and an endless succession of those in search of a billet opened the door to look in and never shut it.

There was not even room to sit down in the hall. Poor Jumbo lay on his bed trying to read *A Life of Richelieu*. Beside him, on Fifi's sacred bed, lounged Kuzma, vainly trying to start a conversation with him. Nor were the Hungarians able to move much. Squint Face and his lot occupied the only stools there were and the entire floor-space free of straw. In the appalling fug that reigned there, Muki's canary softly sang in his cage hanging up near the ceiling in the smoke from the stove and the cigarettes.

Matilda

28th-30th
January

IN MY notes, the morning of 28th January is described as peaceful. Squint Face and his merry men had disappeared unobserved, taking with them their automatic pistols and kit-bags and leaving behind them a stench, a pile of trampled straw and hundreds and hundreds of scraps of newspaper. Then Kuzma came. We were used to his visits by now. He settled himself comfortably in the Hungarians' room, let his bloodshot eyes rove round it, sighed, and beckoned to me with his finger.

"I hate them!" he said.

"Indeed?" said I, on a note of interrogation, not really knowing whom he meant.

"Come closer," whispered Kuzma hoarsely, lookly cautiously about him. "I'm a Tartar. Do you know what a Tartar is?"

"Of course, I do."

"Well, then, a Tartar. You understand. But I believe in God. Do you doubt it? Well, look!" and Kuzma hurriedly, but unctuously, crossed himself thrice. "I have a family in Siberia, you know. They, poor devils, are boiling up grass to eat now. Yes, yes. There's famine there. And here am I soldiering at the other end of the world, the very end, and God knows why."

"How do you mean?" I asked.

"They deported all of us from the Crimea to Siberia. I'm an old Siberian myself, but not those from the Crimea. And there they are now, wandering about in the frost, downtrodden. And who deported them? The Russians! Yes, yes. There's lots you don't know. But I'm telling you, and I'm a Tartar. And I believe in God. But they believe in nothing. Perhaps you think I'm tight?"

"Good gracious, no!" said I.

"Well, perhaps not you, but someone else might."

"They might, indeed," I agreed readily.

"But I'm not tight. Oh, I get sad at times, when I think of my people. And, Lida, do you know I've got a whole two pounds of sugar? Do you happen to know a woman, who——?"

Every moment or two a peasant would come to the house to borrow a knife, axe, or something else, for the Russians were slaughtering a cow just beside the house. Though the Russian Army is the only one with which I have been on intimate terms, I imagine that if one were to ask for volunteers to slaughter a cow from any hundred English or American soldiers, two, or perhaps five, would step forward. But ask the same of a hundred Russians and a good ninety, if not ninety-nine, will offer their services. And it is the same whatever is to be done: if there's a hut to be built, a cart to be repaired, a wounded man to be bandaged, or a sick horse doctored, there will always be plenty of volunteers. No Russian likes to admit that there is something he cannot do.

Whether theirs was the normal military method of slaughtering a cow, I don't know, but several of the Russians laid hold of the wretched brute. Then they summoned the peasants to help, and in a moment the terrified animal was surrounded by a throng of jabbering men. When the crowd had dissolved somewhat, the cow's bloody body was lying there in the snow. The head was cut off and the carcass skinned at lightning speed: all done with instruments borrowed from the nearest cottages. Then they hacked up the meat; the guts and innards were left lying in the snow beside the head, and that was that.

The Russians walked away and in their place came the dogs. Alf and Isa, of course, went too, but being helpless bourgeois dogs they did not know how to begin. There was a heavenly smell, but when you got to it nothing really to eat. The common local dogs chose a good spot and, squatting in the snow, began patiently gnawing the warm sinewy bits of meat that dangled in thin strips from the severed head. The cow, as usual in such cases, just gazed at the snow-bound world with an expression of extreme surprise in her still unmisted eyes.

The door opened and who should walk in but Nicholas, our nice, young hooligan friend Nicholas, who first came to see us to spy out the land and later rescued Fifi's bracelet from some bandits. After him came another soldier, a small, foxy fellow with a cunning, laughing face, who looked round him with great curiosity.

"Come in, friends! Come and sit down!"

Their arrival caused great excitement. "Nicholas has come to see us with a friend. Both from the 'Ensemble.' You remember, don't you? Friends of the Victor-Chaliapin and Alosha who fired their pistols in the General's room." We were really glad to see them, only the Hungarians, once they had discovered that neither Nicholas nor his friend Fedia had the faintest idea of what was happening at the front, had no further use for them, and withdrew to their lair. We others made ourselves comfortable on our bedding and started talking.

Fedia was the first European I had come across in the Red Army. He was a member of a jazz band in Moscow, with which he had gone on tour in Germany in 1940. He also told us that they had been in France, but I am pretty sure that there wasn't a word of truth in what he said. Fedia nourished a deep and sincere contempt for everything Russian. There

were no exceptions. His contempt began with the Russian
air that he was forced to breathe, included all Russian music
and art, and ended with the Red Army. There were only two
things he was prepared to recognize as good: American jazz
and the English language, and he dreamed of somehow or
other getting to New York and playing there, even if he only
played the trumpet or the drum, even though it were in the
worst of all the bands there, even though the pay were
wretched, nothing mattered if only he could have nothing
more to do with Russia. This was an attitude one might have
expected in a Westerner who had spent some time in the
U.S.S.R., but Fedia was a child of the Moscow pavement and
so his harangue struck us as very strange. He spoke of Russia
in such a tone of abhorrence that we were amazed and tried
to catch Nicholas' eye; but Nicholas just kept silent and fixed
his eyes on the metal stove pipe from which a mixture of
water and rust dripped on to our heads.

"Just look how you're living!" exclaimed Fedia. "Like
dogs! worse than dogs. I can see it all. You haven't even a
stove; you lie on a stone floor. And why should innocent
people be ill-treated like that? They turned you out of your
house. I know all about it. First out of the big one, then
from that small one; and now you have to live in this hole.
Innocent, good people! Why didn't you run away before we
came? Why? I can see that you used to have money, though
you're poor enough now. You should have got away before
we came, and not waited for us. What good has it done you?
Ah?" And Fedia clutched his head in his hands and rocked
to and fro in despair at the sight of our wretched lot.

"With whom could we have escaped?" asked Fifi. "With
the Germans, perhaps? We would rather starve here on a bit
of filthy straw."

"You should have fled before that: sold everything and
gone to America. And no looking back."

"It's not as easy as all that to go to America," said Jack.
"You need a lot of money to get there."

"Paris is about as far as we would have got," I added.

"Oh, that's far too near," said Fedia, appalled. "The farther west, the better. Who knows what will happen to Paris yet?" Then, after a moment's reflection, he said decidedly, "No, no, far too near," as though we were in fact proposing to go there. "It would have to be a bit farther. London would be better. Perhaps, after all, Paris might just do, but certainly no nearer. That's the very minimum."

"Just you wait, Fedia," I said. "We'll meet in New York yet. We'll have a party together with the Americans."

"You know, Lida," said Fedia, "we have a saying: a fine place, where we aren't. It's an old, old saying."

We did put in a word for the Russians and try to explain that the Germans were the cause of all our misfortunes, but Fedia wouldn't hear of it. It was all the fault of the Russians. He would not hear a good word for them.

"Now, you see, take me for example. Just an ordinary Moscow 'smarty,' but I know what I'm talking about. I know what tales you are going to tell me. I know our people, and I know what they're like. So you don't need to explain anything. I've got eyes in my head. You're hungry, too, aren't you?" he asked, with feigned carelessness.

"One of the drivers gave me half his duck not so long since," I said, "just because I plucked and cooked it for him. Otherwise, we hardly ever see meat."

"You haven't any potatoes, either, have you?" Fedia went on. "In fact, you're pretty hard up for food. Isn't that it? I know that it is. Well, see you soon."

Both stood up. We shook hands with them at great length, standing in the open door and letting the freezing air surge over Jumbo. Then we translated the entire conversation for his benefit. Jumbo was amazed.

When the two Russians had gone we relapsed into our former lethargy of hopelessness, and sat there silent in the darkness.

The door, as was inevitable, opened again and more Russians appeared. This time it was an old soldier; a cheery, young peasant, and the indolent Kuzma. Kuzma, as a constant visitor and friend of the family, poked his nose into every corner and then flung himself down across Jumbo's legs and made his hundredth, useless attempt to start a conversation. The two strangers, hearing Russian voices in the Hungarians' room, stayed where they were in the entrance-hall. The elderly one came from Central Asia and we nicknamed him "The Nightingale" because of the lovely fairy-tale he told us. The young one was a taciturn, dull-witted country lad of that specific type of Russian who miraculously grows up without an ounce of malice: angelically patient, always smiling, ridiculed and exploited whatever the regime. This was such a one. He radiated goodness, as a stove radiates warmth. He smiled continually, was always moving out of the others' way, knocking against or overturning something as he did so, and he never said a word. But he listened to everything that was said. While Jack and Fifi talked with the Nightingale (though he was not yet called that), I went across to Kuzma who was making mysterious signs to me.

"Listen," he whispered, puffing his breath that stank of garlic and sour wine, straight into my face, "you, Lida, I've got two pounds of sugar, only don't tell anyone. I know you won't tell. You're good. I'm a Tartar, but I believe in God——"

"I know, I know," I interrupted, "but I don't know any women. You must look for one yourself."

"Well, Lida, it doesn't have to be a woman. A watch would do as well. You try and get me a watch, and I'll give two pounds of sugar."

"No one here has a watch."

"Oh, Lida! You don't want to give it me, that's all. And I would have given sugar. Just think, all that sugar for a watch!" And Kuzma stretched out comfortably on poor, long-suffering Jumbo's legs, drew his hand across his eyes, and fell suddenly asleep with his head on Jumbo's stomach.

We talked with our other guests about the bourgeois life in Europe, and in Russia. We tried, too, to satisfy our hunger for the exotic and learn something about Central Asia, but that was impossible. There was nothing interesting about Central Asia as far as the Nightingale was concerned: it was the remote, neglected interior, and that was all. So we returned to the subject of *Kolchozes* and private property, trying to find out what a settler from Central Asia thought of the free peasants in Europe. But the Nightingale did not live in a *Kolchoz.*

"I," he said, "am from Turkestan. It's not true what these young fools say that in Russia no one owns anything. I, for instance," and here he lowered his voice, "have a house in Turkestan. Perhaps, where those others come from, wherever it is, there are only *Kolchozes,* but with us in Turkestan people have their own house. I have a house in Turkestan. Not a big one, it's true, but then it has a veranda. It's warm with us and half the year you sit out-of-doors; that's why I don't need a large house. And then I've got a veranda. And all around," he was speaking quickly now, as though afraid he would be interrupted, "all around grow jasmines. Do you know what jasmine is? Perhaps it grows here too? In Turkestan, when it flowers it's as though someone had sprinkled the bushes with white stars. And that jasmine's mine. All those bushes round the house are mine. They belong to me. And nightingales live in them." Here the old man paused, took breath and said triumphantly, "My nightingales. Trained. In the evening, if I go on to the veranda and whistle, just whistle ever so softly, there's such a commotion in the bushes. I stretch out my arms, and whistle, like this, softly, and they hear me and come flying from the bushes and perch on my arms and sing. Oh, how they sing! It just bubbles in their little throats."

"Nightingales?" we asked, disbelieving and mocking. "Trained nightingales?" But the man from Turkestan was so absorbed in his fairy-tale that he never noticed the tone of our voices.

"Yes, nightingales," he repeated. "I tamed them and trained them to do that. They're my nightingales."

We said no more. Who could compete with a man who owned nightingales? What is the largest herd of horses, cattle, or pigs, compared with something so lovely as a nightingale that comes flying out of a jasmine-bush to sing perched on your arm?

After lunch we received a visit from Victor-the-Hooligan and his friends, Victor Porfirovich, Nicholas and Alosha. They explained that they had come then because they were unable to come to supper. The Hungarians were still all in the kitchen, so we went to their room where we were joined by the Nightingale and his kindly, nit-witted companion. What could we talk about with such a lot? One was an actor, another a singer, a third a dancer, and Nicholas no one knew about, but he must have been something of the same kind, for he also belonged to the Ensemble; then there was a nightingale-fancier and a young nit-wit. You will never guess it, but what we talked about was Hadji and his silly Eastern wisdom, or if you prefer, his wise Eastern stupidity. We set each other first the riddles of Hadji, then others, and Victor Porfirovich knew them all. Then he began setting us mathematical and geometrical puzzles that defeated us all. After that he began talking about art, painting, the theatre, and poetry. There was nothing he did not know. He flashed his teeth, laughed, gesticulated, and talked and talked. I watched him, wondering how on earth he could stand life in the Soviet Union, he, a sort of belated child of the Renaissance, with his strong individuality, his rich mind that was crammed with the most diverse collection of knowledge, his seething, active, youthful intellect: how could he stand it? And yet, he got on excellently with his Alosha and the other, honest or less honest, simpletons. That was the greatest riddle of all.

They went, and Kuzma returned: sober this time and with a piece of paper and an envelope in his hand.

"Give me a pen and ink, Lida. I'm going to write home to Siberia."

The old Tartar then carefully put on a pair of old-fashioned, steel-rimmed glasses; stuck his tongue half out of his mouth and began writing in the dusky room. Every other moment he would lift his head and exclaim, "They're so poor. They eat shavings." "The Russians drove them out." "Oh, my unhappy, persecuted people!" "They're from the Crimea. They don't know the frosts of Siberia. It's different for me, I was born there; but they, poor things, will freeze." "Mine, too, have to cook bark. They're hungry, hungry. And here am I, fighting the Germans!"

Having finished his letter, Kuzma bade me draw him in the attitude of writing a letter. The background was, if possible, to be the canary in its cage. I drew him, very badly, but it pleased him mightily, and he proudly folded it in with his letter. Then he drew the envelope across his huge tongue, and sealed it. At that moment the sound of Russian voices came from the entrance-hall and Kuzma hurried away. For the hundredth time I wondered at the strange way these Russians behaved; just like wild animals. They got out of each other's way, lived in packs, each with its own hunting-ground; they did not trust each other and were more ready to fight than to help one another. Wolves.

I went to the little entrance-hall and there found a young officer, with a grey cap set jauntily on the side of his fair head. I looked him over: was he good, or bad? Friend, or foe? He wanted to take the Hungarians' room as a billet for a lieutenant-colonel. We produced our magic piece of paper from the H.Q., on which it was written that house No. So-and-so was allotted to us, fifteen persons, as our quarters, but it was losing its power now that things were becoming more difficult at the front and the village was getting more and more crowded. We tried appealing to the officer's heart. We showed him Alec and Muki; wailed that we ourselves had hardly room for our poor heads, etc. "All right! All right!" said the officer. "I'll see what can be done."

It was already dark and another of our days nearly over. And what days! The men had to spend them on their beds. If they went outside at all, they had to limp and bow themselves, like old crones. The women never stopped cleaning up after Russians, fetching water, sawing logs, cooking, or, as I, trying to amuse the members of the liberating army with intelligent conversation so as to keep their minds off rape and loot. It was all excellently organized and functioned perfectly, but we never had a second even to stop and think. I was permanently confined to the house. One Russian-speaker was too little, so either Fifi or Jack had to help me. We never even stuck our noses outside, and all day long we talked and talked and talked, smiling even when we were most afraid, turning everything into a joke, and somehow managing. In the village Russians were raping and looting, but with us it was a sort of mad cocktail-party that lasted twenty hours a day. We had no time even to say that our nerves could hold out no longer. And why say it? We knew that they would, that they had to.

Eastern Dance

31st January– 2nd February

THE kitchen had become a barber's saloon for the three lorry-drivers. They were being shaved and having their hair cut by three barber-girls of the Red Army. We were beyond caring what was happening at the front, for a fresh catastrophe had fallen on our heads; an N.C.O. had come and ordered us to clear our one room for the lieutenant-colonel. This time we could not get out of it, and we did not even have Jack or Franzi to help. Before dawn, when it was still dark, a young soldier lad, with an automatic pistol, had come with a member of the local militia and taken them for work. Fortunately, they were not to dig trenches but to work in the local officers' mess.

I do not know how other armies are organized, but I can hardly suppose that it is on the same lines as the Russian. The Russians need substitutes and the assistance of civilians in everything. God knows how they would have got on by themselves in the desert round Tobruk! When their underclothes reach such a state of filth that they offend even themselves, they summon the women of the village and order them to wash their pants and vests for them. And in a few hours the village is full of long Russian drawers and foot-clouts waving in the breeze. If there is a field-kitchen, it is the locals who have to lay the table and serve, wash up and help with the cooking. If a lorry has to be pulled out of the mud, a cow slaughtered, or bodies buried, the civilian population has to help. Even the officers have to be helped to read their maps, and they need an audience for each evening's drinking, for alone they would be bored. And everything is an order, even the social side. They live in groups in cottages, and shoot the dogs, sleep with the women, make the husbands drunk or drive them out with work-parties. They get their provisions locally, each group for itself. There is no official, organized requisitioning, but indiscriminate seizure of what the individual can find. A Grishka or Ivan hears a pig grunt as he walks along, opens the door of the sty, and takes it. In a short while some other member of Grishka's group is flying round in search of a pot; yet another looking for wood. When they have collected all they need, Grishka and his group eat their pig and move on, leaving behind them in their temporary quarters somebody's pot, somebody else's plates, another's forks, somebody else's jar of salt and the bones of the pig. The peasants, if they are to retrieve their plates, knives, or whatever it is, have to search the village, but by the time they have discovered in which house Grishka and his group had their tasty meal, there's already a fresh Grishka seated beside them on a feather-bed taken from next door, eating a goose stolen from somewhere else still. This is a highly specialized and very practical system. The Russian soldier carries nothing but his arms, unless it be a spoon down the side of his boot. He doesn't even have a photograph of his fiancee with him when he sets out, but just steals the first photograph of a girl that takes his fancy wherever he may be, and exhibits that to all and sundry as his fiancee. I have been shown many Rumanian, Hungarian, Serbian or Czech "fiancees" whom the proud Russian prospective bridegroom had never seen.

One would think that the Russians would not admit the civilian population of an enemy country into their lives; but they do. It is understandable that civilians should be made to dig trenches, carry in the wounded, bury the dead, provide carts, food, or straw, but it does not stop at that. Usually

Ivan or Alexy needs three girls to sweep out the floor, and another five to keep him company when he drinks and sings in the evenings; five men will be needed to bury a dead comrade, or two to heat up the bath. They never do a thing for themselves. They will hunt through the entire village to find a cobbler or a blacksmith, instead of making a sole or shoeing a horse themselves. I suppose this is due to their appalling un-European indolence, but why has a man's coffin to be carried to the grave by four hostile foreign peasants, instead of by his friends and companions? And why must a local enemy driver repair a lorry, and not a Russian mechanic?

The method of issuing orders is also a little peculiar. Sometimes the leader of a group, usually a private, goes or sends someone to their officer's billet to find out what is to be done next; but more often the officer himself runs about the village looking for his men to tell them that they must leave for the front immediately. And the way they move! Some, after much parleying with the drivers, will scramble up into empty or loaded lorries going in their direction; others, less astute, will set off on foot and revile those who ride on lorries as traitors of the revolution, as they plod along.

The war for the Russians was a sort of migration, a Grand Tour made in highly dangerous circumstances, but very interesting for all that. Their curiosity was insatiable. Often some who were almost too tired to stand, were still inquisitive enough to ask our ages, names, why we had no children, and whether our husbands performed well in bed or whether they were as weak and sickly as they looked. They asked such things with all the gravity and professional interest of the scientist.

Over and over again we explained to the officer-quartermaster that there were fifteen of us, that we had three lorry-drivers quartered on us already, and that the kitchen was full of someone else's furniture, but it was no use. They even sent—wonder of wonders!—a soldier to help us clean the room, and with him the son of the local interpreter. The only result of their assistance was that Matilda's huge wooden chest disappeared.

First we removed Julie's furniture and things from the kitchen, and so discovered some of our silver that she had stolen from the Manor. The Hungarians shook their heads. We dragged it all up into the attic where we discovered a large part of Marietta's wardrobe. This done, Marietta, Elsie and Dolly moved their lowly couches into the kitchen. Suddenly there was an inhuman shriek, a peacock call that could only have come from Matilda. She had just discovered that the wooden chest containing literally all that she had managed to save in thirty years' service, was no longer there. We searched the adjoining cottages, questioned the neighbours, but no one had seen the chest. Matilda came to enlist my assistance. "Please, Madam! Please! It's my chest," she screeched under my nose. I went off to the cottage where the soldier who had "helped" was quartered.

The entrance was piled high with packs, the room dark and filled with smoke. The fug was indescribable, for there were so many there that they sat literally one against the other. "Who helped us move our things?" I asked. It appeared that no one had. They had all stopped talking when I came in, and now just stared at me like so many animals. In the gloom I could distinguish the interpreter, and beside him his son. "Where did your son put the chest that he took from our cottage?" Silence. "Where?" I repeated.

"He didn't take anything," replied the interpreter and turned to look out of the window, puffing at his pipe. What was I to do? The soldiers kept silent and their looks were not friendly. Then the interpreter's son broke the silence in an attempt to make sure of the Russians' support. Clumsily he imitated their mannerisms and gestures, their type of joke. He was revolting. I walked out. Turning round suddenly in the porch, I saw Matilda's chest under the pile of packs. And at that moment, Matilda herself, who had evidently run after me, saw it too and let out a triumphant shout. I turned back into the room.

"The chest is here," I said, "and it didn't get here by itself. Why did you say that no one had stolen it? Shame on you, stealing all that a poor old woman has. Shame." The Russians had decency enough to say nothing; so, to add to the effect, I went on, "And then the people here will say that the Russians steal, that the Red Army robs poor people!" The old interpreter withdrew his gaze from the window. "No one took it," he repeated impertinently, looking me straight in the face. I turned and walked out.

I was so disgusted with the peasants, with mankind generally, that I was shaking all over. It is different when the Russians steal: they are soldiers waging a war. But the peasants! And I suddenly remembered Julie's sweetly tart martyr's smile and the silver dishes of ours that she had stolen. How she must have suffered, I thought smiling to myself, when we moved into her house and dumped our things on her stolen treasures. But our attitude to her had not changed. Only the dishes had been quietly transferred to our suitcases.

Matilda did not even thank me. She considered that we were to blame for letting things reach such a pitch that her chest could be stolen. Nothing but thieves all about you, I thought, and you're helpless. So much baseness and villainy, everything upside down, and there's nothing you can do.

The quartermaster was urging the Hungarians to hurry. "Hurry! Hurry! The room must be free immediately." In the end it was, and he and his three men made themselves comfortable in it. There was no sign, no mention, of the Colonel. We had our lunch, that is, we ate some bread standing in the kitchen.

Franzi was now going to sleep with us in the porch, for there was no room for him in the kitchen. Elsie would have to sleep half on the suitcases and half on the surround of the stove. There was no room on the kitchen floor at all, for on it were the beds of Rudi, Tacitus, their two wives, the two "girls" (Lina and Matilda), Honono and the two children. Lina was to sleep under the table, and even so her feet would have to protrude into our entrance-hall. The canary we had left in the room, for in the kitchen it would have suffocated. There wasn't even room for Isa. All she could do was to squat on her haunches, whimpering gently, and dumbly begging us to take pity on her. "I'm twelve, an old, faithful dog," she seemed to say. "Can't you make a little room for a dog that loves you?" But there was just no room.

It was growing dark. Someone tugged at the door and in walked a small, middle-aged officer with a crumpled face, a flattened nose, and a cigarette stuck to his lip in the corner of his mouth. He was almost bald. He kept his hands in his pockets. His chest was covered with medals. He peeped through the glass door into the room, heard Russian voices, and walked straight across to the kitchen. We fixed smiles on our faces, such as all photographers demanded thirty years ago, and said in chorus: *"Zdrastvujtie!"* This was Major Blashchuk whom we were to know much, much better.

"What's up here?" he roared. "Corps-de-ballet? You're as crowded as in a *Kolchoz.*"

"Corps-de-ballet" in contemporary Russian slang means an appalling crowd.

"Yes, yes!" said the Poles. "This is our *Kolchoz.* Corps-de-ballet."

We invited the Major to sit down. He settled himself and at once began telling us all about himself. His distrust of us soon evaporated. He had looked in out of sheer boredom and a little curiosity, and had been rewarded with a submissive audience. What luck!

"I," he shouted, thumping his chest, "am Major Blashchuk. I am famous. More than the Germans have reason to know me. Here," he said, pulling out a silver cigarette-case with a dedication in German: *Für Ferry*, "I shot that Hun in the head, and, as he was dying, look what Major Blashchuk found in his pocket: a silver cigarette-case. I'll kill everyone: wounded, expiring, all of them. Let them see what sort of person Major Blashchuk is."

Then he told us the story of how the Germans had murdered his entire family, and we told him our story. Then he wanted to know who was whose wife, how old we all were and what were our names, but his questions were largely rhetorical, for the only person that really interested him was Major Blashchuk.

"I'm in the artillery now," he went on. "Before that I was in the tanks until I got concussion, and before that, in the last war, I was in the cavalry with the Cossacks. But, of course, I'm really a Counter-Intelligence man. I've been fighting for years. I was in the Japanese war, too."

We looked at his flabby face: he could not have been more than forty.

"So you used to be in the navy?"

"And how!" he replied. "And all along in the Counter-Intelligence. Oh, in Russia people know Blashchuk all right. Just ask anybody, he'll know me."

Suddenly he stood up and walked out. We breathed a sigh of relief, and the Hungarians asked what sort of strange creature that had been. We summed up the Major's character in a few words: "Bad, but stupid. Can be humoured." It was already quite dark outside, and the Russians had lit the lamp in their room. They began pestering us about the canary. "Why doesn't it sing? Why hasn't it a mate?" Then they summoned me. "Come here, you. What's it you're called?" "Lida," I answered and stepped inside.

The room looked empty. In one corner stood Julie's bed, ready for the fictitious Colonel, a three-legged table, a night-table and a marble wash-stand. The iron stove smoked against the wall. A young soldier brought some turgid, brown wine in the ewer, on which were soap-suds, not yet completely dry. "Have a drink with us, Lida." I had drunk wine and petrol with men from the armoured corps and with lorry-drivers, so

I might as well drink wine and suds with the infantry. I emptied a mug of the sour-smelling brown liquid at a gulp. Ugh!

Jack came in and told us that he and Franzi had been working in the kitchen. The kitchen was in the garage, the mess in the Manor. Jack had minced meat on Jumbo's XVIIth century Spanish chest, or on what remained of it. "Don't tell Jumbo," I said; then I heard Major Blashchuk's voice and had to dash to the kitchen.

The Major was drunk, and at once collapsed on to the floor across the Hungarians' beds. Then he caught sight of Muki. "Hullo! A fine youngster!" he said over and over again, pulling the child towards him by the leg. Muki squealed in terror and cowered into the corner like a young wild animal. "Don't be afraid of the Major. He's a good man. Go to him," said Rudi, in a flat voice. Curious, but still half-afraid, Muki crawled across to the Major, and there began the dangerous entertainment of a drunken Russian playing with a six-year-old child. His parents looked on in tense silence, never taking their eyes off him. The Major began pretending that he was going to burn Muki with his cigarette, and the child laughed, for he knew that no grown-up would touch his cheek with a lighted cigarette. We, however, could not feel so sure. Every now and again, as though it were part of the game, we would try to take Muki away from the drunken Major. Then the Major pinched him, and Muki gave a piercing shriek that died away as he met his parents' grave eyes. The Major handed round cigarettes, and again we had to listen while he told us how he had taken part in the Japanese War. "Let's ask him if he was in the Crimean War, too," I whispered to Fifi. Then the Major again seized hold of the child, who was now thoroughly frightened and looked quickly from the Major to his mother. But Dolly gave no sign; she just sat there, afraid to move. Had she been able she would have throttled our visitor, and the world would have known the famous Major Blashchuk, pillar of the Counter-Intelligence since 1905, no more. "He must have been nought-years-old when he joined it," I whispered to Fifi. However, as that organization had not existed then, that was possible.

Seeing that the Major was obviously so fond of children, we now tried to turn his attention to Alec. Alec was older, already nine, and a pinch or two, even a burn, would not do him any harm. Blashchuk, meanwhile, had picked up his automatic pistol and was waving it about threatening to shoot every German and Hungarian that existed. (You mothers, whose children sleep peacefully in their beds at night, unpinched and unfrightened by a famous Major from a liberating army, you do not know how lucky you are.) However, it was still Muki the Major wanted, and when the child tried to get away from him he gave him a fierce pinch and a brutal jerk that made him scream like a wounded animal. Dolly suddenly became a tigress, snatched her child away and clasped him to her, her eyes blazing.

"He's sleepy and ill," I said, in an indifferent tone of voice, to the Major who, with a drunkard's stubbornness, was looking round for his toy.

At last Major Blashchuk stood up and we said good-bye effusively. As we saw him to the door, for we were horribly afraid that he might turn back and not go, he informed us that we were a fine lot, the sort that he, Major Blashchuk, liked. He reeled against the door, told us that he never drank, was a teetotaller and had never so much as tasted alcohol; then at last he lurched out.

We hurried back to the kitchen. Perhaps, now we might be left in peace for a moment and allowed to get something to eat. We never dared eat in front of the Russians unless they were our particular friends, for they would snatch everything from us. We had just managed to swallow something when one of the three in the room, a young lad with his hair cut close to his head, came swaying out and sat down on the only stool of which the kitchen boasted. The moment he emerged all our food disappeared from view.

"Food! I'm hungry, and you're bourgeois."

"What is your name? Where do you come from? How old are you?" we asked quickly, anxious to respect the ceremonial of a Russian introduction.

"Shenka," he muttered gloomily. He was obviously drunk. "And give me something to eat, —— you, or I'll search the whole —— kitchen and take everything."

He got a piece of bread.

"God Almighty! I'll shoot the lot of you, like dogs. Bacon! Where's the bacon?" he roared, groping for his automatic pistol.

He got his bacon. As he slowly chewed, he gazed at me out of fuddled, drunken eyes.

"And why are you pretending to be a woman?"

"I'm not pretending at all. I am a woman. My husband's lying there in the entrance-hall, ill. The Gestapo had him in prison."

"Why lie, when I know you're a man?"

Importunate, impertinent and drunk, Shenka was a bit of a hard nut. Why is it that the Russians almost always turn dangerous when they are drunk? Why does drink turn those good-natured, generally decent peasants, into degenerate criminals? We struggled with Shenka for a good two hours, and in the end he went back to his friends without either shooting at us or searching the kitchen.

Another day was over. Franzi lay down between me and Fifi. Jack, tired with chopping meat on Jumbo's Spanish chest, was already snoring in a corner of the little hall. The door into the kitchen was open and through it protruded poor Lina's legs. The open door made the porch warm, but the rusty stove-pipe above our heads kept dripping drops of icy water on to us. The Russians had made their room so hot that the wall against which Jack was curled, glistened with wet. What was to become of us?

About eleven o'clock we heard footsteps and loud voices, and a horde of people swept through the door into the dark

hall. "To the left! To the left!" we shouted, and they barged
their way into the room, knocking their pistols against the
wall, stumbling and cursing. We could hear the typical shrill
voices of Russian women. The door could not be shut, for
the Russians kept running in and out with straw, and we
might just as well have been lying out in the open. "The door,
Comrade, the door!" we kept shouting, but they never shut
it. In the end, peace returned. It was, perhaps, one o'clock.
I could hear the even breathing of Franzi and Jack. A small
lamp was burning in the kitchen where the Hungarians were
still awake. With thirty persons in that small cottage, it smelt
abominably, but all the same we should be able to get to sleep
now. What a terrible day it had been! How awful it is having
to live in constant fear. Sleep is God's greatest gift. Or is
death, perhaps, greater? No, one must not let oneself think
like that. One must go on being a queen to the end. And
then, when death does really come, pretend that it does not
matter, that it is quite all right, as though one had a hundred
lives and not just one.

The outside door was quickly opened, but this time only
one came in. Jumbo switched on his torch, and in its beam
we saw a fine-looking, clean, tidy young soldier.

"The Colonel and the Major would be glad if Lida would
kindly go to them," he announced.

"What for? In the middle of the night. Which Major?
What's happened?"

"You're to come at once. I'll take you there. And alone.
Only Lida is to come."

"But what for?"

Was this the Counter-Intelligence again? Was I being
arrested, or being sent up to the front as an interpreter perhaps? Jumbo was appalled, and begged me to get Jack to go
with me, or to creep along behind.

"You are to banquet with our Colonel," said the young
soldier.

We just did not believe him. A banquet at one o'clock

in the night. Which Colonel? How did he know my name? Jack pulled on his high boots, cursing and swearing. I kissed Jumbo. "Keep that chin up," whispered Fifi. Franzi turned over in his sleep, able at last to stretch out full length.

In a small room in a cottage down near the river was Major Blashchuk, still drunk, and a grey-haired Colonel I did not know. That was a nightmare "banquet" I can assure you! Between the two Russians sat a village girl, her set face veiling all her suppressed hatred and fear, afraid to move. I saw at once that she was in no danger; both the Russians were too drunk for that. The Colonel was a Lesghian and his Russian bad. He had a good face and was obviously a man of breeding. With his white mop of hair and swarthy face he made a striking figure. The room which was furnished on urban rather than village lines, contained two beds with a sofa along the end. A table by the window was loaded with food and bottles. Jack cautiously followed me into the room. Our greetings were very formal and official: the two officers stood up, shook hands, and waved me to a chair. "Hey there!" roared Blashchuk. This was addressed to his men sitting outside in the entrance. He shouted at them as though there had never been a Russian revolution, nor a French one either. In a moment the Major's men humbly brought us plates full of fat meat, cabbage, and potato. The Colonel filled my glass with a mixture of champagne, vodka, and liqueur. "I think that should be all right," he observed, holding the glass up to the light and proudly inspecting his cocktail.

They tried to make the girl drink as well. Blashchuk took her head, bent it backwards and poured the filthy stuff on to her clenched teeth. I ate as much as I could and always selected the greasiest bits. The appalling mixtures we were given, champagne and rum, wine and liqueur, vodka and cognac, soon had their effect and Jack began to feel unwell. I began making excuses, my nephew was very ill and I must take him home. Anything to escape and get out of there. However, they just sent for a doctor. Jack collapsed outside the cottage and lay in the snow in the pale light of the setting moon. He was green in the face. The doctor came and pronounced him "perfectly well, but dead drunk." I kept applying snow to his forehead, while the two Russians raged at me for not going back inside. I was beginning to feel slightly dizzy now and implored Jack not to leave me alone. Suddenly, on the snow between two cottages, I saw Alf looking horribly like a wolf. He heard my voice and came running up. I cursed the others for not keeping the door shut, but there was nothing to be done. I could not take Alf home, for Blashchuk was again trying to drag me inside. Jack staggered back with me and slumped heavily into a chair. The girl was still sitting there motionless in the clouds of smoke, her eyes shut. What did a Hungarian peasant girl make of a Russian holiday? Major Blashchuk began dancing, contorting his whole body and singing out of tune. And all the while the Major's men came in and out quickly and humbly with more food and more drinks. Their two officers treated them like Eastern slaves.

The Colonel and I began talking politics. Though neither of us spoke good Russian, we understood each other all right, chiefly thanks to the fact that a Lesghian who comes of a good, ancient family is closer to the European than is the Russian of no ancestry at all, like Blashchuk.

"No, Lida, nothing will happen to you with us," the Colonel assured me. "To-morrow we'll come and thank your husband for letting you come to us and make our night so beautiful."

"Nonsense," I said. "There's nothing to thank him for."

"But, of course!" the Colonel went on with true Eastern courtesy. "We must thank him for his great kindness, and ask him not to begrudge us so charming a companion in the future."

Meanwhile, Blashchuk was still leaping about, now on one leg, now on the other, and singing the nostalgic songs that he had learned from his dead wife, a Jewess. From time to time a soldier would come in with fresh bottles and more food, and walk past his dancing Major without paying any attention to him. Jack still sat on in his chair, green in the face, and doing his best not to faint. Opposite was the snow-white mop of the Lesghian, whose face, in the dim light thrown by the little lamp, seemed as though carved in bronze. Between the Colonel and me sat the village girl, like a statue. Her eyes were closed and she might have been thought asleep, only the joints of her fingers were white from the force with which those red peasant hands were clenched.

"Lida, please tell her to have a drink," said the Colonel. "What does she think she's doing? High-ranking officers have invited her to supper and not a hair of her head will be touched. We're cultured people and she's sabotaging our supper. Her behaviour's almost subversive. I ask her once again, with no ill intent: have a drink."

I turned to the girl and said in her own language, "Drink; or at least pretend to. Nothing's going to happen to you, unless you make them angry. And you don't want that. I, too, would much prefer to be asleep instead of sitting up all night, but we've no choice."

The girl's head spun round towards me. It was as though I had trodden on a snake. She gazed straight into my eyes with a look of utter hatred; then she relapsed into immobility. Her finger-joints cracked. I turned back to the Colonel. "She doesn't want to drink. In Europe people don't drink as much as they do with you. It isn't our custom."

"But it's ours," said the Colonel, with a smile. "If it wasn't for our drinking, the Germans would have been beaten a year ago. But our men, once they get hold of alcohol, you might as well not have them. You won't get a thing out of them as long as there's a drop left."

"But that's bad," I said. "I don't mean only for the war, but for the whole nation. If the rest of the Slavs are to model themselves on you——"

"Ach!" exclaimed the old Colonel, with a contemptuous

wave of his hand. "There's always been vodka in Russia. And what harm's it done? We've done more with vodka and will do so, than without it. And what if it does make the war last longer? We've plenty of time. So much time."

Blashchuk was still dancing, but more and more slowly now, and his singing too was growing softer and softer, as though he were a clockwork toy that was running down. Conversation ceased. It must be five o'clock, I thought. I stood up, took Jack's arm, and said good-bye. The old Colonel recovered his liveliness. "Please come again to-morrow evening. There'll be champagne every evening. Every evening a banquet."

Outside the night was starry and frosty. The cottages seemed to crack with the cold. Stupid peasant-girl, I thought. With a little cleverness she would have got away, but as it is she'll sit there till dawn. I could hear Alf barking, then there was a burst from an automatic pistol. The Major's men humbly bowed us out; an officer's lady is no mean personage. Blashchuk and the Lesghian were strong personalities and kept a tight grip on their men. Treat a Russian like that and at once he is all obedience and submission. It was hard going uphill on the crunching, slippery snow, but at last we reached the cottage. Alf was crouching by the door.

The moment we were inside Jack collapsed on his bed and was asleep. I whispered to Jumbo, "Nothing. It was all right. They were decent," and in the darkness he happily stroked my face. Poor Jumbo, what he had had to suffer! He had heard from the villagers what happened in their cottages and how, when the women resisted, the Russians shot both them and their husbands. But the peasants, I told him to comfort him, are stupid. You must be nice to them, smile at them, and have the cunning of the serpent, and everything is all right, as it will be with us. Smiles, politeness and good nature do not, perhaps, pay with other nationalities, but with the Russians they do.

Tired as I was I could not get to sleep, for the girl-soldiers were beginning to leave and had, of course, to cross the hall on their way out. It puzzled me rather that they were going so early and behaving so quietly. When morning came, I understood; they had stolen all the bed-clothes put there for the mythical Lieutenant-Colonel. Not that I cared about the bed-clothes! They belonged to Julie anyway; but the Russian girls knew that they had been prepared for a high Russian officer, and yet they had stolen them! They had only just left, when an armed soldier came to fetch Jack and Franzi.

When it was light, still not having slept, I got up to have a look at Alf, who never stopped licking himself and did not come when I called. There was a bullet hole right through his back. The bullet had luckily missed his spine, but it had torn away a piece of the flesh. It was a big, deep wound, full of his dirty, sticky hair. So, instead of sleeping, I had to set to and bandage Alf.

It was not quite noon when the rest of the soldiers who had spent the night in the room left, calmly taking with them the iron stove. I shouted after them that the room was being kept for a Colonel and that a room without a stove was useless in the cold we were having, but they just laughed, "To hell with your Colonel. Perhaps he's dead anyway." I ran to the sentry, one of whose duties was to guard our house, now that part of it was to be a billet for a high officer. The sentry galloped after the soldiers, his automatic leaping about on his tummy. He roared till he made himself hoarse, stamped his feet, waved his hands, and swore. It was quite moving to see him get so worked up over our stove. The soldiers, however, just loaded the stove on to a lorry, and paid no attention to him. And why should they? There were four of them and they, too, had automatics. Let him shout there in the cold. Seeing this, I tore down the hill to Major Blashchuk and the Colonel. They had been so decent the night before, that perhaps they would help me rescue the stove; especially as it had been removed from a room requisitioned by the Red Army.

I found them both standing in the doorway, packed and ready to move off. They never even looked at me. Either they did not recognize me, or they were pretending never to have seen me. In a stifled voice I related the story of the stove. They listened reluctantly, walking slowly uphill towards the lorry. As we got nearer we could hear the uproar as the sentry and the others quarrelled.

"What's all that?" barked the Colonel. "Who dares shout like that here? Are they drunk, or what? I'll make them give you your stove back." And the now furious Colonel set off up hill almost at a run.

"Stealing under my very nose, are they?" said Blashchuk. "I'll give it them. They'll know Major Blashchuk again, when I've finished with them. Have they nowhere else to steal, except under my very nose? I'll show them."

Highly delighted, I hurried up the hill after the two Russians, already seeing myself returning proudly home with the stove. When, out of breath, I caught up with the Colonel, he was just on the point of getting up into the lorry in which the stove stood blackly, and his face was wreathed in smiles. I stopped, thunderstruck. Turning round, I saw Blashchuk just coming up, and beside me the sentry still foaming with impotent rage. "Wait," I said to him. "There's the Major coming, and that other's a Colonel. Tell them that they've stolen our stove." The sentry ran forward and began swearing at the two of them, cursing them up hill and down dale for a couple of thieves.

The Colonel clapped his hand to his automatic pistol and roared in a voice that shook Half-wit Hill, "Silence! Shut your mouth, you harlot's son." His was the real tone of command. The sentry walked away.

There was, of course, an explanation. The stove had been stolen by Blashchuk's men, perhaps even on his orders. The famous Major walked up and climbed into the lorry, chuckling to himself. I did not wait to see them go. After that we had two sentries to guard our plundered cottage, and we had to cook fritters for them both.

Later, in the afternoon, a Lieutenant came and locked the door of the room. He gave the key to me, but that was to be a great secret, and I was to tell everyone that the key was at the Commandant's office in the village. The Lieutenant was followed by a train of jackals sniffing after the room: a woman Lieutenant and several soldiers. They went wherever he did, possibly hoping that he might get drunk and then let them have the key, or tell them where he had put it.

Shortly after the Lieutenant had departed with his train, a soldier rushed in and told us that we were to go and clean out straw. Where? Why? How? I went out to investigate, and a few cottages away was caught by my arch-enemy, Mahomet. The work was for him! I had to clear the straw out of his stable with a pike and, though I worked like a Stachanovist, Mahomet did not even have a word of thanks for me. He was in a bad temper because a new Major had arrived with a horse which was to be housed in Mahomet's stable, which he had let get into a state of indescribable filth, and he had been ordered to clean it and to do so quickly. Mahomet poked me in the ribs with his pike and showed me by gesticulating what I was to do, for he spoke very little Russian. Not once did his face, that was like an illustration from the Arabian Nights, lose its gloom and expand into a smile. Mahomet was angry.

Time after time I plunged my pike into the straw that was heavy with dung and bore it outside into the sunshine. It smelt of horses. The sun was on the point of setting and the broad sweep of the evening sky framed a truly wintry landscape: the dingy wretched village, a few bends of the river imprisoned under the ice, trees stripped of their leaves, yet all the same it seemed to me that there was already a scent of spring in the air. Ungrateful though he was, I even enjoyed working for Mahomet. I am sure he regarded me as an un-

clean infidel dog and was happy that he, faithful follower of
the Prophet, was once more able to trample on the giaour.

When I got back to the cottage I had to see to Alf who
had developed a high fever. A sick dog is the worst torment
I know. A person, even a small child, can tell you what he
needs and you can explain what you are doing to him, but not
a dog. Alf howled when I cut the matted hair out of the
wound, having sterilised the scissors in a flame. Then I
poured vetol over the wound and Alf growled. But he did not
bite: he knew that I was doing something to cure his wound,
only it hurt dreadfully. He could hardly get at the wound
with his tongue, and his continual efforts to do so were cracking the skin and making the hole larger. There was a pink
fluid there already which showed that by the morning it
would be suppurating. As I stroked his poor head, I could feel
even through the hair how high his temperature was.

That evening, too, the Russians took all our bed-clothes;
but at least they did not steal them when we were not looking
but requisitioned them, promising that we should have them
back in the morning. Naturally, we never saw any of it again.
That's the Russian system. No one can quarrel with an army
of occupation for requisitioning things, even bed-clothes, but
when the officers of that army tell you in minute detail where
and when you can go the next morning to get it all back, and
then drive off with it half an hour before the time they told
you to come, then you do want to explode. But the Russians
will only laugh: that is what they call a successful joke.

After a supper of bread and some miserable potatoes, we
lay down on our bare beds. Then the Lieutenant came for
the key. We begged him to spend the night in the room,
offering to leave the doors from the kitchen and the hall open
so that it would be warm, but he would not: it was too boring
to sleep alone. During the night a fresh lot of three arrived.
It was a shame that the key had been taken, for it meant that
they had to spend the night on a stone floor, despite the fact
that there was a large room vacant. The three new arrivals

were young: one was a Polish Jew from the neighbourhood of Sanok, the other a Mongol from Tashkent, called Wolodja, and the third a Ukrainian. Each represented a different world, but as a group they worked in well together. They were, indeed, close friends: sensible, honest, quiet and with plenty of charm. The little Jew talked with us in Polish, observing the polite formalities of the language. The Mongol was a tiny person, slim, with beautiful, narrow little hands that would have graced a Persian Princess. His face was as smooth as though it were cast in bronze, almost girlish, and in it his black eyes with their drooping lids gleamed like jet. The Ukrainian was a lumbering, fair-haired lad with innocent blue eyes. All three hated Russia. The little Jew despised it, and the Mongol from Tashkent spoke of the Russians as the East speaks of dogs. Quietly and without trace of bitterness they told us that in Russia to-day there is no question of Communism, and that after the war what was left of it would disappear.

"The heroes, the high officers, are going to be a separate class. If we don't get rid of them after the war they will grow up over our heads and become our future bourgeoisie."

"I've a wife waiting for me," said the Mongol, "but no one waits for the Russians. Their wives are just—bitches. They don't know what God is, or what it means to give one's word; they don't know the meaning of faithfulness; they're just dogs."

The Mongol had the strongest character of the three, and so it was his personality that coloured the group. We were horribly disappointed when we discovered that he was called Wolodja: we had been expecting some lovely Eastern name. We wanted him to tell us something about Tashkent, but he was not talkative. However, when I asked him what "water" was in his language, he replied that it was "ob," and proudly added, "The Russians have made that the name of the whole river all the way to the White Sea. We Asiatics will one day have a voice in affairs. We don't change every five years like the Russians. We have our own laws, very good, old laws.

We don't need to be taught something new every five years."

These three were continually begging our pardon for disturbing us; and they would not even pillow their heads on our beds, but slept sitting upright in a corner of the tiny entrance-hall on the stone floor. In the morning they bade us a dignified, courteous farewell. It was amusing to see the Jew from Sanok and the Ukrainian peasant imitating the easy, polite, rather ceremonial mannerisms of their youthful leader from Tashkent.

2nd-8th
February

THE priest was coming to give the Hungarians Communion, so I sat down to breakfast alone. Later, I had a great piece of luck: Tacitus found that a sausage was high. We had so little food by then that we had developed a mania for keeping everything for the so-called "rainy day," and it was one of those "rainy day" sausages that had gone bad. Tacitus, feeling sublimely benevolent and Christian because of the coming Communion, made me a present of the sausage. Fifi watched in horror, as I greedily feasted on the disintegrating meat. I cannot live without meat, and I had eaten none for a long time and before that only in insufficient quantities. That sausage tasted so superbly that I was quite certain that it would do me no harm. And it did not; though Fifi averted her eyes in horror and looked up at the ceiling while I ate it.

All day the Russians, officers and men, struggled for our empty room. Some tried to break in; and the scenes they made were as horrible as their curses. We referred them all to the commandant's office, laughing spitefully to ourselves.

Nicholas, the Hooligan, was another visitor. He brought a toy aeroplane of chrome-nickel for Muki. It was a moving thing to have done, for it was obvious how greatly that aeroplane appealed to Nicholas himself. Muki, however, was not there. There was not even room for him with us now, and he was every morning sent to one of Tacitus' old servants, Frank, and spent the day with his children.

The days passed quickly, for nothing interesting happened. There were just the eternal visits, from which we were slowly going mad. A soldier from the officers' mess came every morning now to fetch the two boys to their work. As soon as it was light off they would go with their armed escort, all because the cook was afraid that another unit might steal them for trench-digging. It would have been no use getting a written order from the Commandant that they are to work in the kitchen; the only way of making sure of two such exceptional kitchen-hands as untidy Jack and dirty Franzi was to send an armed escort for them.

Domestic quarrels had broken out again, as always happened whenever life became a little less hectic; we quarrelled about who was to chop the wood, who fetch the water; quarrelled because Elsie washed her hands too often; because Alf and Isa would get on to the beds; because the canary had been locked up in the empty room and was starving to death; we quarrelled because a sausage had gone bad; quarrelled over whether or not we Poles ought to share anything we managed to steal, and so on. And all day the sentry put on the Colonel's quarters sat warming himself over the stove in the kitchen, where, without him, there was hardly room to move.

The sentry was so bored that he began learning Hungarian. Russians pick up languages quickly, like children, whose empty heads and unburdened minds they have. It is almost unbelievable how quickly they pick up not only individual words but whole sentences. After that they never stop introducing local expressions into what they say, even when talking among themselves. I suppose, though, that they forget what they have learned just as quickly as children do.

The boys' escort from the officers' mess brought us a present of a bag of dried apples. For this he was given a pocket handkerchief which pleased him mightily, though he tried not to show it. After lunch a new hooligan, Pietia, made his appearance. Pietia was on the hunt for sheepskin coats and, despite our protests, he was just about to gather up ours when Jack's head suddenly emerged from under one of them. It appeared that Jack was already acquainted with Pietia from the officers' mess kitchen. "What do you want?" Jack demanded sleepily. The words "lousy bourgeois" that Pietia had been repeating interminably ever since he walked in, died at his lips. He was fearfully ashamed. Steal, yes, but not from those you know personally, not from those with whom you are on terms of friendship; I repeat, friendship. That is the unwritten law of the Red Army, and, as I have already mentioned several times, it is observed. Pietia was covered with confusion and made a very clumsy effort to try and turn the whole episode into a joke. "I did not know that this was your house," he muttered to Jack, and then sat down on our beds to make friends with the rest of us, which, of course, meant asking the usual obligatory questions. That over, he pulled out his pocket-book, which contained the usual collection of fiancees. He must have stolen an album of family portraits taken in the 1880's from some country house. The photographs themselves were stiff and faded. The women they portrayed young, and all different, but that did not deter Pietia from assuring us that they were all the same woman, and she a labourer in a Ukrainian *Kolchoz*.

"Very prettily dressed," said the Hungarians, pointing to a string of pearls and the tulle covering her bare shoulders.

"Isn't she?" said Pietia calmly. "She always dressed well. Our girls are always dressed like that. This one she gave me on Kharkov station. She was crying so much, that she threw it through the carriage window." The mere recollection of this mythical parting almost reduced Pietia to tears. "And this one she gave me before that. Went and had herself photographed when we were already betrothed."

"She looks older here," observed the sober-minded Hungarians.

"Too much hard work," explained Pietia, and proudly restored his collection to his pocket-book of cardboard imitation crocodile skin.

Shortly afterwards Nicholas came in, and again Muki was not there. Pietia must have had a bad conscience, for at the sight of Nicholas he got up and slipped away. Nicholas was leaving Mora. He stood there holding his beautiful model of an aeroplane delicately in his fingers. It was obvious that not only did he consider it lovely, but that in giving it to Muki he was parting with a real treasure, which made it all the more moving. Nicholas fidgeted, talked and then went out again, still clutching his aeroplane. It never even occurred to him to leave it behind: either he would give it to Muki, or none.

Russians love giving presents and they give them in the most delicate manner imaginable, passing them over as though they were from somebody else. When you thank them, they become embarrassed and look as though they wished the ground would swallow them up; they act as though your thanks did not refer to them, but you can see their hearts swelling with happiness. Thank a Russian and he will blush to the ears, crack his fingers, gaze at the ceiling, and behave generally like a lying dog. How charmingly dogs lie! Call such a dog-fibber, especially when he has something on his conscience, and immediately his fleas will start biting him and he has to sit down and scratch. Call again, and that just happens to be the moment when he must sniff, and he sniffs and sniffs to the right and left, and goes on sniffing with scrupulous care. Call again, make your voice as grave as you can, and the dog will move in your direction, slowly, stopping, looking round, going on, stopping, in other words, pretending that your calls are not meant for him. That is how a Russian behaves, when you thank him for a gift. I cannot make up my mind whether that is *savoir vivre* thousands of years old, or the East's sense of tact, but at any rate it is a charming habit and a very winning one to the recipient.

The fourth of February was the first day of spring. Such mistakes happen in Hungary. It's mid-winter and suddenly spring is there. Nature's influence was so great that I sat at the door of our cottage, quite forgetting that a blue sky meant before all else favourable flying conditions for the Germans. There were plenty of them about. Those Bashkirs were right to dig their zig-zag trenches, and Tolbuchin would no doubt go and sit in them, for it was he who was supposed to have moved into the Manor. That's what the priest said, and it was also our opinion. The Russians, of course, were like oysters, and we never learned from them who was in our house. The sun was hot, the wood I had stolen from Julie came away beautifully beneath my axe; all the eaves were dripping. Could anything bad happen on such a lovely day?

A strange officer approached the cottage, caught sight of Pietia lounging in the doorway and drove him away. It appeared that there was an order against troops visiting cottages, though apparently no one knew of it. Among the millions of that Army only one officer had been told about it and was trying to enforce it. And poor Pietia was the victim. He shambled away, cursing to himself.

As I sat there peacefully in the sunshine, two of the Red Army girl-barbers came to ask if the Colonel's room was free yet. They were not in uniform; buxom, thick-legged, their hair greasy, their faces round and shiny, they used to come a dozen times a day. They would poke their heads into the kitchen, sigh deeply at the sight of the filthy old straw which served us as beds, and then return to their work of shaving the men. They wanted that room very badly.

A sky like silk was stretched in a huge, blue dome across the white, sparkling world. Chuckling brown streams poured down Half-wit Hill, smelling of dung and spring, and furrowing twisty troughs out of the dirty black ice. A row of crystal drops dripped regularly from the eaves, dashing themselves into silver on the half-rotten timbers of the porch. The caress of the sun was that of a warm soft hand. In front of me a young, red-cheeked soldier was playing with snowballs. He laughed as he threw his balls of sticky, melting snow at the half-naked gipsy children who were our neighbours. "Come and play, too," he suggested, his eyes glittering, as he squeezed yet another ball of snow and mud in his huge, red paws. "No," said I, "I'm too old for that."

Everybody seemed excited by the continual murmur of the thousands of little streams, by the sound of monotonously falling drips that came from everywhere, by the exaggerated heat of the sun, and by the battles of the 'planes in the air. It was the sort of day when it would be easy to die, the sort of day, however paradoxical it may sound, when it is easier to reconcile oneself to the idea of death. I would have been safer sitting inside, but I wanted to be outside and to watch man hunting man; it amused me, even though it might have cost me my life. My old thoughtlessness that I thought had left me for ever during those dull days of frost and wind, had returned.

Round the corner of the cottage staggered Jack, bent double under the weight of a sack of peas given him for his labours. Hunger was beginning to show in our faces, and here was a sack of peas. Providence watched over us, as Matilda said, turning up the whites of her eyes.

Oh, those eternal visits! Normal soldiers would have found some girl or other and gone off for a walk arm in arm; then they would have taken her to the inn for a glass of wine and flirted a little. Or, they would have had an exercise, or some sort of training to do, or they would have been told to wash their clothes, or sew on missing buttons. The normal soldier has a thousand different things to do, and, when he has nothing to occupy himself any normal commander tries to find some way of keeping him busy. It is only the Russians who don't worry about such trifles. They don't flirt: either the girl comes to bed, or several of them take her by force to a safe place and rape her. They practically never read books, have no sports or games. With all the beautiful snow there was that winter, no one stole our skates, or our skis. Of course, sport exists in the Soviet Union: in fact, it is under the patronage of the State and on a high level, but it is not for the masses. When the snow melted, as it did later, normal European soldiers would have played football or basketball, especially as the front had by then receded a long way; but I never saw a Russian soldier playing any game whatever. They wandered about from place to place, accosted the girls, usually frightening them so that they fled in terror, sat in the doorways of the cottages cracking their fingers and yawning with boredom or whittling senselessly at a stick; or they lay in the sun, usually falling asleep like dogs the moment their heads touched the grass; or else they got drunk without rhyme or reason. They were so appallingly bored that it was pitiful to watch them.

The door opened and in walked Lieutenant Nina Alexandrovna followed by her pock-marked orderly, Reda. We knew them both well by sight. Nina was the mistress of a Major. The Lieutenant had evidently given her the precious key to the "Colonel's" room and she installed herself comfortably. So far we had not been able to get to know a Russian woman properly, for our acquaintanceships had been limited to short conversations; but now that we were to share a house with Nina, we should have an opportunity of doing so.

Nina objected to the pane of glass at the top of the door: the Major, she said, did not like people looking into his room. "But who would look in?" we asked in surprise. "What's there to look at?" But Nina just seized our last towel but one and, mounting on a stool, with it veiled the tiny pane of glass. As she said, she liked things to be cultural. She did not relish the idea of people watching her and the Major and, of course, did not believe that we preferred sleeping to playing at Peeping Tom. Nevertheless Nina saw no harm in the fact that Reda, her orderly, should sleep on the floor beside their bed.

Actually, when the poor Major was too busy defeating Hitler's armies to come home, she would call upon Reda to act as a substitute. Having installed herself to her liking—and made an infernal noise with her shrill voice—Nina and her shadow departed "for the town" as she put it.

It was raining and raining, and by evening the mud was over our ankles. A fresh horde of Russians seemed to have descended upon Mora, for there was no end to those who came wanting the room. We repeated what Nina had told us, that the room was reserved for a Major from the General Staff. Late in the afternoon Victor-the-Hooligan, *alias* Chaliapin, remembered our existence and came to see us. Being friends we got news of what was happening at the front. Even the stupidest Russian soldier will not talk about such things, so well has the lesson of the "war secret" been hammered into his head, but with a friend it is different. The friendly Russians were those who treatd us like Russians, and not like foreigners. The Russians, it appeared, were retreating all along the line: in fact, they had been retreating ever since we left the Dower House. Victor never even noticed how thunderstruck we were by the news. He sat on for a while chatting, and then he left.

Nina and Reda returned in the best of humours. They were incredibly proud of having got the room, for the village was so full that some of the peasants found themselves literally in the street, and there was not a spare corner to be found in any barn, stable or woodshed. That night all our neighbours were turned out into the mud, and they shouted and called to each other through the darkness as they staggered along under their bundles, while the women lamented loudly and the children howled. We took a young peasant girl in for the night, which annoyed Tacitus, but we somehow or other made room for her in the tiny entrance-hall.

That night Alf again had a high temperature. His wound was bothering him and he could neither find a convenient place for himself, nor walk about except over our bodies.

Once Nina opened her door slightly and, calling Alf, gave him a huge piece of bacon. I was glad to see him wolf it down and obviously like it, for that meant that he could not be at death's door. Nina liked dogs, which as a rule Russians do not, especially the men; but it does happen with the women. In the same way, in Europe it is usually women who like cats, canaries and gold fish. Nina's mysterious Major appeared during the night. He jumped over our bodies as though they were corpses on the field of battle, triumphantly reached his mistress's door, and disappeared behind it without having uttered a word.

Mist again! The two boys went off into it before dawn, and even before that the Major had left his mistress's side and gone back to the Staff. What a melancholy, grey day! There were potatoes to peel for Nina and her Major; then I went to fry them. I was so obliging, only because I hoped to be able to steal some of Nina's bacon. She was all over the cottage, ordering us and poor Reda about in her shrill, squeaky voice. She was most masterful and obviously despised us: she, a Lieutenant in the victorious Red Army, a doctor, mistress of a staff officer; and we, members of a subject people, squirming on dirty straw.

A soldier sauntered up. He had the same ideas as Nina. Stretching out the pair of filthy drawers he was clutching in his hand, he barked at me, "Wash these!"

"Not I," I replied. "Take them somewhere else. Why should I, an ally, wash your dirty clothes?"

"Will you wash them or not?" roared the soldier, almost foaming with rage. "Who do you think you are? You'll remember me yet!"

Then he assumed a threatening attitude and began cursing me. Although I was afraid that the consequences might not be pleasant, I never even touched his filthy drawers.

The Russians are quite inconsistent. They try to frighten you with shouts and threats, and if they do not succeed just

go their way. How different from the Anglo-Saxon method,
which never threatens unless the threat can be carried out,
which will never demand what is most unlikely to be
given, which never tries to frighten those who are not afraid.

The soldier walked off with his drawers. How quiet it
was! The guns were silent and everything was drowned in
the grey mist. I began chopping my wood beside the cottage
door. Two soldiers came up and stopped to watch. After
whispering together for a while, one of them approached me
and held a bottle to my lips. "Have a drink?" It was spirit
mixed with wine. I drank, and it warmed me and lifted a
weight from my heart. They were a decent-looking couple.
They watched me a little and then walked on, leaving me
with half a litre of their mixture as a present. The Hungarians were never moved by such gestures, and whenever I said
anything their answer was always the same: they have robbed
us of millions, are we to be moved now when they treat us to
some of our own wine? I never knew what answer to make.
It was the truth, but not the whole truth. There was a different truth in those gestures, less official, less tangible, but
more human, a truth not concerned with the law of loot, but
with goodness of heart. However, not being able to explain
this simply and quickly, I preferred to say nothing.

I was in a good mood. I was glad that there was not so
much firing, and that life generally could have been worse.
And then the door opened and in walked my enemy, the one
whose drawers I had refused to wash. Vengeance had arrived,
thought I, wondering what would happen now.

"Off to the kitchen. You're to scrub the walls," shouted
the soldier. "Come along now, every woman here off to the
kitchen."

There was no getting out of this, so I changed my tactics.

"The kitchen? But of course. Excellent. Come along,
Marietta, Elsie, we're going to the officers' mess to scrub."
And to Fifi I whispered, "Hide! Someone who speaks Russian
must stay behind."

And so Dolly, Elsie and I went to scrub out the kitchen, in other words, the old laundry of the Manor.

We got back at dusk, exhausted, but in a good mood. At home I was told the awful news: the N.K.W.D. was looking for me. A soldier had come to fetch me an hour before, and, finding I wasn't there, had taken Jack instead. He had been interrogated and released. They had promised to come for me again. What was I to do? I wanted to run away, to hide, but Jumbo maintained that it is only people with something on their conscience who run away, and that I ought not to hide. That was all very well in the days when only the guilty were punished and the innocent were set free, but where were they? Perhaps I had been denounced; perhaps they would again take me away to another village: better hide. I was afraid, just ordinarily afraid, but I admitted that Jumbo was right. What had to be had to be; so without waiting for the soldier to come for me, I set off by myself for the lion's den.

There was no difficulty in finding the house. Although this unit of the N.K.W.D. had only reached Mora five hours before, there wasn't a soldier who did not know where it was.

"The Major in?" I inquired haughtily of an N.C.O. at the door.

"Who're you? Why're you here?"

"The Major sent for me. Go and tell him that I've come on my own."

"Why did he send for you?"

"Go and ask him. You'll find out."

The N.C.O. disappeared, and a moment later was back again.

"It's not true. He wants to banquet with you. He hasn't time now. He'll send a soldier to fetch you in the evening. Go home and wait."

The tone of his voice was polite.

I reached home to find a furious quarrel in progress. The

little officer from the Commandant's office was taking away Miss Alexandrovna's table and lamp.

"How dare you," screeched Nina. "This is the Major's. You can't take them. Give them back! What do you think you're doing? The Major'll show you!"

"This is not his billet," the Lieutenant interrupted. "He doesn't need either a table or a lamp to sleep here. He has a room with a table at H.Q. And, anyway, you shut up. He'll find you in your straw without a lamp!"

Later on I was sent for again. The Major politely seated me opposite him. He was a nice, placid person. We already realized that not everybody was a devil in the N.K.W.D. Perhaps the Major would have been awful had he suspected me of anything, but he did not. I apologised for my bad Russian, then I had to tell him the whole story of my life. I explained that, as a Pole, I had avoided all contact with the Germans and had no information to give him. He was a man of one idea and gave me nothing to drink, and, what was worse, nothing to eat. Then Jack came, as arranged, to say that Jumbo was ill, and I took my leave.

Whom should I see outside but Nina Alexandrovna and the miserable Reda cursing as they staggered with their bundles into a wretched little cottage.

"What are you standing there for?" screeched Nina. "Come and help with the bundles. Carry them in here. Into this room."

But out of the room emerged some soldiers. "Taken, Comrade Lieutenant," they said.

Nina gave them a charming smile. "I'm so sorry for you, but it's for a Major from the Staff. Move your things out." And with much waving of arms, shrill squeaks, and shouts at Reda and me, she turned the six out. That done, she squatted in the middle of the empty, dirty room, and wrote on a piece of paper, "This billet is taken for Major Balyga of the Staff."

"I'm going with Reda to get the rest of our things," she

said. "You stay here and guard the room. If anyone comes in, show him this paper. Understand? Is that clear? And sweep the room out. I want to find it clean when I get back. If anyone tries to take the room, curse them, shout, and say that a Major is going to live here." With that she ran off up the hill, her short, wide boots plunging deep into the sticky Hungarian mud.

So she's been turned out of our cottage, I thought, as with hands and feet I brushed the filthy, stinking straw from the floor. The owner of that hole, a young peasant woman, watched me out of angry eyes, and I felt sure that she was planning vengeance because I was "helping" the Russians.

The peasants, guided only by their own interests, hated the Russians. The Germans looted less, that was the peasants' only view-point. People of the middle-classes just regarded it all as the logical, time-honoured sequence of events. Having been taught history they knew about it, but the peasants did not, and it was because of this attitude of ours that they hated us most of all, and, whenever they could, tormented us and denounced us. And we were helpless, because the Russians who see everything as either black or white, will always believe the tatterdemalion with dirty nails. We were in the peasants' hands.

I did not wait for Nina but went home. Fifi told me how Nina had been turned out, and shamed. (The mythical Colonel had proved to be a real person after all.) Actually I was sorry it had happened. She had made a lot of work I know, and it had not been easy to steal food from her, but she had at least kept Alf going with biscuits and bacon.

Whilst we were having supper I heard a rustling noise outside. Opening the door I saw the cowering, shivering shape of an emaciated English setter. The Russians must have taken it from some country house and then lost or abandoned it, in Mora. What was to be done? Alf would forget his wound and tear it to bits if he saw it. The setter gazed tearfully at me. Its eyes were appallingly trusting, for setters seldom lose the faith in mankind with which every puppy comes into the world. Even in the darkness I could see its ribs and spine and thigh bones. Its tail was tucked tight beneath it, its ears drooped. I went back to the kitchen.

"I'm still hungry. Give me a bit of bread."

Tacitus grumbled, but gave it. I took it outside, but at that moment they discovered the dog. When people are hungry their senses are sharpened.

"She's giving the bread to some dog or other! We've got to go hungry so that she can feed strays!"

In the end it was decided that the Poles would have no bread at all the next day. We suggested that ourselves for the sake of peace. That decided, silence fell upon us. Both sides were in the right; and both sides felt slightly ashamed of themselves. But what was I to do with the setter? Then I had an inspiration: I would take it to Nina. Nina liked dogs.

The setter obediently pattered after me. It was as light as a shadow, and delicately picked its way through the mud at my very heels. Poor dog. Nina's room was in darkness. I opened the broken door: silence. I groped about the straw in the corner: nothing there. Nina and Reda were obviously amusing themselves elsewhere. We knew by then that Nina was also living with two Lieutenants, who took it in turns to come to her during the day. She was probably with them.

"Come here," I said in Polish to the Hungarian English setter. "Here you are, fresh straw; it'll be nice and warm. Here, make yourself comfy here. That's it, tramp a nice bed for yourself! Don't be afraid when Nina comes back. Perhaps, she'll give you some more bread. Go to sleep."

The setter shoved its nose in among its paws. I patted it in the dark. What a good thing that the intonation of the voice is international. It had understood everything.

Shouts from the road summoned me outside. Two of the Red Army women were standing there: was I the one who drew? Indeed I was, and I felt proud that my fame should have spread so quickly. "Come with us," said the two Russians. "We would like you to sketch a dress for us and act as interpreter."

A tiny room in a neighbouring cottage had been turned into a *salon de modes*. A Hungarian woman sat there cutting a length of sea-green satin. Beside her on the bed groaned the mother of the seven half-naked children who were outside playing in the mud. She was in labour. The Russians took off their belts, leaned their automatic pistols up in the corner, took off their skirts, and began measuring and trying the satin, while their eyes gleamed.

A Russian woman-soldier's figure has to be seen to be believed. Indeed, it is almost beyond description. Nowhere in Europe can you see such huge breasts, hitched almost up to their chins, such thick, short legs, such broad thighs, such shapeless arms, such grey skin that has not been washed for weeks! And their hair: whether long or short, it is always filthy and pinned up with hair-pins four inches long. The eyes of the two peasant women sought mine for confirmation of their disdain for such complete lack of beauty and grace. The woman in labour, already mother of seven, for all the pains and sweat standing on her forehead, had a face that was delicate and almost spiritual in comparison with those of the two Russian girls. What have the Soviets made of their race? Have they killed off all those who even approach the European type? I looked at the intent faces of the two girls: deep-set dark-blue eyes, wide mouths, lumpy noses, thick lips looking as though they had been stuck on. And their fingers, as stubby as though they had been chopped off short with an axe.

After lunch we learned that the child had arrived, a girl. Lina stole some of Muki's and Alec's soup and took it to the mother, while Fifi and I extracted two of Jumbo's table-napkins, the only clean ones left, that were being carefully kept to be used as towels in the future. We wanted to take them to the mother so that she might have something in which to wrap her babe, but at that moment two soldiers arrived from the Commandant's office: Potemkin and Basil. So they had not forgotten about the room!

Potemkin and Basil had brought with them an iron stove, which they began installing where once had stood the stove stolen by Major Blashchuk, whose fame is known to all Russia. There was no stove-pipe, so the two ran to the next cottage and tore the stove-pipe from the wall; then they went to another cottage and knocked the little iron doors that their stove lacked, off its stove. A little clay to cement the pipe into the wall, and ten minutes later the last of our wood was roaring in the stove. When the Russians like, they can work quickly and well.

"Some officers from the Staff are coming to live here. Moving in at once," announced Potemkin, wiping his clay-covered hands on his trousers, and with that they left.

The road was now clear, and Fifi and I stole some of the mead that was being kept against the time when the children might need it, and, with the two table-napkins under our arms, walked across to the cottage where the mother lay. She was just as she had been that morning, lying on the same dirty rags, only some kindly neighbour had placed a clean table-cloth beneath her. We apologised to the poverty-stricken wretch for not being able to give more, but she and her husband, of course, knew all about that. The two table-napkins were immediately hidden away safely and, as we learned later, the babe never so much as saw them. They were too valuable for her to use. (Both mother and child died when the spring came.)

We walked back feeling rather pleased with ourselves.

9th-14th
February

IT WAS just beginning to grow light and the mist was slowly lifting, revealing more and more of the landscape with which we were now as familiar as a prisoner with the walls of his cell. I went out for my morning constitutional with Alf. His wound was no longer festering, but it was healing very slowly. Every morning at dawn I used to go for a walk round the cottage with Alf and smoke my first cigarette. That first cigarette smoked on an empty stomach was the best of all. And then the early morning calm! As I splashed through the mud trying to collect my thoughts and calling to the dog, I pretended to myself that I was leading a normal life. In a moment or two the village would wake up, and with the sun the artillery would start up again and my illusions would have to give way to reality. But those few minutes of solitude were wonderful.

Most people do not realize how important it is to have a few moments to oneself each day, because they do have them, either while sitting in the bus or walking to their work, or being left for a moment by themselves in a room. It makes no difference if you are in the middle of a swirling crowd. Even there you can be alone, because all over the world people are divided into strangers and those you know. We do not accost strangers, nor they us, and in a strange crowd we can enjoy complete privacy. We can, but the Russians cannot. For them no distinction between "acquaintances" and "strangers" exists. The Russian feel that they "know" the whole of humanity. They will walk up to anyone and begin a chat with him, and the wretched European is quite helpless when confronted with their effusive familiarity. They are like very small children who accost everybody, like dogs who will not let another by without first sniffing him over.

How pleasant it was with the village still asleep and the front still quiet! How silently the dawn pierced its way through the mist. Alf was crunching some old horse bones; I inhaled my cigarette. A wonderful moment. I had time now to assure myself that I did exist. During the day there was no time to realize that one had a separate existence, and to do so now was a wonderful feeling. To think that I was I, I!

The little son of our neighbours at the Dower House came running in, out of breath, yelling, "Our houses are free, come on. They're empty, hurry, quick!" I tore down Half-wit Hill towards the river, walked over the rickety bridge which was full of holes, and ran on up the hill, hardly able to draw breath. Leaping over broken pieces of furniture, fences, coils of wire, rotten potatoes, heaps of carpets, I finally reached the house. Soldiers and peasant children were busy looting. "What are you doing here?" I shouted at the soldiers in Russian. The peasant children looked jeeringly at me and went on pulling things out of the wardrobes with their dirty little simian hands. I ran on, then an officer barred my way.

"This house is still occupied by the Army," he said. "You may move in, but there will always be a sentry here to see that nothing disappears. You will be responsible. If anyone should want to take anything, the Commandant's Office is opposite. Run and report there immediately, or else send the sentry. I'll send him over immediately. Now, go and throw out the soldiers."

Throw out the soldiers! Wouldn't I just. Squaring my shoulders importantly, I ran into the first room.

"And what are you doing here. Aaah?" I shouted, trying

to imitate a Russian officer, especially that long-drawn-out "Aaah!" "Out with you. Get a move on! This is the General's house!"

The soldiers began to move out. The peasant children could not believe their ears; the old order had been overthrown, the new one begun, and now, all of a sudden, the old one was back again.

I went to the drawing-room and then to the bedroom. The disorder and the dirt were simply fantastic, in fact quite surrealistic. The whole floor was covered with stuffing from the chairs and cushions, and the stuffing was besprinkled with pepper, laurel leaves and lavender from the little bags we used to keep in the linen-cupboards. Why? I don't know, and I shall never be able to guess. And here and there, like sultanas in a cake mixture, were pickled cucumbers. And out of it all emerged a broken marble Venus. Beside her were neckless champagne bottles. Some of the panes in the windows were broken—a good thing, too, because otherwise it would have been quite dark, so filthy were those that remained. Also the stench would have been even more unbearable. In the next room the carpet was crumpled up in a heap. Why do they wet carpets and then roll them up, I wondered, because I remembered that I had seen others like it outside. I investigated, partially unrolling it. It looked as though the whole Staff had been sick on it. I opened the drawer in a bed-side table, there lay a piece of rotten meat. I kept slipping on bits of pickled cucumber as I wandered round with no idea what to do first. I looked helplessly at the young guard standing quietly in the doorway. He just gazed dully at that fantastic scene. It never entered his head that there was anything unusual about it. He saw nothing wrong.

It was a depressing sight. Where on earth could one begin? I kicked aside a mound of furniture stuffing and there underneath was a heap of torn photographs; torn into tiny fragments. Why? And right beside it was a glass bookcase, the books untouched. A miracle.

Through the window I saw Jumbo approaching, dressed in his trench-coat and leaning on his stick.

"Send Honono to help and the rest of you pack," I shouted to him. "Tell Jack to ask the Lieutenant, The-One-in-the-Specs, for a cart. We are allowed to move in. We even have a guard, because if the Russian offensive fails, the General will perhaps come back."

The Lieutenant gave us the cart, and the kind old pockmarked driver who was one of the "friendlies," made three trips. Honono arrived, and shortly afterwards Matilda. We began clearing up. And what a job it was! My diary contains a detailed description of all that we did and feared, because at the time it was that which appeared important, and not the fact that Elsie went straight to the shelter and discovered that it was all dug up and that we had lost all our money, gold and jewelry. There is no mention of that.

In the yard outside stood a moribund horse, its saddle loaded with sacks of potatoes. Beside it stood Jack and a young N.K.W.D. man. What was happening? I quickly glanced at the soldier's face: are you good or bad? Then I looked at Jack. His expression was reassuring.

"This is my friend, Victor Klimof," Jack said, "I have invited him to spend the night with us because he has lost his unit and he and his horse will only be able to catch it up tomorrow, for it's too late now."

That is how we met Victor, one of our best friends and one of the nicest boys under the sun.

Our room was still very dirty but pleasant. Jack lit the stove, and at last it was warm. It was probably no more than 50 degrees F., but I felt hot, so unaccustomed had I grown to having a stove. Jumbo was in bed. On the table burned a small lamp, for which Jack had made a chimney out of an empty jam jar. He and his friend occupied the sofa. I produced the cocktail that we had been given by the Ensemble. It was the last of our reserves, but we felt we ought to drink it now with our friend Klimof. There was to be no supper. We had only potatoes, and no one had either the time or the strength to cook them. However, I still had some dry bread and a piece of "rainy day" bacon, and this was all set out on the table. Victor sensed that this was all "rainy day" stuff and would not have any at first. But he was young and hungry and had nothing of his own to eat, as he had lost his unit and no strange lot would ever have fed him. In the end we managed to persuade him, and everything was divided equally, although the result was not much more than a toothful.

Klimof came from Moscow, his father was an architect and his only sister had married a Colonel. They had a two-room flat in Moscow and a two-room *datcha* in the country. Victor was twenty-one, but with a mischievous smile he told Jack that he was officially nineteen and had only been fighting for two years. Jack, who appreciated these problems of age, told him in his turn that he was seventeen, and then they both burst out laughing. They understood each other as human beings, over the heads of their governments so to speak. Both of them were doing their best to get into the army as late as possible, and, once in, to get out as soon as could be. They were both Slav individualists, and Prussian discipline which had succeeded in keeping a hold on the entire youth of Germany was quite alien to them. Both boys were patriots and praised the valour of their respective nations, but theirs was a sentimental patriotism of no use at all to the machine of State. Both would at once have become American citizens if given the chance, and would have wept as they listened on the other side of the Atlantic to "The Wild Geese" or "Into the Darkness of the Night" on the wireless.

Victor wanted to become a diplomat, but he obviously could not if he were to get killed in the war, so he had done everything he could, and his father had pulled what strings he could, to get him into the N.K.W.D. where the percentage of casualties was very small, because the N.K.W.D. kept to the rear. Victor had no use for the institution of which he was a member. He always carried an English grammar in his pocket which he would study whenever he had an opportunity. His heroes, he said, were Maisky and Litvinov.

Then we had an English lesson. Klimof was delighted that he had hit upon people who knew the language, and I had to listen to him reciting "the table," "the sugar basin," "the chair," over and over again. While this was going on I was several times summoned to the kitchen. Matilda could not remember that we now had a sentry and whenever any strange soldiers came into the kitchen in search of billets, she would automatically shout, "Lida, Lida," as of old. However, on each occasion the sentry sent the intruders away, looking very secretive and whispering something into their ears. Probably some "war secret" about the General, who had reserved our house in case the offensive should fail.

When night came they changed the sentry, and in place of the tall, quiet Great-Russian we got a stocky, impudent Siberian. Instead of patrolling round the house the Siberian wandered into our room. He saw that there was vodka on the table, heard us talking Russian, and obviously said to himself, "This is something for me."

"What do you want, Mishka?" I asked.

Mishka, jealous that a strange private was drinking with us and not he, adjusted his automatic and stalked up to Victor.

"Your papers!" he shouted.

"I won't show them," said Victor to tease him, for he had all his papers in order.

"Your papers!" Mishka repeated glumly, satisfied that he was spoiling our party.

I did not know what sort of papers Klimof had, and, fearing that he had none at all or that they were not in order, I said to Mishka,

"The bottle's empty. Nothing for you, I'm afraid. Why didn't you come in earlier?"

"I did not come for vodka. I'm after deserters. Come on, you there, give me your papers. Let's have a look. I'm the Commandant's patrol."

Lazily, Victor pulled out his N.K.W.D. pass. Mishka was covered with confusion and was out of the room in a moment. And Klimof laughed and laughed till we thought he would burst.

"Now you understand why I am in the N.K.W.D.?" he asked.

Yes, we certainly did, and we laughed with him. But it can't be at all amusing for the Russians to have the N.K.W.D. hanging over their heads like a sword of Damocles all the time. In the Red Army everybody is under suspicion of being a deserter, and mobile patrols are always out demanding to see the papers of all and sundry. Even officers have to show their papers, when asked, to privates and N.C.Os. of the N.K.W.D. They must be terrified of desertion in the Russian army. Such methods do not offend the Russians because they know no others. They have grown up under that system and consider it normal, whereas we cannot help finding it distasteful that an ordinary private should shout at an officer, stop him, and inspect his papers in order to make sure that he is not a deserter. Sometimes the officer humbly produces his documents, but others roar an "Aaah?" at the private, and the private retires in a panic, realizing that he has tried to stop some untouchable personage. Mostly, however, this searching for deserters is very reminiscent of poker. If you can bluff, you can get away with it.

It was time to get ready for bed. Victor was deeply touched by our hospitality and did not know what to offer us in return. He took off his jacket, which had once belonged to a German airman, and offered it to Jack; then he started emptying his pockets and distributing their contents. He was not drunk, because he had only had two glasses, the same as everyone else. No, he was not drunk, just decent. The first thing

that emerged from his pocket was some electric wire, which
he gave to Jack. This was followed by a pair of artificial silk
stockings very badly torn.

"Take them, Lida, take them. I was going to send them to
my sister, you know, the Colonel's wife in Moscow. But the
war's not over yet; I shall bring her another pair from Berlin.
So you take these. Really, I mean it, please take them." He
saw that I was hesitating, because in point of fact I was wondering what I would do with such a terribly torn pair of
stockings. "I know," he said. "You don't want to take them,
because you think that I stole them. I swear I didn't. I found
them in an empty house. There wasn't a living soul there, and
if I hadn't taken them somebody else would. Word of
honour! Now, will you take them?"

I accepted the stockings. Victor was seized with a real
frenzy of generosity, and in the end he was left standing there
barefooted in only a short, and a very insecure, pair of padded
trousers. His young, pleasant, open face beamed with happiness. He had already given away everything that he possessed,
despite our protests. Suddenly he turned round, delved into
the pocket of his jerkin and produced an enormous, ancient
watch and chain.

"Take this, Pa," he said to Jumbo, and, going up to the
lamp, he added, "Here you are. It's written that the watch is
from Tula. From Tula, not stolen. A real one of ours." We
flatly refused to accept it, because we knew what it means to
possess a watch in Russia, but the negotiations were very moving and protracted. Victor sat down like a child on Jumbo's
bed, stroked his hand and tried to persuade him to accept the
watch. Jumbo kept shaking his head and saying "*spasiba*"
over and over again with the accent on the last syllable. In
the end Jack and I managed to calm Victor down and get him
on to the sofa. The Russians get these attacks of kindness
fairly frequently, that is frequently in comparison with Westerners among whom such behaviour would be regarded as
insanity. Even in Russia, of course, there are not many who

will suddenly give away everything they possess, including
their watches, for no particular reason at all. I kissed Victor
good-night.

We still talked on for some time after we had put out the
lamp. I kept wondering why in the Red Army the other ranks
are more intelligent than the officers. Or, rather, why it was
only among the other ranks that you met people who could
easily have been turned into Europeans, while the officers
were mostly hopelessly "Soviet," so I asked Victor.

"Victor," I said, "why are you, an educated member of a
cultured family, an ordinary private?"

"You see," he replied, out of the darkness, "it's the same
as with my age. If I had given my real date of birth I would
have been four years in the army already. If I were an officer,
there would be a good chance that I would not be demobi-
lized at once but would have to attend God knows how many
officers' courses. I would get stuck in the army. But as a private, once peace is signed I shall, with any luck, get sent home
soon. Before, our officers were kept in the army for ten years
or so. They just would not release them. Made regulars of
them. So you see, if they were to keep me for another five
years after the war, when would I ever have time for my
studies?"

It occurred to me after this that it was mostly the unam-
bitious and unintelligent type which in present-day Russia
adopts an army career. This, of course, must suit the regime
admirably. Such men obviously do not become generals or
field marshals, but instead of promotion they get decorations.
In no other army have I seen such a profusion of decorations.
Every private had at least three, while the officers had at least
a whole row, sometimes one on the left side and one on the
right. This, presumably, explains why most of the pleasant
and cultured people we met were not officers. That kind of
person only joins the army because he has to, and wants to get
out as soon as possible. All the Russians we met who in any
way approached being what we term "Europeans" were quite

uninterested in Soviet principles and had a cynical approach
to their regime, or else were frantically afraid of it. They
were afraid of their own regime: that surely is the essential
difference between a democracy and a tyranny.

The next morning we started scrubbing. We scrubbed
everything that we could lay our hands on, for everything was
sticky with dirt, except the W.C. It had never been used. Or
if it had, as a drinking fountain. However, we found another
W.C., or rather a latrine made out of an old peasant wardrobe, in the yard opposite the main door. Presumably Tolbuchin had shared the views of a certain Russian officer who
had told our priest, "We're a cultured nation, not pigs like
you. We don't stool in the house we live in."

The cart made another trip with the rest of our belongings. We gave the pock-marked driver three cigars and a
pocket-book stolen from the Hungarians. "I only did all this
for you Poles," said the old driver, stuffing his present away,
"I wouldn't lift a finger for the others." After that Fifi and I
secretly took a bottle of Tokay to the Lieutenant, the One-in-
the-Specs. The Hungarians considered that they owed the
Russians nothing for their help. "They threw us out, so now
they can give us a cart to move our things back, can't they?"
they said. I am afraid that there will never be any real understanding between that nation and the Russians. Perhaps the
two Governments will come to an agreement and officially be
friends; but not the citizens. Whenever the Russians come
into contact with a Western people they say of them suc-
cinctly, *sukhoy narod*—dry, or heartless, people. The whole
egoism and materialism of the West is contained in that
description, *sukhoy narod*.

When we arrived there, the Lieutenant-in-the-Specs' billet
was full of soldiers, many of them strangers. The poor wretch
was afraid to talk to us, afraid to accept the wine. He was
chilly, indifferent, almost rude. Our own friend, the Lieuten-

ant, the One-in-the-Specs! That is how fear can change people.

That afternoon our sentry left his post for a few minutes. The instant he had gone an officer, who must have been waiting for the opportunity, rushed in with his herd and grabbed our curtains and mattresses. When the sentry came back I told him that a captain had taken the things, saying that he had come from the Commandant.

"He was lying," said the sentry calmly. "Some stranger or other. But I also need mattresses."

"Listen," I said, "if it goes on like this, what is that General of yours to sleep on?"

Elsie spent the whole day in the shelter. With a single candle to light her, she sat for hours over the hole in which our treasures had been buried, poking about with a stick. In what? I have said that our W.C. had been the only clean thing in the house. The wardrobe of the widow from across the road must have been for "officers only," and the other ranks used the shelter. So Elsie, with great self-sacrifice and with a spotted handkerchief tied over her nose and mouth, had dug for hours by candle light with her little stick. Her efforts were rewarded. She found some pearls, a priceless first edition of the works of some famous ancestor of Rudi's, the remnants of her son's clothes, and some gold knick-knacks. Thus encouraged, she dug on. We called her the Gold-digger, or another, less printable name.

Towards evening we received a terrible blow: the General was coming back. The sentry came to tell us. Had it been Mishka we would not have believed him, although it was really our turn for vengeance, but it was another who brought the news. Also Honono came back from the village with the story that the Russians were again retreating on Mora. In view of this Jumbo went to the farthest room to prepare it for the mythical General's reception. Poor Jumbo carefully swept the floor, made the bed, our only one except for his, and covered it with the curtain from the servants' room, because we noticed that the Russians liked lace.

Although it was still dark I could see that it was snowing outside. Alf crept out of his corner. Dogs always know (but how?) when you wake up. I was still undecided whether or not to go to sleep again and had not yet opened my eyes, but all the same my cough or the conscious way in which my fingers moved, told Alf that I was awake. A soft muzzle nudged my hand up and it descended on Alf's head. Slowly, he started to climb on to my mattress. First, just the front paws; then it became apparent that there were two more, because a third was suddenly pressing on my thigh and finally, very timidly, the fourth. Alf had come to be petted. Somehow he had realized that life had returned more or less to normal and was demanding his rights. I scratched him in all his favourite places. I teased him by drumming his black damp nose with my finger. He suffered it patiently, well aware that consciences can prick, and that you should not take everything literally. Then to make things right again, I scratched the curls on his chest. Alf had now forgotten the treacherous way that he had got on to my mattress, and was resting his whole weight on me. The last paw which till then he had kept just touching the floor for the sake of decency, was now pulled up. Oh, my beloved dog! You survived. Together we cured your wound and your blood-poisoning. God helped a bit, and we did all that we could. And we succeeded! You're well and want to be petted, do you? My dear, dumb person. God only knows to whom you belonged when I found you homeless and masterless. A war dog. But now we're together, sharing the one mattress, helping each other.

That morning Elsie, with the perseverance of a born sportswoman, again plunged into the contents of the shelter. This time she found my platinum ring which had rather a big diamond. For that, I kissed her poor work-worn hand. Elsie had made a sport of going down into the shelter. We really were unconquerable. I began wondering what it would take to exterminate people like us. I should think murder would be about the only thing. And in this respect the leaders of the Russian revolution were right. The only way (this for the benefit of future revolutionaries) to get rid of bourgeois, *i.e.*, people who have had the means to learn life inside out (and for this you need "means" in the other sense) thanks to tradition, travel, or their development of all their latent possibilities, is to murder them. Their sense of humour, cynicism, sense of superiority, and the elegance with which they suffer and die, are very dangerous. So, my advice to you is: murder them. Time will teach you the things that will disappear with us. I am not referring here to the rich or the aristocrats, but to those whom the French call *"des gens bien."* Just wait, and you too, in time will become *"des gens bien,"* and then you will be hunted in your turn.

A dreadful day. It was still thawing and the sun was shining. The gun-fire was incessant, and so close that it shook your inside and the whole house trembled and rang with it. Suddenly Franzi rushed in shouting, "Budapest has surrendered! No more digging trenches!" Great jubilation: then the chilling thought, were any of our friends still alive? Were our houses still standing? How many friends and relations had been killed?

Later on we had a visit from Victor-Chaliapin and his friend Wolodya, the one that once fired his pistol in "the General's room." I would not have mentioned the visit at all were it not for the lovely story that Victor-Chaliapin told us as he sat on Jack's bed. I give it here word for word, because it is of political importance.

So many secret documents have recently been published, so many mysteries explained, that it would be a pity if the real story of the Anglo-Soviet alliance were never to come to light. Particularly so, as it is unknown to anyone in Britain, and in Russia only the singers of the Moscow Ensemble choir and the captain and crew of a certain Leningrad ship are aware of it.

"What do you know about us?" Victor-Chaliapin began. "Not a thing. But we have been abroad. Our Ensemble, for example, was invited to sing in Berlin in nineteen thirty-nine. You think that we Russians stay at home all the time. It's not true. But our Stalin knows who can be let out and shown to the world. That was why we were sent. Two hundred of us.

"The Germans, there's a wise, cultured nation for you, only they've gone stupid. When they made a pact with us, they thought we were savages. So we had to show them that it wasn't true. The boys in the Kremlin hit on the idea of sending our Ensemble over to Berlin. The Germans know all about music, I'll give them that. They can play all kinds of instruments, but they've no notion of real singing. So the boys in the Kremlin said to themselves, 'we must show the Germans whom they've made a pact with.' We knew that the Germans could also sing, but not properly. It's only we who can do that, you know. So off we went, two hundred of us, the whole Ensemble, to Berlin. And did we show the Germans what Russian culture was? They couldn't stop listening to us. The poor creatures had at last heard real singing, and realized that they had made a pact with a cultured nation. When our boys in the Kremlin heard about this they thought to themselves, 'Aaah, we'll have to take advantage of this. The Germans now know what sort of a people we are, what a pity the British don't.'

"What I am going to tell you about now was at the beginning of nineteen forty, when the British really knew nothing about us at all. They thought, as the Germans had: the Russians?—a lot of savages. It was only later that they gradually came to see that we're cultured, and they at once made an alliance with us for the British are a sly lot and always want to have what's best in the world on their side. But at that time, in nineteen forty, we'd not yet made a pact with them. So our boys in the Kremlin put us on a ship in one of the

Germans' ports, and off we went to England to show the British what they'd missed by not signing an alliance with us.

"The ship had been specially ordered for us, sent all the way from Leningrad. So we went. However, our commanding officer knew all about international law and so did the captain of our ship. They said, 'The British are not our allies, so we have no right to land on their shores. We are a cultured nation and we respect international law. We must stop by the shore.' We replied, 'All right. We'll do what we can for Russia, and we'll respect international law and we won't land.'

"So we travelled by sea, but not so very long, till we spotted England. You could see the coast easily from the ship. The captain gave the order 'Halt!' and the ship stopped. We all happened to be on deck at the time. Every single one of us. Then our Commander came and said, 'Now boys, sing! You're singing for Russia. This is propaganda. One, two, three!' And off we went. There were two hundred of us, and everyone knows what two hundred Russians singing at once means. The water carried our voices. The very air trembled. If you haven't heard Russians singing you can't imagine what it was like. When only two sing, it's lovely. But two hundred! There were one or two people standing on the English shore and as soon as our voices reached them they started muttering to each other and came quite close down to the water so as to hear better. Every new Englishman that came to the coast at once joined the others and listened to us. By after lunch the shore was black, there were so many people. Those of the English who had their wits about them ran off to town to get their wives and kiddies. So the women and children also came and listened. Word was sent to the town, to the English port that was there, and by the evening the entire population was down on the shore, some up to the ankles in the water, so as to hear better. And we kept on singing from the sea, standing on deck. The order was: 'Don't stop! Sing all the time. It's for Russia.' And we sang. During the night

they sent word from the port to London that the Russians
were singing. So the English began coming down from London as fast as they could. They were told, 'Hurry up! They
started singing this morning and it's night now. They'll be
getting tired soon and will have to stop.' So the English were
in a tremendous hurry to get down from London. The trains
were so crammed that they couldn't get in and so they clambered on to the roofs, they were so afraid they wouldn't get to
the sea in time. Towards morning the management of the
English railways had to order special express trains, for when
it was known in London that the Russians were singing they
all wanted to hear us. So the first special expresses began
arriving in the morning, but there was such a crowd on the
shore that you couldn't stick a pin in. We were very tired
and hungry by then. To stand like that all day and all night
and sing without stopping, it's enough to give you a sore
throat. But our orders were not to stop, because it was propaganda for Russia. So we went on singing. And of course,
we could not land because we respected international law.
We're a cultured nation. But the English were making
signs to us to come off and sing on the shore. But not
we! We pretended not to see. Then they began to see
what they had missed by not finding out about us before
and by not having a treaty with us. They saw what real Russian culture was. And all the time they kept sending wires to
London from that port and telephoning, 'Come quick, because the Russians are still singing,' so that those who were
left behind in the offices and factories could get off and come
and listen. We could see from the deck how they were pushing and wading into the water to hear us better. It was black
as far as you could see. They hadn't room to move their feet.
We were getting a bit short of breath; but they had said, 'It's
propaganda for Russia,' so we went on singing. And the
English listened spell-bound. They listened, listened and
couldn't hear enough. So beautiful is Russian singing. And
all the time express trains kept arriving from London because

everybody wanted to hear us. And those who were on the shore kept telephoning to their friends and relatives who lived farther away from London and told them, 'Come quickly to the coast, to such and such a port, because the Russians are on their ship but they won't come off, so you can only hear them sing from the shore.' We sang like that for two days and two nights, without stopping. And when in the end we had no strength left and our voices had grown quite hoarse in our throats, our Commandant said, 'Well, all right, boys, enough. We're going back home!' So our ship turned round without once touching the English shore, because we knew international law and the English were not yet our allies. Although they made signs to us and invited us, we knew better how to behave. And we went straight to Leningrad. So that was how the British found out we were cultured too, and they were sorry that they had no treaty with us. But the papers published nothing about it, because it was a war secret. That's why nobody knows about it yet."

I don't suppose that Victor believed a word of his story. Nor did Wolodya, although he chipped in with a lot of details about express trains from London. They were both conscious artists.

AGAIN some soldiers of
the "hooligan" variety, although not of the worst have swept
through the house. Although only wanting some hay, they of
course poked their noses into everything, and, as usual, there
was no sign of the sentry when they arrived. They inspected
the house as calmly as though they were thinking of renting it
for the summer, and, of course, asked our ages and who was
whose husband. Having satisfied their curiosity they felt
thirsty and demanded wine and, finally, a pair of trousers that
was drying in the bathroom. I could not get rid of them.

"And why is your husband so old, aaah?" one asked me,
"and ill? You must find it very dull. If you like," he suggested politely and in rather a condescending tone of voice, "I
can sleep with you."

"No thank you," I replied, "he isn't so very old and ill
yet."

"You know," went on the soldier, but obviously only out
of simple politeness and the wish to do me a favour, "if you
like, I will. I know how it is. An old, ill husband, it must be
very unpleasant and boring for you, as you are still fairly
young."

I again thanked him politely. He did not insist, for I did
not attract him in the least; he was just a well-brought-up
young Russian ready to do me a kindness. Meanwhile poor

Fifi had run to the Commandant's office for our lazy sentry. The two of them arrived panting, shortly after the hooligans had left.

We had just sat down to lunch when the cry "Lida, Lida!" rang out again. Three soldiers had arrived and were demanding to see the papers of all the men. Our sentry had suddenly grown blind and deaf, and was pretending that nothing was happening. The men showed their documents but, of course, none of the Russians could understand the Latin alphabet. Only Jack managed to clear himself. He was lying in bed and showed them a card, signed by Major Sergey, certifying that he was employed at the veterinary hospital. "You're all right," said the soldiers, dismissing him with a wave of the hand, but they drove the others like a lot of cows to the Commandant's office. The sentry turned his head away and let them past without a word.

Creeping cautiously through the garden we followed to see where our husbands were being taken. The worst thing about the Russians is that you can never be sure of anything. You never know what they are going to do. We could see that the soldiers driving our men away had only pretended that they were taking them to the Commandant's office, because they calmly walked past that building and disappeared round the corner. We ran out into the road and questioned some peasants. We were really worried by then, knowing as we did that the soldiers had lied to us and had not been sent by the Commandant at all, so we returned home to hold council.

We were still talking when Franzi and his father appeared back again. They had been interrogated and set free, but Jumbo and Rudi had been detained because the peasants had denounced them as officers, or so Tacitus alleged. It did not matter that neither Jumbo nor Rudi had ever served in any army, because the Russians were in any case unable to read their documents. Nor did we know whether what Tacitus and Franzi had heard in the village was not just a rumour. How were we to find out what Jumbo and Rudi were charged with?

The interpreter, a local Communist, would tell us nothing. Tacitus was afraid that they would not be interrogated in Mora at all, but, if the denouncement were serious, they would be sent to Counter-Intelligence headquarters at the front.

I tore off to the Commandant's office, but they knew nothing about it at all. It was none of their business. Their job was to run the village. This was a job for the N.K.W.D. I went further, and discovered to my amazement that there were several Commandants in the village, each of them independent and authoritative, no unusual thing with the Russians. But where to look for the one in which my husband was detained? I ran to the doctors, because I was told that there was a Commandant's office there. The women doctors said yes, they were it. Then some peasants told me that there was another Commandant's office at the home farm. I went there. "Quite so, quite so," a soldier informed me, "that's us, but we haven't caught anyone to-day. Go to the priest's house, there's a new lot there, and they are probably out arresting, because they only arrived this morning." So I ran on to the priest's house. There at last I found out from the priest's housekeeper that the new Commandant was next door. I was there in a second. The sentry would not let me in. There was an officer walking about. I implored him to take me as an interpreter. He would not listen to me. He said they already had an interpreter, a local man, a very decent fellow with a red arm-band. And the officer disappeared. Then, as so often happened, the sentry forgot that he had refused to let me in a moment before, and so, panting and trembling with anxiety, I found myself inside. There in a small glass veranda sat the two innocents, Jumbo and Rudi. They did not know of what they were accused, nor what was going to be done with them. They had already been interrogated, but that had been no more than just translating their documents for the Russians. There was nothing I could do. I was afraid for them.

I began joking with the sentry. My "nice pussy" method again. Perhaps poor Jumbo's fate would depend on that man. Stealthily I took a piece of bread out of my pocket and tried to hand it to Jumbo, but the sentry jumped up and stopped me. I tried to soften his heart, but he was adamant. There was obviously nothing I could do, so I ran back home to let everybody know where Jumbo and Rudi were.

That done, I ran back again across the fields. I had been on the run ever since the morning and was so exhausted that I could hardly get my breath. In the distance I could see Tacitus and Franzi on the road; they were going to see the local interpreter and try to find out what it was all about. All of a sudden I spotted Jumbo and Rudi, escorted by two armed guards, walking down the highway that led to the west. Oh, Lord! Now I would have to turn back and, instead of making for the cottage, run to the highway. That meant the ditch and the path. I slithered down the slippery slope followed by a shower of muddy stones and with mud spattering over me as the plants at which I clutched came out by the roots. Then, splash, into the water. I emerged on the other side wet and covered with mud. I must have been a sight. Another few yards of mud and then I was pounding down the highway, my heart thumping in my throat. This was becoming a Marathon: I had now been running for two hours almost non-stop.

I caught up with them. The guards took no notice of me.

"They're taking us for interrogation to the next village, seven miles," Jumbo shouted.

"All right, I'll borrow some bread somewhere and catch you up. We'll go together. I'll tell them I'm the interpreter." With that I turned round and made for the nearest cottage. It was the last one in the village and belonged to one of Tacitus' labourers. I burst into the room. A young peasant woman was standing glumly in a corner looking with loathing at a laughing and rather nice little Mongolian.

"Lend me some bread," I gasped and then explained the position.

"Listen you," said the little Mongolian, "tell her not to be afraid of me. I shan't bite her. I just gave her a pat, and now I'm supposed to have been beating her. She can't see a joke."

The girl hurriedly cut me a large hunk of bread. I seized it and dashed out again. I must catch them up. But were they really being taken to the next village? Or would they be led aside into the fields and robbed? I imagined all sorts of horrible things happening to them, and began reproaching myself for having left them at all, but, on the other hand, in a famished country you cannot move without bread. I wallowed on through the mud which was now coming in over the tops of my boots. It splashed up in every direction and my face was covered with a rapidly drying crust. Who does not know real mud cannot even imagine what it is capable of, for real mud is an element, like fire or water.

I had almost reached the high road when some soldiers stopped me. "Soldier, soldier!" they called, taking me for one of them. Only then did I realize what a sight I must have been. No sooner had I got rid of them than a Russian jeep drove up, splashing me all over with thick, brown water. "Soldier, can you tell us the way to Mora?" Again I had to stop, chafing at the delay. Finally I reached the highway. Looking round, I saw Franzi pounding along from the direction of the village, his huge feet sending the mud spurting up like a tank, and there, in the west outlined against the sky, were the silhouettes of the two prisoners and their guards.

I caught them up almost at my last gasp, and thrust the bread into Jumbo's hand. The two soldiers paid no attention to me. After that I followed them like a shadow, keeping five yards behind them.

Jumbo turned round.

"You still here?" he shouted in French. "I forbid you to follow us. Go back home at once."

Then ensued a discussion, carried on, because of the distance between us, partly by signs and partly by shouting. I did not want to go home and Jumbo intended that I should. In the end the soldiers grew sick of it and probably also a bit suspicious.

"Be off, go home," one of them yelled to me.

"I want to be with my husband," I said.

The sound of his own language made the soldier alter his tone.

"Now, old girl, what do you want to come with us for? You should be glad to be free yourself. You keep away from us, and that's good advice. You're only asking for trouble. Go back to the cottage, to the children."

I walked stubbornly on, and then the soldier lost his temper.

"Be off, before I make you. Can't you understand what I'm telling you?"

The procession halted and the soldier assumed a threatening attitude.

"I implore you, go home!" said Jumbo.

I turned back.

On the way home I scraped the mud off my face and hands. I was deadly tired and hungry. When I got home I found that there was more trouble. In the kitchen were five soldiers and the son of the Communist interpreter.

Here I must make a small digression. It should be realized that among simple, primitive people who have never read anything, there are two conceptions of Communism. The least popular of the two is that it means that everybody ought to be equal as regards his standard of living. Not many hold this view. The majority of primitive Communists consider that Communism just means a reversal of roles: I used to scrub her floor, so now she, my former mistress, can scrub mine. Whenever I heard this expressed, I used to suggest that to be really equal we ought to take turns to scrub, but the response was never encouraging. All that these "Communists'" communism amounted to was class vengeance, and, unfortunately, all the Communists in our village were of that type. All they wanted was a reversal of roles, and the fact that that would not change the economic system quite apart from its having nothing to do with Communism, did not worry them in the least. Any order that would have allowed them to sit in the manor and drink black coffee, while we mowed the lawns and raked the paths, would have been Communism to them. That was their ideal, and nothing will ever convince them that that is not Communism.

These were the people who put on red arm-bands and went about stealing, looting and demoralizing the Russians by telling them any old nonsense. Taking advantage of the Russians' credulity (they will believe anything a poor person tells them), they denounced us as a matter of principle without even knowing us. That was why they were so very dangerous. A considerable proportion of them had worked in with the Germans and benefited considerably, and now they had changed sides and were all for the Russians. This was the type of person with whom the Russians mostly had to deal in Europe. What for us were the dregs of society they had to use as the mainstay of their order.

The five soldiers were standing in the kitchen shouting that they wanted billets and that they didn't care twopence about any General because they had been sent by the Commandant. The interpreter's son, who was wearing a red arm-band and had an evil, wolf-like face, was explaining to Marietta that by refusing she was getting herself into trouble, because he, too, had been sent by the Commandant. He was self-assured, impudent and threatening. I had the feeling that it was he who had denounced our menfolk. There is no knowing how long this unpleasant business would have lasted if our happy-go-lucky sentry had not suddenly turned up and driven them all away. They went off with their tails between their legs, but all the same the interpreter's son had lost face and we were afraid of his vengeance.

With them out of the way we were at last able to sit down to the cold, wretched meal we called dinner. With our supply of wood, a hot meal was out of the question. There wasn't even bread, because the little we had would have to be given to the peasant girl who had lent me the piece for Jumbo and Rudi. After dinner I went to take it to her, but she refused to accept it. I shall remember that cottage. Whenever I dream of one day finding myself rich, I always think of the nice present I shall buy that girl: a pig, or perhaps even a cow.

What a terrible day it had been!

Looking through the window it was obvious that someone was creeping stealthily through the bushes. The priest in his underwear! What was this? What else had happened? Fortunately nothing bad. The priest sank panting into an armchair. He was covered in mud and tightly clasped his unbuttoned cassock about him. He had come to tell us that a relative of his, an engineer, had seen Jumbo and Rudi safe and sound in the next village. The engineer had just returned from being interrogated there. He had arrived from Budapest two days previously, so the Russians had at once arrested him and taken him off to be questioned. So perhaps Jumbo would be back soon.

In the evening Dolly slipped into the "Polish room." She wanted to know whether Jumbo had remembered to take off the watch which Rudi had lent him. A chorus of voices informed her that of course he had not taken it off: how could he have known that the Russians were going to arrest him? Dolly wrung her hands. "That's the end of the watch!" "Let's hope that it's not the end of him!" said Jack angrily. Jack's remark hurt Dolly, and she walked out of the room without saying good-night, slamming the door to let us know what she thought of us.

The next day began with a tremendous commotion in the house. The Hungarian militia forced their way in and took our bed: our sacred bed, straight from under our noses! The Hungarians, who were as afraid of their own countrymen as of the Russians, had been unable to stop them. Shame had fallen upon our household. I was furious, because in that con-

founded village I had to be as careful of my prestige as any
sahib so as not to lose face. I ran to the Commandant's office
to see the Lieutenant. He was a small, dark, sleepy little man.
His men always said of him, "You can't figure him out," and,
indeed, throughout the time we knew him we were never able
to fit him into any known category. He was a classic example
of the famous unfathomable soul of the East. Shouting at the
top of my voice, I explained the situation. I began my speech
with a few juicy oaths aimed at the entire Hungarian nation,
the first time I had ever been so disloyal to my hosts as to
curse them to a Russian. "You'll never be able to deal with
that lot," I screeched. "Either you will become like them or
you will have to liquidate them." I told him the story of
Jumbo's and Rudi's denunciation and its sad ending. "It's me
you should trust, and not just anybody," I roared at the unfortunate Lieutenant. I also told him how the peasants kept
sending soldiers to us for billets or food, and that but for them
our sentry could have slept all day long, and the whole lot of
them in that office too, because I was perfectly capable of
defending the house myself. But I could not struggle against
the peasants if the Red Army were always to favour them. I
then demanded that he summon the new headman immediately, new because the village had just staged a local revolution of its own and declared itself independent of the
neighbouring town.

The headman was sent for and came at once, together
with the interpreter's son. Now my anger had found the
victim for which it had so fervently longed. I began banging
the table with my fist, a thing I had never done before in my
life, but I knew that was what was needed on such occasions.
I shouted at them in Russian. Whether they understood anything I don't know, but the Lieutenant did, and he kept
motioning to me to calm down. He did not like the Hungarians either, "*sukhoy narod,*" a dry nation, but those two
were the mainstay of the new Red regime, and here was a
bourgeois cursing them up hill and down dale just as in the

old bourgeois, blood-sucking days, and that in the Russian Commandant's office. The Lieutenant assumed the expression of a Pontius Pilate, not knowing with whom to agree. Then that sly, old man, the new headman, chipped in.

"I don't know which is the real Commandant," he said, "there are several Commandant's offices in the village and they all tell me to billet the soldiers on the gentry."

"What, you don't know which the real Commandant is?" I interrupted, setting my arms akimbo. "What do you think of that?" I said, turning to the embarrassed Lieutenant with the Pontius Pilate look, "he doesn't know that you are the Commandant. Just think of it, the headman, and he doesn't know!"

This touched the Lieutenant's self-esteem and the odds were turning in my favour. The headman realized that he had made a gaffe and might any moment see the ambitious Lieutenant turn against him, so he changed his tactics.

"I know," he continued, "that this is the only office that counts, but what am I to do? I am an old man. Strange officers come to me, shove their automatics into my belly, and yell at me: find quarters, find a bed, tell us where the spies are hiding. What am I to do? Let them shoot me?"

I waited patiently for him to finish, like a good chess player who gleefully sees his opponent making a false move. I let him finish, then said, with an irony which he was unable to appreciate, "So they wanted to shoot you because you wouldn't give them a bed? They held an automatic to your belly, did they? Fancy that!" As soon as the headman stopped, satisfied he had got himself out of the hole, I began again, this time in a sort of duet with the Lieutenant.

"What, you such-and-such? You're lying! The Russians don't shoot at civilians. Ugh, you son of a bitch, you'll remember this. Is that the way you speak of the Red Army? You are to return the bed this instant! Get out of here. What impudence! Look at him, they threatened him with a gun. How is it you're still alive?"

The headman and the frightened interpreter's son withdrew as quickly as they could. My anger immediately ebbed away, like water after a flood. I turned laughing to the young Lieutenant, and he laughed back. It had been a very successful game of "frighten your neighbour," one of the most popular in Russia. Without many words I had achieved an understanding with Lieutenant Vanyusha. Why mince words: we had enjoyed ourselves. When I left we shook hands. Vanyusha disliked the Hungarians intensely.

Supper was a miserable meal. With us, however, all our meals, irrespective of whether we had peasant chicken or just plain unsalted potatoes, were a family ceremony. No one was allowed to be late, because otherwise Tacitus would fall into a silent rage, visible only to those who knew. That is what keeps nations going. The table was always properly laid, and although it was often only three or six degrees above freezing in the dining-room, it was there that we always ate because that was what the dining-room was for. (Provided, of course, that the house was free of Russians.) The boys or Marietta handed the things round and so we created the illusion of the good old days. But Tacitus was not a romantic who fed himself on illusions. He did it so as to continue certain fundamental customs, among which he had grown up and which he termed culture. Perhaps he was right.

Immediately supper was over we returned to our room. The Hungarians without Jumbo bored us horribly. Jumbo was the link that united us. Where was he now? What was happening to him? Where were they driving him?

I woke up the next morning with a very sore throat. My throat was in fact so sore that I stayed in bed. I could hear the burr of the engine of one of those little planes the Russians used behind the front lines for distributing their mail. It was a symbol of the receding floods. Those little toy planes used to fly about 200 feet above the fields and very slowly, so that one could see quite plainly the pilot's face, red with the frost. When they appeared anywhere it was a sign that the front had moved forward, because they could only fly in safe places. To me it was as joyful a sound as the swish of the wings of his dove to Noah. "A good omen," I thought, and at that moment I heard a commotion in the house although no one was calling "Lida, Lida!" The door of my room opened and in walked Jumbo, and behind him I could see Dolly embracing Rudi.

Jumbo sat down on his bed and bathed his feet in a basin of hot water. Jumbo who was fifty and inclined to be delicate, took six weeks to get over that trip which gave him bronchitis and a high temperature. He spent all morning washing, shaving and talking. They had been accused of being officers. Or at least that was what they thought. They had hardly been interrogated at all, because the Russians had been in a great hurry to move on after the front, and that was why they had been set free. The Counter-Intelligence men simply had not known what to do with them. They, of course, had pocketed all their valuables, except the dollars, because the officers had not known what they were. And Dolly's famous watch was gone. Jumbo got into his wretched bed and we sat round him proudly, enjoying having him back, instead of getting on with our work.

Jumbo told us to invite Vanyusha and the warrant officer, Sashka, for supper. Elsie had found a bottle of champagne among the Marshal's rubbish and we thought we would give a party for the Commandant's office and so get some protection against the constant denunciations of the peasants. Jack, however, said that Sashka hated his commanding officer, Vanyusha, so we decided that Sashka should come by himself that evening and Jack would invite Vanyusha separately for the following day. Jack walked across to the Commandant's office and returned beaming because Vanyusha had accepted our invitation and promised to come on Sunday, that was the next day, together with his friend. We waited patiently for Sashka to turn up but he never came. Perhaps he had taken offence when he learned that we had invited his officer separately.

The bells were ringing for Mass, which was to be celebrated in the school for the first time since the invasion. A solemn occasion. Only the Poles had breakfast, because the Hungarians were going to Holy Communion. Then the house emptied and I was left alone to guard the house and Jumbo. After Mass, Jack looked in at the Commandant's office to find out why Sashka had not come the evening before. Sashka, it appeared, wanted to come with his officer. All right, let him.

Jack had found out in the village that all the Russians were leaving and that only our Commandant would remain. He was to be our only hope. After the Russians left, the peasants went quite crazy. They took no notice at all of the new Provisional Hungarian Government. They, or rather a handful of them headed by the new headman, owed their authority to the Russians and they decided to take full advantage of it. They began to set up a collective farm. We called this playing at Robinson Crusoe, because those peasants behaved as though they were on a desert island and had absolute power. They terrorized the whole village, took no notice of the regulations issued by the new Government and invented new laws of their own as though they were the only people in the world and Mora the only village saved from a flood.

After lunch Franzi returned from some peasants whom he had been visiting. Franzi told us that he had seen a new batch of Russians arriving, so Jack was sent to investigate. He came back in an hour. "You know who it is?" he asked. "The Commander of our Ensemble, the manager of the Odessa Opera. Grigory he's called. He's a friend of Victor Porfirovich. He told me that Russia had put forward further demands at the Crimean Conference, but that's possibly not true because he was a bit drunk. He also told me that the famine is much worse on the other side of the river. You can

get a woman there for a pound of salt or a hundred cigarettes."

Lieutenant Vanyusha and Warrant Officer Sashka either
forgot about our invitation or were drunk, because they never
came. As evening fell, a crier was sent round the village calling upon the peasants to return all looted property. We could
hear his monotonous voice through the window. Matilda's
favourite sentry, that horrid Siberian Mishka, was tucking
into the remains of our supper in the kitchen. Jumbo had
fallen asleep. The silence made me feel sad, and I dreamed of
getting away to Budapest.

19th-25th
February

NOW began a succession of dull, domesticated days. The difference in temperament between the "impossible" Poles and the more pliable Hungarians became increasingly accentuated, and led to much bickering. We Poles discovered that they were cheating us over food. Honono would bake some miserable little cakes behind our backs, and we would be offered none. That was what happened last night, when the three of us sat in the dining-room vainly waiting for the Commandant. As Poles we felt it our duty to do so; but while we sat there the sly Hungarians ate all the cakes. The story of how we incited the unfortunate Jumbo to defend our rights takes up most of my notes for that period. All the same, don't forget that we were all permanently hungry then, and even our cigarettes had given out.

Jack went down to the Commandant's office where he learnt that Vanyusha was still asleep, having been drunk the night before, while Sashka had gone to Budapest. That was why they had not turned up. The Russians never bother to tell you if they are not coming when you are expecting them; but we already knew that habit of theirs.

All of a sudden four Russians walked in, "just to have a look round," as they said, and proceeded to inspect the place.

There ensued the stereotyped conversation about our private lives. I noticed that no Russian could ever understand how a woman of my age (thirty-five) could choose a husband of forty-nine, yet they understood perfectly if it were the other way round. Whenever we told any of them that eighteen-year-old Jack was the lover of forty-five-year-old Elsie, they accepted it as a normal occurrence. It would appear from this that in present-day Russia the only prerequisite for sexual relations is difference of sex, as is the case with animals. Age, looks, etc., are of no importance. Thus a young boy will enjoy himself just as much with an old woman as with a girl of his own age; but it is quite different for a young woman. Of what use to her is an old man? A woman is, so to speak, never obsolete, but a man becomes useless after a certain age. Thus the Russians would have accepted Jack as the lover of Lina or Matilda without demur, but they could not understand what I was doing with a husband thirteen and a half years my senior. A Russian of fifty is an old man, a spent machine, and so many a nice young Russian boy shook his head pityingly over me, when he learned that Jumbo was my husband. How could I have chosen such an old husband? Incredible. On the other hand many of those nice young boys wanted to force themselves on Matilda. She knew three words of Russian, was kind to them and was in charge of the kitchen. Seeing that, many of the Russians took her for the mistress of the house, for to them to reign over the pots and pans was to rule the whole household. As they had no notion of class, of types of faces, or of our way of dressing, they kept making the same mistake, especially as they would sometimes hear Matilda, with the familiarity of an old retainer, shouting in her shrill voice at Marietta, who would reply to the tirade politely and with a smile. No European would have doubted for a moment: the one was a lady, the other a typical elderly cook. But the Russians would rock with laughter: hark at the old mistress telling off that young one! What to us was obvious was to them a closed book; they crossed Europe feeling their way in the dark, as it were, with the ten fingers of Soviet propaganda keeping their eyes tight shut.

Fifi and I entertained our four guests, while Jack ran for the sentry. Fortunately, however, no help was necessary, because the officer and his three men, having found out our names and ages and told us everything about themselves, were just going. The guard whispered into Jack's ear, "Those are not Counter-Intelligence, but frontier guards. If they want to make a search, it can't be helped. But if they start looting, just you let us know at once. We'll soon show them." Now you know what being really "friendly" means. A really "friendly" person does everything to help his friends.

We spent the rest of the morning inspecting the remains of our fortune, the things that had been deposited with the gardener and the mechanic. Everything was broken and useless.

A peasant woman, kind soul, brought us some potatoes. Someone else came with the news that 2,500 Cossacks were due to arrive in the neighbouring township the next day. Oh, Lord! we moaned, what was three miles on horseback? We would have them all day in Mora. The sun shone after lunch, but it was very dull at home. The priest came to chat with Jumbo who was still in bed, and they amused each other with stories about popes. In another corner of the room, Dolly was confiding to Fifi that she was convinced that Elsie was in love with Rudi. "She keeps crying all night, the lunatic," she whispered indignantly. Our men had now become sufficiently bold to go out and chop wood in the yard. Lunch was excellent: potatoes and peas, and there was even a sliver of meat for everyone, because the peasants had grown kinder since the Hungarian administration across the river had started functioning. But our greed was not so easily satisfied and we often dreamed about cakes, or steak and onions. We even went so far as to sit down to a game of bridge after we had washed up, but it had to be interrupted as Marietta discovered that she had a louse. However, the fact that our troubles were such

things as lice and unfortunate love affairs, was merely proof
that the war was far away and would return to us no more.

Matilda dragged us out of our beds in the early morning
because a strange soldier had strolled into the kitchen. However, it was only the new sentry come to boast of how well he
had defended our house during the night. And indeed he had,
for 1,500 Russians had descended on Mora in the night, and a
Lieutenant-Colonel had wanted to force his way into our
house. In spite of this new catastrophe the Hungarians all
trooped off to the school for Mass. It was Marietta's birthday.
While she was out I drew a silly birthday card for her, with
wishes in eight different languages. We put some unroasted
coffee beans in her cup and decorated her place with privet
leaves. To add to the effect we put on the table a china
nymph minus one arm and her Greek bun, and a statuette
of Napoleon bestriding a prancing horse with no front legs.
While we were proudly regarding our work, in walked Sashka.
The sight of so tastefully decorated a table, and the terrible
drawings on the birthday card evidently filled Sashka with
cultural jealousy, for he pulled a sacred picture out of his
pocket to show that he, too, was interested in the arts. The
picture represented the infant Jesus patting a lamb.

"It's a little girl," he explained, proud to have us crowding
round him, "you see, she's playing with a lamb. Pretty, isn't
it? Look at those eyes and her hair, well done, aren't they?
Isn't she a pretty little girl?"

We admitted that she was. Sashka sighed and left us.

After lunch, for which we were hardly able to wait because
it was better than usual, we received a visit from Grigory,
manager of the Odessa Opera and chief of our unforgettable
"Ensemble." He brought with him the pale Major who had
once sent us a soldier to defend us against the hooligans. This
visit was to convince me how truly polite the Russians are.

We never for a moment believed that Captain Grigory
was manager of the Odessa Opera. Whatever the opera in

Odessa was like, neither it nor any other could ever have had
a man like Grigory as its manager. But we were already accustomed to the polite routine lies of the Russians, and so we
listened, smiling politely, to his stories about the opera. The
two were so effusive that we switched the subject to the situation at the front. They readily produced a map and showed
us that the front had hardly moved at all, and that the chief
town in our district was still partly in German hands. The
Hungarians looked at me triumphantly: so, in spite of all that
I had said, it was possible to get information about the front
out of the Russians. But was it? Grigory was no Vanyusha,
but a sly Ukrainian, and every time he opened his mouth he
lied. Also it was very obvious that he wanted something
from us.

Having lied enough to satisfy the requirements of the
Russian *savoir vivre*, Grigory got down to business: all he required was china and plate for twenty for the Red Army Day
celebrations of the staff in the neighbouring village the next
day. He said that he would come later to fetch the things and
that he would bring them all back on the evening following
the banquet. Tacitus asked that in return for the loan of the
china and silver we might be given even just a handful of tea,
as for weeks we had been drinking nothing but lime flowers or
hot water and flour. Grigory promised us mountains of the
best tea, and departed with the Major after a most courtly
leave-taking. They came for the crockery just before dinner,
and promised to return everything in excellent order the next
evening and to bring us some food. I made a drawing for the
unknown staff officers, depicting a group of Red Army men
drinking wine, with the caption "To Victory" in block letters.
Then, with many "till to-morrows," Grigory departed, and we
were never to see that charming man again. He probably
passed through Mora a hundred times after that but, tactful
man that he was, he was careful to avoid our house. Captain
Grigory, manager of the Odessa Opera, could easily have
robbed us of all our china and silver, but he preferred to ac-

quire it politely. He was a cultured man, as he had so often told us. I went outside to see the lorry off. "Greetings to the Ensemble," I shouted, "and best wishes for the whole staff on the occasion of Red Army Day." "Till to-morrow!" cried the officers happily (now I know why so happily).

As the lorry disappeared it occurred to me that Grigory had probably never even seen the Ensemble, just as he had never seen the Odessa Opera. He had probably never been in the N.K.W.D. either, although he had told us, as a great secret, that he had been working with it for the past twenty years. That would just have been to frighten us, so as to make sure of getting what he wanted, but we were not Russians and those four letters were not our bogey. Tacitus, meanwhile, was rubbing his hands in anticipation of the tea. Moreover, he had only packed nine forks and twelve plates, which in point of fact was all that we had.

Jumbo got up for the first time since his "interrogation." He still had a temperature, but he was so bored that he decided to take a walk in the garden. We strolled round sedately and slowly, my husband leaning on my shoulder with one hand and on a stick with the other. Dinner was a true birthday dinner. We madly ate all our good things, taking no heed for the morrow. There was carrot soup, a slice each of hot but smelly ham, pease-pudding, potatoes, and soufflé with the rest of the jam.

At dusk Franzi and Jack crept into the Manor to retrieve the remains of our treasures. They brought back a few pictures in broken frames and the remnants of Jumbo's XVIIth century Spanish chest on which the Russians had once chopped meat for their rissoles. That's all there was. Jumbo gazed in horror at the beautiful woodwork and the wonderful iron clasps wrung from their hinges. "God alone knows," Jumbo said, "how the hinges could have hindered their rissole-chopping!" But there it was, Spanish hinges were evidently an obstacle to the oriental mind's approach to mincing. Jumbo had taken a step forward in his acquaintance with the great Slav family, and emerged from the experience with a heavy sigh.

Jack wasted the whole of the morning at the commune and the Commandant's office in an attempt to get out of being sent to dig trenches. We received a visit from the priest and Tacitus' young agent. You could tell from their faces that they knew something. They did. Two German tanks had penetrated into Orla the day before. That was the extreme end of the wing of the Germans' counter-attack. The centre was aimed at the county town, which they had succeeded in occupying. Thus they were advancing on the whole sector. Where would the Russians stop them?

Lunch was a very gloomy meal. Only Jack was in good spirits, because he considered that with Sashka's help he had done the Crusoes in the eye, and would not now be required to dig trenches. Muki had a high temperature. He was the first victim of the muck we were having to eat. The potatoes were partly rotten, the flour was mildewed and either the meat or the fat not fresh. We were all of us later to succumb, except me. Even a hyena would boast if it had my stomach. Muki was so ill that Jack and Franzi went for the Russian doctor, but she only said "*Nitchevo*" and would not come. Dolly sat by the side of her child, gazing at him as though she were trying to suck the sickness out of him with her eyes. That was the only medicine we had. Sashka dropped in bringing us a handful of tobacco. Slowly we gathered round the outstretched hand, like moths round a candle: Fifi, Rudi, Jack and I.

We were smoking in the dining-room, inhaling slowly and devoutly, when suddenly the door opened and revealed the new headman and a Russian soldier. To what did we owe this unexpected honour of a visit from the chief Robinson Crusoe, who had hitherto avoided us like the plague? He had come to arrest Tacitus.

Sashka and the strange soldier at once began quarrelling.

Sashka, however, was not really a hundred per cent "friendly," and, as the strange soldier belonged to the Counter-Intelligence, the odds were against us. They took Tacitus away. He did not even have time to take food with him. He returned half an hour later. What had it all been about? We asked, clustering round him. He had been taken to the priest's house where a new mobile Counter-Intelligence unit had just established its headquarters. Tacitus' young agent had been arrested and spirited away somewhere on a vague charge, and Tacitus had been summoned by mistake. But we knew that this was the headman's work, for he was most anxious to have Tacitus taken away; preferably deported straightaway to somewhere beyond Tomsk or Omsk. Though unsuccessful this time, he would not lose hope.

"Stupid fools!" was all Sashka had to say, and he dismissed the matter with a contemptuous wave of his hand.

Sashka was still with us when a soldier came demanding billets for a hundred and thirty men. What, a hundred and thirty men in this little house? Having made sure that the ragged creature had no connection with Counter-Intelligence, Sashka quickly disposed of him: in other words he threw him out. That done he himself stood up and left to inform his chief of the impending visit of the three Poles whom he had invited to supper.

As there was still some hot water in the kettle, I even washed my hair for this occasion. We took a bottle of Tokay with us. It was a magnificent meal. Fritters, sausage, rissoles, jelly. We toasted the Red Army. Vanyusha, however, was not feeling well and hardly opened his mouth and left Sashka to keep the conversation going. In a corner sat Stepan, smiling inanely each time we praised his culinary accomplishments. Russian cooking is tasty, but in the army confined to three or four dishes, which are filling, heavy and extremely primitive.

We returned home to find a cousin of Marietta's, a lady of about sixty, who had trudged all the way from the capital,

covering twenty-seven miles on her poor old feet. It was an
unexpected and an uncalled-for visit. In the first place the old
lady was a countess, of which fact the peasants were well
aware. A title those days was a curse. Secondly she was a
well-known reactionary, and thirdly, she was lousy. She
laughed at us for attempting to fight our lice. She had given
up long ago, and just let them bite her. She was too old to
tackle them, she said, and we, too, would soon find out that it
was a hopeless business. She said that there was famine in the
capital, and typhus. "Aha," said the Hungarians to themselves, "we must get rid of this woman as soon as possible."
"Not our relative, not our house," we said to ourselves, "let
the Hungarians do as their conscience tells them."

Franzi was to go off before dawn to dig trenches. Franck,
one of Tacitus' former servants, came to ask Jack to stay in his
cottage, because he too had to go digging, which would leave
his wife, mother-in-law and small daughter defenceless against
the Russians who would inevitably start raping the women the
moment the men were out of the village.

In the night some peasants brought back a camp-bed
which they had previously stolen from the Manor. They
brought it secretly, because they were again not sure whether
it was a good or bad thing to return stolen goods. An old
groom, Joseph, also came during the night and brought gossip
and some food. He whispered mysteriously into Tacitus' ear,
insisting that a Russian offensive would be launched in ten
days' time.

We had supper very late, not till we had put up the barricades and no longer expected any callers. It had been a very
tiring day, for we had grown unaccustomed to so much excitement. We ate in silence, glancing stealthily at our guest and
automatically looking for any signs of lice on her neck and
collar. We'll throw you out to-morrow, we thought to ourselves. Who told you to meddle with politics, anyway? We
had grown hard. And all the time she ate greedily and in silence,
unaware that on the morrow she would have to resume her

wanderings. Tactitus had had enough conscience not to say anything to her yet. Let her at least eat her potato-noodles in peace and quietness. A hard day. Jack came back from the Franck's cottage quite late.

We were awakened an hour before dawn by a Russian soldier and one of the village militia-men. Jack's triumph over the Crusoes had proved short-lived. The commune had won and Jack was to go to the front to dig trenches for five days. That the Commandant had exempted him made no difference. The Crusoes had found another lot and now, in the middle of the night, Jack could not go and drag Vanyusha or Sashka out of bed to confirm that he was exempt. Furious, Jack dressed by the light of a candle, while I chatted with the soldier and, out of sheer boredom, exerted myself to make him into a "friendly." And how useful that friendship turned out to be! Jumbo lay as still as a dormouse. He had no idea what it was all about, but he knew that it was best to pretend that he did not exist, as certain beetles do in the face of danger. Somehow nobody discovered him in the darkness, so he escaped being taken away, which was lucky as his bronchitis was at its worst. Meanwhile, Marietta had got some bread and a piece of bacon ready for Jack. It was some good bacon that we had never touched even when we were most hungry, because it was earmarked for those who might be arrested and taken away.

Before Jack was ready a Russian officer swept in with another Crusoe and started a man-hunt. After inspecting everybody the officer decided that I was the only one of any use. "Come on," he said, "you're going to the front for five days. You'll do a little digging for us!" He was rude and angry that the peasant had brought him to a house where no one was fit for heavy physical work. The Crusoes had all sent their families away to a neighbouring village the day before, they being the only people left with the horses and carts to do so, thus all the local Communists had managed to avoid being sent to work. I explained to the officer that there were several people ill in the house, and that someone had to be there to chop wood and fetch water, that you could not leave a dozen or so people without help for so many days. But the officer would not listen. He had been told at the commune that he ought to take the people from the bourgeois house, and so he insisted. My little soldier, hearing the shouting, came running out, forgetting that he was supposed to keep an eye on Jack, and took up the cudgels on my behalf. He whispered something into the officer's ear. Evidently the officer considered that *"les amis de mes amis sont mes amis,"* because he at once altered his tone, and taking the soldier tenderly by the arm walked off, followed by the wretched Jack and the two militia-men.

Dawn was just breaking, so no one bothered to go back to bed. I put out the lamp in our room, threw on a coat and cape and went for the water. While I was at the well our unwelcome guest from the capital was sent on her way to the south. Rudi gallantly saw her as far as the main road, down which the old, lousy woman shuffled on her blistered feet. During the siege she had fetched water for the people in her shelter every day, often under fire, and had been given bread for her services, and now she had become a tramp. Rudi came back looking like someone who had just had to shoot his old dog. But what else could we have done? As we learned later, Countess Elisabeth got no farther than nine miles from Mora. Then she was arrested for her notorious anti-Communist attitude, and so was the priest who had taken her in. I believe she died in prison. If not, she must still be there, because she would never be let out.

In the afternoon the priest came as usual with the local gossip. I would have liked a rubber of bridge, but was too tired and sleepy. My hands were all raw from chopping wood. Tacitus was down with stomach trouble and Rudi also in bed, to avoid being taken for trench digging. Elsie spent the whole day bringing back the things that we had given the game-keeper to look after. It was a long job, because she did not dare carry large parcels through the village which was full of soldiers. At four o'clock I went to bed, wrapping myself up in a sheepskin coat. Jumbo had a high temperature and was asleep. Then I, too, dozed off.

It was evening when I woke, and already quite dark. The wind had risen and was howling outside. I felt quite warm, so it must still have been thawing. Eight degrees above freezing in our room, but we considered that warm. I woke up slowly under my sheepskin. I could hear the rattle of knives and forks in the dining-room, where Marictta was laying the table. Enjoying that moment's peace, I thought to myself: Where am I? Why was I there? I could hear Jumbo breathing heavily in his sleep. Was my family alive? What was life? I, for example, was alive. And I repeated over and over I, I, I am, in order to confirm the fact of my existence.

25th
February–
10th March

THE sun was peering out from behind the clouds. Old Isa was warming herself on a heap of leaves and twigs in what had used to be the rock garden, and Alf was stalking about on stiff legs, all because an old peasant woman had brought along Tacitus' wire-haired dachshund which he had left behind in the Manor. The dachs would have liked to say "Hullo" to Isa, but he was afraid of Alf, and ran from one corner of the courtyard to the other, whimpering quietly and waiting for Alf to find a bone to occupy his attention. Meanwhile Isa pretended to be asleep and not to know what was going on, and I chopped my wood.

At about ten o'clock a Russian officer appeared, accompanied by two soldiers and a militia-man from the commune.

"What do you want?" I asked.

"Ah, you can speak Russian, you're a Slav," said the officer. "We've come for dogs, my dear. We want some big dogs."

"What for?" I asked, the blood draining from my face.

"That's none of your business, but you see that little hairy one over there, he's no use; but we'll take the two big ones. They're the sort we want."

There was only one person who appreciated how I suffered during that conversation and that was the Hungarian peasant, the militia-man. It never entered the Russians' heads that they could encounter any difficulties. I am neither quick-witted nor good at lying, because life has seldom forced me to resort to untruths, but at that moment, sensing the mortal danger that threatened our dogs, I felt inspiration enter into me.

"Those dogs are old and weak and of little use," I said to gain time.

"We don't mind. It doesn't matter if they are very old, even sick," said the officer.

"That's fine," I said gaily. "I've got still more dogs," and I whistled for Alf.

"Where are you going?" shouted the officer, reaching for his automatic.

I was already standing by the steps leading from the rock garden, with Alf at my feet and Isa, her gentle, nut-brown eyes bulging out of her head, following behind. "To fetch the other dogs," I said. "Big, hefty ones," I added, and began walking backwards up the steps, keeping my eyes on the officer and feeling for each step with my heel. The militia-man had not understood what we had been saying, but seeing that there was to be no fuss considered me beaten and smiled jeeringly.

I whistled gently and ran across the garden with Alf and Isa bounding along behind me. I reached the field. It was terribly muddy, and my feet were soon so heavy with mud that I could hardly lift them, but in the end I was across. Then I slithered down the bank of the little ravine through which flowed our river, and here we were joined by the dachs, completely out of breath but very proud that he had found us. I walked on, bent double like a child playing at Red Indians, and every now and then whistling quietly to the dogs to keep them from straying. So far I had met no one, but I was now

coming to a break in the ravine where it was cut by the road
to the ford. Should I run across the open bit, or stroll across
as if I were out for an ordinary walk? There were a few cottages beside the road there. The militia-man must have long
ago realized that I had run away and reported it to the officer,
so by now they were probably already searching for me in the
village. It was a dangerous place and I had better take it at a
run. I scraped some of the mud off my shoes and took to my
heels.

What did the Russians need the dogs for? I had no idea;
yet I knew that death awaited them, and I was right. I continued along the ravine which now began to broaden. Both
banks were thickly covered with young acacia trees. I still did
not feel safe. When I reached the point where the river takes
a deep sweep round the village, I crossed the little bridge and
found myself in the long meadow where we always used to
gallop when out riding in the autumn. I waded through the
mud until I reached the row of old poplars, and in the cover
of them I was able to walk on quickly. The dogs were delighted: walks again at last! At last people had remembered
to give poor dogs their due! They were so grateful that,
instead of hunting on their own, they kept running up to me
with their tails wagging furiously, and Alf tried to jump up
and lick my face whenever the ground was dry enough for me
to break into a trot. I was still heading for the farm which lay
a few miles from Mora, as yet undecided where to try and
hide in that confounded plain. Houses were out of the
question, for everybody would give me away. The row of
poplars came to an end and across a large field I could see the
farm buildings. Our neighbours' bailiff lived there, a recent
convert to Communism who already had many deaths on his
conscience, for he was denouncing people right and left. Two
months later we were to discover that he had been sheltering
German officers all through the war, and that he had denounced people not only to divert suspicion from himself but
also to settle accounts with his personal enemies.

I purposely kept to the swampy rough ground, often sinking up to my knees in icy water, and having to fight my way through thick bracken. I won't meet anyone here, I thought to myself, and indeed it was the sort of place to which no one went. I found a relatively dry place in a drainage ditch. The snow had not yet all melted and the ditch was only half-filled, so I lay down on the slope of the bank, where I would be out of sight. The dogs sniffed round for mice among the heaps of sugar beet in the field. There were so many of those heaps that I decided that the dogs would scarcely be visible among them from a distance, and nobody could possibly see me where I was. The only snag was that it was damp. I sat there for hours without moving, feeling temporarily safe. I had no idea what I would do in the evening, but for the time being the dogs had been rescued.

What should I do? Return home, I suppose. Perhaps the officer had forgotten about me and the dogs by now. I reached the house *via* the ravine before it was quite dark, and crept carefully up to the door. There was no sign of Russians. Proudly I walked into the kitchen, followed by three panting, muddy dogs, only to be met by decidedly hostile looks. I went straight to our room. Jumbo, instead of rejoicing and congratulating me on my daring, merely remarked dryly, "A good thing the dogs are back, because they must be handed over to the Russians to-morrow."

I turned to Fifi for an explanation, and gradually it all came out. My disappearance had led to a tremendous row. As soon as the officer had discovered that I had tricked him and that he was wasting his valuable time waiting for me, he had rushed into the house foaming with fury and threatened to arrest Tacitus unless the dogs were handed over within an hour. Nobody had the faintest idea where I was, and anyway there was no one who could go to look for me. Tacitus himself had a high temperature from food-poisoning, like poor little Muki, and so had Rudi. An hour later the officer returned and, seeing the glum look on Fifi's face and no dog in sight, had pulled out his revolver. The whole house was searched for dogs. The officer fumed and ran around flourishing his automatic, while his men looked into the wardrobes, under the beds, and even searched Matilda's room. There was no sign of the dogs.

Hissing, "You just wait," the officer had run out, followed by his two men. They were furious at wasting all that time, and also at having lost face, for to spend an entire morning looking for two dogs was no occupation for members of a victorious army. However, just as they were leaving, the smaller and nicer of the two men turned to Fifi with a conciliatory smile and said, "Our officer is a bad man and a fool."

After all this fuss the Hungarians began to get really worried about me and despatched a punitive expedition, consisting of Elsie and Alec, to look for me. The expedition returned empty-handed. The suspense reached its climax when the officer was again seen coming down the drive, clutching his inseparable automatic, and followed by an angry, pock-marked soldier. They all thought that Tacitus' last hour had arrived. They had come for him. Cursing his thoughtless sister-in-law, Tacitus prepared himself for the journey. While Marietta, her face stony with terror, was stuffing bread into her husband's bag, one of the Crusoes rushed in with the news that he had seen me and the dogs from his window, near the river. He had not thought anything of it until he found out that half the village and the whole of the militia were looking for me. Tacitus then begged the officer to postpone his arrest. He swore that he would hand over the dogs, that if I were hiding in the village they would soon find me. The whole family guaranteed that they would catch me themselves and take me, together with the dogs, to the commune. The officer agreed to give Tacitus half an hour's grace, put his automatic back into its holster and stalked off. In a matter of minutes the pock-marked soldier was back with a sixteen-year-old comrade, demanding dinner. The Hungarians, relieved that that was all they wanted, gave them their soup, but before the soldier had time to lap it up the officer was back again, still in a roaring temper. It appeared that the Commandant of the village was going to arrest Tacitus and now Marietta as well because the officer could not spare the time, and there were technical difficulties in the way of his taking Tacitus to the neighbouring town where he was quartered. He had wasted the whole day over our dogs and could devote no more time to them. With that the Russians left, and the Hungarians heaved a sigh of relief. However, they were still very anxious, this time about me. Then I had returned.

Fifi ran to get Sashka and we held a conference. I told Sashka the whole truth. Everybody was moved by my touching story, but Sashka being a man of action shook his head:

"Why didn't you send for me at once?" he asked.

"Is it true," I said, "that you make soap out of these dogs?" for that was the rumour circulating in the village.

"What?" exclaimed Sashka, astounded. "Soap? What would we need soap for? Who would go to all the bother of boiling dogs up into soap? Who wants soap, anyway?" he added. "Now, if one could make vodka out of them, that would be different."

The rumour about the soap had probably arisen through the peasants hearing that the Germans were supposed to make soap from dead Jews. Why then should not the Russians, as a more humane nation, make soap out of dogs? But Sashka only laughed.

"Soap," he kept on repeating. "Soap! They drive the dogs on to the minefields. If a big, heavy dog steps on a mine, it goes off. You can clear a whole minefield that way."

"Sashka," I asked, "is it true that your Commandant is to arrest the 'Master' and the 'Mistress'?" And that was how it came to light that no one in the Commandant's office had so much as set eyes on the lot which had been collecting dogs, and that the officer had been lying. As we were talking, two militia-men came in with an order from the headman that I was to report with the dogs at the commune the next morn-

ing, and then take Isa and Alf personally to the neighbouring
town and hand them over to the officer.

"I'll go," I shouted angrily, "but alone and straight to
town. And they can arrest me instead of Tacitus and Marietta. I'll gladly do time for this, but I'll not send the dogs to
their death. I'll go to the minefield myself. Cowards, that's
what you are: refusing to spend a few days in prison for the
sake of an old, innocent dog!"

Part of this tirade was in Polish, so that Sashka could not
understand all of it.

"Come on, Lida, calm down and stop shouting. I'll go to
the commune myself right away and settle everything. I'm
your friend," said Sashka, and proudly pushing his cap still
lower over his eyes, he adjusted his belt and walked out, driving the two terrified militia-men ahead of him.

It was only then that we calmed down and stopped beginning every sentence with the word "dog." Tacitus, however,
still refused to speak to me. Elsie's peregrinations in search of
me had proved of some use after all. She had seen the Czech
mechanic, who told her that several sacks full of our silver
were hidden at the mill where he was now working. It had
been stolen by the chief mechanic, a Communist whom the
Russians had brought from a nearby sugar-beet factory to get
Tacitus' mill working again. We all began talking about the
silver, but I got more and more anxious because Sashka had
not come back from the commune, and in the end I decided
to go to the Commandant's office myself.

Vanyusha was hopelessly tight and very effusive, so that,
instead of looking for Sashka, I had to sit down and drink
wine with his chief. He also gave me cigarettes, which I
greedily smoked one after the other in the vain hope that it
would kill my desire for them. Vanyusha was charming. He
kept talking thickly, drinking, and filling up my glass, and in
so doing he spilt half on the table-cloth and then tried to wipe
it off with his hand, but only succeeded in rubbing it in. Then
Sashka came in and gave him his post, a letter from his fi-

ancee. Vanyusha causually remarked that his fiancee was
Polish, which I knew was not true. He was just boasting because, as we discovered, in Russia even the worst Pole was
considered better than a Russian girl, and besides Vanyusha
considered it polite to tell me that he was engaged to a
countrywoman of mine.

While Vanyusha with considerable difficulty and in a loud
voice was spelling out his letter, I held a whispered conversation with Sashka. It was all settled. I would not have to go
to the commune nor hand over the dogs. The officer had lied
when he said that he had been to the Commandant, because
Vanyusha had only just got back to Mora.

It was still dark when I went for the water. I had been
counting on a morning frost, but in places the mud reached to
my calves and I kept getting stuck with my heavy pails. The
dawn came glum and watery, and the sky looked as if it was
painted in water colours. I made three trips for water, then
threw the pails into a corner in the kitchen with a clatter, and
went to bury the silver which we had recovered from the mill
the day before. Fifi announced that she intended to beg for
some bones in exchange for a little salt that we had been
given and make *borsch* with them and the beetroots she had
found beneath the refuse in the cellar. On the whole our
minds were a bit easier. One couldn't keep dying of fright day
in, day out, and the gun-fire now sounded farther away.

When the priest arrived with his news, it was to tell us
that there had been seven German attacks on our sector in
the last few days, and each time the Russians had driven them
off. At one time the Germans had been only seven miles
away, but now, apparently, the Russians had the situation
under control, having at last slept off the results of celebrating
Red Army Day.

It cleared up after lunch, and glorious spring weather en-
veloped the entire world. The whole family went out into the
yard. We had cut down a large, old tree, and we now sawed

and chopped it up. Rudi and Tacitus did the sawing, and Elsie and I the chopping. Marietta and Alec made a pile of the twigs and small branches. The dogs lay on the stones in the rock garden and basked in the sun. How lovely it was to be able to work in the garden! The sky was blue and velvety, like a delphinium. The saw sang softly and the sawdust poured down like a stream of muddy water. Our axes came down with little hollow thuds and the splinters flew up glinting merrily. We laughed at anything. We were happy.

Dawn. A strong gale was threshing among the leafless branches of the trees, crumpling the surface of the puddles and drowning the distant sound of gun-fire. Dolly opened the windows in the dining-room, and went for her mop and duster. Hers was the duty of keeping the dining-room clean. I looked out of the window. Suddenly I heard a blackbird sing: dew translated into sound, the same purity, coolness and freshness. What a wonderful sound!

The Hungarians went again in a body to the school for early Mass. There was less of religion in their attendance at Mass than a demonstration of the dissatisfaction of the gentry with the present state of affairs. I had just been waiting for this moment to make my way to the larder, and despite Matilda's animal roars, steal some "rainy day" lard which Elsie and I smeared on some bread stolen in the village the day before. Why should Tacitus have been the only one to have "rainy days" as he did whenever breakfast appeared? It was my turn now and my "rainy day" started at half-past six on 2nd March.

The door opened and in came the two boys. They were both ill and looked terrible. Franzi had wasted to next to nothing with fever and dysentery, and Jack, who had influenza, looked just as ghostly. They were at once packed off to bed, or to be more precise, Franzi to his mattress and Jack to the sofa. I took off Jack's boots and threw them behind a

heavy corner cupboard as a safeguard. Apparently the Russians were again hunting for men for trench digging, as conditions were so frightful that as many as possible ran away,
but they could not take a person who had no boots. You
could not dig frozen earth with bare feet.

Jack said that they were going to dig anti-tank trenches
in Mora, and the news put us into a panic. There were two
schools of thought, one that we should try to escape to the
capital; the other, headed by Tacitus, that we should get
across the river some thirteen miles to the south of Mora, and
this latter was the one we decided on. But then Franzi in a
faint voice reminded us that the Russians were holding
manoeuvres along that road, and our excitement subsided.
Once again we decided to wait, and at last sat down to lunch.
Lunch was unusually large because Matilda wanted to celebrate the return of the boys, but luckily neither of them was
able to eat, and I could at last see myself being able to eat
my fill for once. However, no sooner had the large plate of
cream cheese appeared on the table than Jumbo called out
from his bed, "Cossacks, Cossacks!" I ran to the kitchen and,
through the window, saw three Cossacks jumping off their
horses and making straight for our door. They had come to
arrest Tacitus, and wanted to take him away at once. We
then embarked on a piece of sly, oriental cunning. Weren't
the Comrades tired? Wouldn't they care for a rest? Please,
wouldn't they come in for a while? The Comrades graciously
consented, and I took them straight to our room. Jack had
to help me talk with them. We had to be very careful what
we said, for at first the officers were off-hand and rude. However, warmed by our synthetic home-atmosphere, which we
developed in such situations to the limits of our capacity, the
officers thawed and became more amenable. They now no
longer wanted to take Tacitus away, so we called him in and
then we all began talking about agricultural machinery. From
what the officers said, it seemed the Red Army was going to
take over all agricultural production on our side of the river.

The front was moving forward so slowly that it had not been possible to set up a local administration and spring was just round the corner. Then the Russians began offering us cigarettes. By now they were quite at their ease and looked about them interestedly. Having come into contact with Europe, the Russians' Communism was beginning to take on local colour, and just like every Hungarian Communist, they now dreamed of becoming bourgeois themselves. They were no longer shocked by "historical injustice," but were rather dreaming of taking the place of those who had dispensed it.

When the Russians left, there was, as I might have expected, little left of that wonderful lunch. As I greedily gobbled up the cold remains, Tacitus came to thank me for preventing his arrest. My mouth was still full when the telephone operators arrived. They were nice, simple lads and lived in the granary. They sat down in the dining-room, filling it at once with the familiar Russian stench. They were beaming all over their unwashed, but dutifully clean-shaven, faces, and said that they had come for billets. We puzzled our brain to think what they were really after. After the inevitable chat, we discovered that this "something" was a remedy for syphilis. The Russians used Ultraseptyl, which was a remedy against influenza, taking it in vodka. It was the telephonists' C.O. who was the sufferer, and they had some Ultraseptyl which, as they explained, was very good, but not the vodka. Where could they get some? Wouldn't one of us go to the capital and exchange some flour for vodka? Otherwise their captain would be eaten away by the disease. Vodka was essential to kill the microbes, and besides, the healthy would be able to have a drink too. We arranged to go with them in a lorry the next day. They chatted a little longer, laughed a great deal, and left.

I was awakened at five the next morning by Sherozka, the telephonists' driver. We were to get ready, for the cart would be coming in a few minutes. Jack and Rudi dressed as quickly as any firemen. In the twilight, on a Russian cart they would avoid the man-hunt. Sherozka sat down beside my bed, poured some black tobacco into the palm of my hand and gave me a piece of newspaper. We smoked in silence. "Well, I'm going for the horses now," said Sherozka, after a few minutes, and walked away. Just before six, when it was still dark, he reappeared, and Rudi, Jack and he, each with a sack of peas for our hungry relatives on their backs, set off looking like smugglers. The cart was hidden behind the mill. Evidently the whole expedition, the object of which was to cure the Captain of his syphilis, was being kept secret from him. How I envied Jack that he would see the great city, still smoking after the siege and its wounds still open!

We were having our morning soup of flour and water and eating yesterday's noodles, and had just remarked that it was already after eight and no one had yet come to collect the boys, when in came the "man-hunters," accompanied by a militia-man from the commune.

"Where's your son?" barked a little soldier, with the impertinent face of a petty criminal.

"What do you mean: son?" I asked innocently and with justification, because I had never had one.

"You know very well," said the soldier, and made straight for our room where Jumbo sat regally in his bed looking like a sick Dalai Lama. However much they tried, no militia-man could pretend that Jumbo was my son. Jumbo, whom I had coached well, gave the Russian a gracious, polite smile and then turned his head towards the militia-man. His eyebrows rose slightly and his enigmatic smile vanished completely. Jumbo was surprised. A Russian was one thing: he could come and disturb Jumbo in the middle of the night, for how could he be expected to know about our famous privacy and what we called normal life? But a Hungarian? And the Hungarian understood what these raised eyebrows meant and withdrew hurriedly from the room.

Then it was Marietta's turn to fight for her son. Driven desperate, she ended by seizing Franzi's chamber-pot, which was full of blood, and ran with it to the commune. When she marched in, the Hungarians nearly fell over with surprise, and the Crusoes must have thought that she had lost her reason along with her fortune. Marietta explained what it was all about, and this was translated for the Russians, who one by one came and peered into the chamber-pot to make sure that she was not lying. Luckily Sashka from the Commandant's office happened to come along, and he spoke to the officers, pointing now at the chamber-pot, now at Marietta, and thus Franzi was rescued from what would undoubtedly have meant his death.

Meanwhile, the little soldier raved and ranted and demanded wine. He delivered a whole speech against his Allies, and from time to time ordered me to get ready, telling me that I would have to take the boys' place. "One is in hospital in the capital, and the other is dying, as you can see for yourself," I said, "so you leave me alone." In the end he left, informing us that we were a lot of rotten bourgeois, and promising to return for me later.

Within less than a quarter of an hour a new tormentor came looking for suitable men. I must admit that the wretched Hungarians were quite right to try and evade this trench digging. The Russians marched them through the snow and mud for more than twenty miles to where they were to work, and all the time one empty lorry after another tore down that very road. Many of the men had no boots or warm clothing, having been robbed of everything, or otherwise having lost them in the war. The Russians did not supply them with food, and quartered them in ruined mud huts. There was not the slightest effort made to help them or to alleviate the atrocious conditions in which they worked. They did not even have clean drinking water. Don't think that there was any malice in this; it was just the result of the ordinary Russian *laissez-faire*. In Russia people do what they are told, whereas in Europe, deprived of the benefits of centuries of Tsarist rule, people still stupidly consider themselves entitled to certain things. Such complete revolutions as have taken place in Russia and in Germany were only made possible by the fact that both those peoples have servility in their blood. It is not an identical servility and it has been reared on different soils, but it could be utilized for the same purpose.

The second "man-hunter" was much tamer. Once he felt convinced that there was nobody in our house suitable for digging trenches, he sat down, lit a cigarette and started to chat with us. The next place the Red Army would conquer, he told us, was Switzerland.

"Go on!" I said, pretending to be surprised. But as a matter of fact, I knew from the Red Press that the Soviet caricaturists had for some time been venting their venom not on the now almost vanquished Hitler but on Switzerland. Ever since we had become friends with Vanyusha, we had borrowed newspapers from him every day. Hitler was now always depicted as lying under a Swiss cow and sucking milk from its udder along with Ribbentrop, Goebbels, and Goering. Sometimes all the four of them would be shown sitting in a pretty chalet captioned "Hotel Switzerland," while the Swiss, represented as very servile waiters, would be offering them tasty foods, chocolate, condensed milk, watches and other objects dear to the Russian heart.

"Oh," said my new friend, "all the Fascists have gone and hidden themselves in Switzerland. They're a sly lot. They will not wait for us in Berlin. We'll have to fight on and on until we catch them all. And I bet we'll find them in Switzerland."

"Very likely," I said.

It was still early when the Commandant's office sent us word that we were to have an officer with a war bride billeted on us for the night, and we began to quarrel about where the Russian captain was to sleep. A little later Vanyusha arrived with a very plain, elderly woman in uniform and her lover,

the self-same officer who had prepared the house for the Staff
when they threw us out and sent us to Julie's. No, the officer
said, he would not be staying with us. He had changed his
mind and had only come to have a look. "Oh dear," we
sighed, "Tolbuchin must be coming back." Elsie cast a
poisonous look at us. We had thrown her out of her room
unnecessarily. The officer told us of the occupation of Kol-
berg and we discussed the Soviet offensive. Then we began
reminiscing about the old days when the Staff had been sta-
tioned in the village. We talked as though that was ancient,
almost legendary, history, although, in point of fact, we were
still living in those great and heroic times, for the front had
hardly moved forward at all. Yet somehow we felt that times
are great only when seen from a certain perspective and we
instinctively relegated them to the past so as not to deprive
them of their glamour. Suddenly there was a commotion at
the door, and Jack and Rudi burst into the room, flushed
with frost and vodka. The Russians took their leave, while
I hurried Jack off to my room, like a dog with a bone. There
was famine in the capital, Jack told me, but all our nearest
relatives were alive. Our enemies, on the other hand, were
receiving rough treatment at the hands of the N.K.W.D.,
which fact, as we were only human, pleased us mightly. But
anyway, what was a punch or two in the jaw in comparison
with the kind of treatment one got in the German concentration camps?

There were all kinds of Russians and all kinds of things
you can say about them, but I never saw a single sadist among
them. Russian history is full of cruelty, but Russia has so far
been ruled by its upper classes whose bad example the lower
perhaps merely copied. I never noticed any tendency towards
sadism among the ordinary Russians. I think that the difference between the cruelty of primitive peoples and sadism is
that the sadist gloats over the reactions of the victim, while for
the former the victim's reaction is of no interest. When once
I asked some Cossacks to shoot a sick horse, they refused

because they did not feel like leaving a warm room. They were thoughtless and accustomed to worse sights than that of a dying horse. On another occasion, a little girl had been raped: but they had to, they were compelled to do it, they explained. They, too, would have preferred an adult, but all the grown-up women had run away and the few that had remained had syphilis, so what else could they do? God willing, nothing would happen to the little girl, but they had had no choice. They had been all these months fighting and fighting, and never able to get a woman.

A peasant we knew was once arrested and got punched in the face several times during his interrogation. But that was not systematic torture, but merely the result of hurry and impatience. This much must be understood: Russian manners are harsh, just as harsh as Russian life. They are the manners of barbarians, of Vikings, or of the very early Middle Ages. Slyness and subterfuge have the same value as courage and physical strength. To steal something cleverly is just as much a feat as to throw a grenade under a tank. These Russians had left home to get booty and for that they had to kill a lot of people. That they used an ideal as a pretext for this is nothing new, for was it not in the name of an even higher ideal that the Crusaders set out to loot the Middle East?

Having found out more or less what was happening in the capital, we inquired whether the expedition had been a success, and whether they had got enough vodka to save the nose of the captain of the telephone operators. "Eh," said Jack, and went on undressing, for he again had a high temperature and was going back to bed. "What do you mean by 'Eh'?" "Well, what we managed to get we drank on the way because it was so darned cold in the cart. Twenty-seven miles in such a wind is no joke, I can assure you."

"Well, what about the Captain and his syphilis?"

"Perhaps it will help him to get over it," Jack suggested, and went into a dead sleep.

All was quiet so I fetched a lot of water and had a good wash. For half an hour I was stark naked. What a wonderful feeling!

The next day the Russians started a three-day feast to celebrate we don't know what. The offensive evidently wasn't to begin until the celebration was over, or so we were told at the Commandant's office. It was quiet all day because the Red Army was busy preparing food and decorations.

All of us, except me, were ill and in bed. Jack had the highest temperature. We prayed that it was merely due to drinking dirty water because otherwise it might be typhoid. I started writing this book today, and wrote all day instead of working. Why write, they all said, the sooner we forget this nightmare the better.

All night long we could hear gun-fire, and towards morning it was coming from three sides. The Germans probably knew the Soviet calendar and had started a counter-attack because of the festival. I went to the Commandant's office in the hope of finding some newspapers.

"But everybody has gone to the feast," said the driver, who had been left on his own. "That is also why the front is not moving forward," he added in all seriousness.

"Will there be papers?" I asked naively.

"But how?" said the driver, astonished at my imbecility. "It's the eighth, don't you understand? They're human, too, the ones who take the papers around. They want to amuse themselves as well. What else did you think? There are no papers, and there won't be. And that's that!"

11th-17th
March

A MIGHTY north wind was almost blowing the roofs off. We were practically all ill, and we had no medicines. I came off best because I was able to eat five lunches. And I needed them, for I am over five feet eight and weighed only ninety-two pounds. After lunch I went to the Commandant's office to ask whether we would have to give Russians billets in the house, for the village was again full of troops. "You may take whomever you like," said Vanyusha, yawning.

"Have the Germans started another offensive?" I asked.

"I won't say as they haven't," replied Vanyusha, turning his back on me, "and you can take in anyone you want, Lida. It's no more any business of mine. Take thirty, if you like."

When I got back, I found in the kitchen the inevitable soldier who came every day to borrow our mincing machine. Minced meat seems very popular in modern Russia and I never ate any other kind of meat with the Russians.

"Yes, yes," said the soldier, "more fighting. Ugh, we're all sick of it! The plague take them. They've lost anyway, so what do they want to go on for?"

I did not want to hear any more, but flew to Jumbo.

"Let's try and get away across the river to the capital. It's all going to start all over again here." And I told what I had heard. The house became a hive of activity: let's get away,

away! Jumbo sent one of the gypsy children to fetch his former manservant, and we told ourselves that we would leave in two days' time, for it was too late to start packing that day.

We sat on in the dusk, waiting for the Major who was supposed to be coming to us for the night. Fifi made up the bed and covered it with the regulation lace curtain, but there was still no sign of him. Lorries were thundering along the road: a dark, endless snake of lorries, roaring and rattling, with gears grinding as they changed down on the hill by the church. Supper was a gloomy, silent meal. The rumble of lorries went on. Then the others went to bed, and our room waited for the Major.

There was a sudden noise, the stamp of feet, then someone opened the door and the beam of an electric torch began jerking across the walls. I ran to the door. The Major had arrived with his officers. "I'll come later," he said, "I only wanted to know where the billet was. When I come in the night, you will recognize me."

"But I shan't be able to keep it for you if anyone else should come."

"Oh, that's all right! I'll leave a boy with you to look after it." But he did not leave anyone, and consequently lost the billet for that night, because at half-past one there was another knock at the door that jerked me to my feet. This, however, was a strange Lieutenant.

"Come on, open up," he commanded, with a smile. "A good thing you're dressed. I know you speak Russian. Listen, you're to make supper for fifteen. And quickly, get another woman, and both of you come to the kitchen."

I woke up Fifi, and we made our way to the kitchen which was infernally cold, and dragged a terrified Matilda out of her lair. The Lieutenant went off to get the food, for he knew he would not find any in our house, and I went out to chop some wood.

The Lieutenant came back with some meat and the fore- and hind-leg of a pig. As he handed over this treasure, he told me to cut off two helpings of meat and to fry them separately so that they should be fit for a Marshal to eat. He also told us to make noodles for fifteen and promised to replace the flour and fat before dawn. Then he went away and the bored soldier, who was supposed to be on guard-duty, followed him. He knew that no one would come to see if he were looking after the place, so thought he might as well get some sleep before his relief came. Fifi and I looked at each other and, without saying a word, I ran for the chopper. "Wait, I'll get some paper. The floor's dirty," Fifi whispered. She gave me the ham wrapped in a newspaper, I laid it on the muddy floor: crash! went the chopper once, and then a second time. The whole end came off and the frozen meat rolled noisily across the muddy flags. I seized the smaller piece and gave it to Matilda with a whispered, "Please hide it safely, this will be for us." Then I set about lighting the fire. Fifi put on the water, while Matilda, cursing and grunting, got the flour for the noodles out of its hiding-place. A little later the new guard arrived, yawning. He was about sixteen. He was chewing sunflower seeds and politely asked where to throw the husks. That was the first and last Russian we met who was at all interested in that problem. He was pleasant to talk to, for he was nice, childish and talkative. It was gradually getting lighter. The meat leaped merrily in the pot. We were very tired. Another day had begun.

Soldiers and officers were now swarming all over the house. The narrow beams of their electric torches intersected in the darkness of the kitchen. They were all thirsty and one and all demanded water. I went with some of them to the well, to show them the way. Down there by the river it was still quite dark. We kept stumbling, and one of the soldiers took a toss with an awful clatter of empty pails. The others laughed. I left them by the river and went back. "The stables! Where are the stables?" someone was calling. "Take them to the stables," Fifi said, "I've got my hands full here."

So once again I stalked out into the darkness beside a small officer.

Clouds had massed in the east and the devil run off with the dawn. We made our way along the ditch, for the road was blocked solidly with silent lorries. Everywhere soldiers were clambering out and bedding themselves down in the frozen ruts. The whole place reeked of petrol and dirty bodies. The officer began to suspect that I was not taking him to the stables at all but leading him into some sort of trap. "It's quite a way," I had to explain. "I'm not lying, I'm a Slav. You'll see that I am speaking the truth."

The sky was pale by the time I got back to the kitchen and learned that terrible things had been happening while I was away. First, some Colonel or other had walked into the hall, sat down on a stool among the horrified Hungarians and gone fast asleep. Then the Lieutenant, who had meanwhile been inspecting the whole house, decided that Tacitus' room was the one he would take for the Colonel's quarters. Tacitus had said that he had no intention of moving out of his room and that the Lieutenant must wait till I came back, when I would explain to them that they must choose another room. At this the Lieutenant had flown into a rage and ejected the Hungarians from their rooms in no time. Fifi had brought the bedclothes which had been waiting for the unfortunate Major since the day before, but these it appeared were not elegant enough. What was good enough for a Major was not good enough for a Colonel, said the Lieutenant, and began searching for something more suitable for the higher ranks. He had gone into Rudi's room and pulled the pillow from under Dolly's head (it was the only one in the whole house that was in a pillow-case), then he had torn the quilt off Elsie, who was sleeping on the floor, and taken from the other rooms anything else he considered suitable for a Colonel's bed and carried them all to Tacitus' room. When I arrived on the scene, Tacitus was helping Marietta to take her pathetic little bundles to their new quarters.

"Don't touch anything," yelled the Lieutenant, "leave everything as it is. A Hero of the Soviet Union will be staying here! Nothing will be taken. Do you think a Hero would steal your miserable rags?"

"Let them take their things," I said from the door, "they need them all."

"And you, you daughter of a bitch, what the hell are you yapping about?" roared the Lieutenant. "I'll teach you people to respect our army! Look at this; trying to give a Colonel a pillow without a pillow-case! You just wait, I'll have the house blown up, if you're not careful; who do you think you are? Do you want to go to Siberia? There's plenty of room there. Enough for plenty of the likes of you . . ."

At that moment a Russian voice behind me said, "She's all right, she's a good girl. She showed us the way to the stables and before that to the well." Attracted by the shouting, several Russians had congregated behind me in the doorway. It was almost incredible how quickly the expression on the Lieutenant's face changed. The Russians' anger seems almost artificial so rapidly does it pass, leaving not the slightest trace. The Lieutenant came across to me, his face beaming, and patted me on the shoulder. "Now, now," he said, "it's all right, all right."

Meanwhile Tacitus and Marietta, eternal civilians, had taken advantage of the commotion to carry out the last of their suitcases. "I've rescued everything," whispered Marietta, breathing heavily under the weight of the suitcase she was carrying, "there's only my evening dress left in the wardrobe," and she smiled a happy, if tired, smile. There was only the Lieutenant, Fifi and I left in the room, and we had a final look round: what else might a Hero need? "I know," exclaimed the quartermaster, striking his forehead, "a cloth for the table!"

I told him that we had no such luxury in the house, but that as the table had a marble top (Louis XVI, the property of my late mother-in-law) that did not matter.

"But it's horrible. Just look, horrible!" The Lieutenant insisted. "It must be covered with something. You can't expect a Colonel to eat off a bare table!" Suddenly his eye lit on the ancient grimy lace curtain which used to hang in a servant's room, and which we now used as a bed-spread for the more important Russians. "There we are!" he cried triumphantly, and the dirty bed-spread went on to the freshly washed table, covering it completely with festoons of holes, torn fringes and filthy stains. "Now it looks nice," said the Lieutenant, and, stepping back, he surveyed his work with a smile on his face.

We then went to waken the Colonel. The hall was the scene of indescribable confusion. The Russians had already penetrated into every room, and were poking into every corner and, like mischievous monkeys, fingering everything in their dirty, horny paws. The Hungarians were like ants whose hill has been stirred up with a stick, running backwards and forwards with bundles, calling to each other, emptying all the drawers and cupboards, and removing every object weighing less than fifty pounds on the assumption that Russian laziness was greater than the Russian urge to steal. Amid this infernal bedlam, the Comrade Colonel, the Hero, slept on a tiny stool, doubled up like a penknife. The Lieutenant shook him like a pear tree, but the Hero slept on. "I've already made the bed," yelled the Lieutenant, "all high-class linen," he added, thinking that perhaps that would penetrate the Hero's sleep. At last the Colonel woke up sufficiently to let himself be conducted, staggering, to the bed.

Meanwhile, more and more soldiers and officers were crowding into the house. It had grown quite light. From the kitchen door I could see in the morning mist that the slope that my late mother-in-law had made into a rock garden was littered with bodies, like a battlefield or a fashionable beach. It was freezing hard and a little cloud of steam was rising from each body. The men must have been absolutely exhausted and just gone to sleep where they were.

A cook came and installed himself in the kitchen, a shameless blackguard called Victor. He ordered us to peel potatoes, and Fifi once again dragged Marietta and Elsie out of their beds and made them help. It was about six o'clock. The Russians had installed telephones in the dining-room, brought in a typewriter and counting-machines (they never attempt a sum unless they have an adding-machine), and in the midst of all that crowd, two telephone operators sat taking down cypher messages from the front with the most infernal din going on around them. The floor of the hall was covered with wooden crates filled with papers. A glance showed us that they were papers from some local government office, probably from the prefecture. Two soldiers, who by some miracle knew the Latin alphabet, had been detailed to look through them, but as they did not know Hungarian they were no nearer finding out whether they had got hold of important secret documents, or worthless bits of paper. There was another crate filled with Russian documents, on the top of which lay a huge picture of Lenin framed in red tissue paper. More and more soldiers kept swarming in, peering into the crates, coming in and walking out again.

The meat earmarked for the Hero had meanwhile cooked itself dry, and when I heard a thunderous shout of "Breakfast for the Colonel!" from the Lieutenant, I took it and some of the noodles into Tacitus' room. The Hero had already got out of bed and was sitting at the table, his dirty shirt unbuttoned and his elbows propped on the filthy curtain. His breeches were unbuttoned, the ends of the legs thrust into black socks. Beside him sat a young, thin, fair-haired little officer. The Colonel himself was short, dark and stocky, and looked somewhere between thirty-two and thirty-five. I was invited to join them for breakfast, but that did not prevent me from having to help the Lieutenant serve at table with all the humility due to a padishah. The Colonel, being a Hero, belonged to the new war aristocracy. He had invited me to breakfast because he thought I was the mistress of the house.

The Russians invariably took any woman who served them at table to be the mistress of the house. Wine was brought in the bathroom jug (embellished with the dried suds of somebody's shaving soap). I sat down on the chair offered me by the Lieutenant. First the Colonel helped himself, then his guest, and finally me. The Lieutenant got nothing at all, and after a while was even turned out of the room. I began to feel uncomfortable. Why had they turned him out? Perhaps they wanted to rape me? But then I remembered that no Russian soldier ever minds how many people witness his sexual acts. In that respect they are like dogs. The two officers were so taken up with their own conversation that they paid not the slightest attention to me. They did not even know that I spoke Russian, and informed me by signs when they wanted me to pour them out wine, or to take a glass myself.

"You should have seen it," said the Colonel, slapping the thin little officer's knee. "Nothing but corpses. And every door I opened, every cottage I went into, more corpses, children, women, men, one or two in every house, even three and four. The whole village in ruins. It must have been some battle! In one cottage there was a woman. You understand, in the whole village only one living thing, and that was a woman. Wasn't I lucky?"

The Colonel then went into details, while I sat saying nothing, staring out of the window, and sipping the soapy wine. The two officers finished their meal and signed to me to clear away, at the same time summoning the Lieutenant who was waiting outside the door for further orders. We cleared up in no time, like a pair of expert waiters. Back I went to the kitchen to help. The kitchen was an inferno even more crowded than the rooms, and the smell of frying competed with that specific stench of the Russians that we knew so well. The cook was opening tins of American canned meat, one after another, and emptying them into the sizzling fat. Dolly, wearing a sepulchral expression, was already on her second pail of potatoes. Her grey flannel suit was splashed with water, and she asserted that Fifi was purposely throwing the potatoes she peeled into the water so hard as to splash her as much as possible. Next to her, her coat and skirt equally bespattered, sat Marietta peeling another pile of potatoes with all the joyful ardour of the born martyr. Every now and then one or other of them would shove their unruly pearls back under their pullovers with a nervous push, looking carefully round to see whether anyone had noticed. Matilda had not come to help. She was lying, teeth clenched, lips tightly pressed together, on her virgin bed. An hour before, some exhausted Russian had suggested that she might let him have a sleep on that sacred bed. Nothing else, he swore that was all, but it had scandalized Matilda, who with peacock shrieks and frantic gestures had refused even to entertain it. Now, seeing that her bed was in danger, she refused to get out of it, although she was consumed by the most horrible anxiety about her kitchen which was just as sacred to her as her bed. In the end her nerves could stand it no longer and she summoned Lina to relieve her. Within a few moments of the exchange, the exhausted Russian reappeared and, as the bed was now less stoutly defended, calmly stretched out on it alongside poor Lina. And Lina lay there, pressed against the wall, terrified of what Matilda would say and not daring to move.

Meanwhile in the kitchen the meat was being minced for the eternal Russian rissoles. It was so crowded that one could not move; in fact you could have lifted both feet off the ground without falling. The stench was indescribable and the noise such that you could not hear yourself speak. Nevertheless, fresh waves of soldiers kept pouring in and out, and, since the door was never closed, an icy wind raged above our heads.

"Fifi and I must get some sleep," I said to Marietta. "It's your turn to look after things. Steal everything you possibly can, and tell Matilda and Lina to pinch whatever comes their way."

It was all Fifi and I could do to push our way through the

hall and the dining-room. In the dining-room the telephone
operators were still roaring at the tops of their voices.
"Danube, Danube," I heard them shouting, as they tried to
get some field exchange to answer. The adding-machines and
the typewriter rattled on without a pause, and soldiers pushed
their way laboriously through the crowd. In the end we
reached our room and immediately flung ourselves on our
beds, without waiting to explain things to Jumbo.

When we awoke they were already carrying in pails of
boiling water for the Hero's bath. His adjutant, the Lieutenant, stood beside the bathroom door at attention, and remained like that all the time the Hero was having his bath.

At about five o'clock they began serving supper. We
noticed that the telephonists had stopped shouting and that
they were now dismantling their apparatus. The typewriter
and counting-machines had disappeared. Perhaps they were
going?

"This," said Fifi, "is the time to try for loot, if we're to
get any." And she was right. I went to the kitchen and
sauntered about wearing my most innocent expression, in the
hope that that would make it easier to steal from the sly
Victor. Then it occurred to me that it might be easiest just to
beg. "Give me a piece of meat," I asked, "you might let me
have a tiny bit." I got my punishment. Victor gave me the
knife, with which he had been cutting up tinned meat, to
lick. There was not very much on it. But what could he do?
He was only the cook. Meanwhile Marietta, Dolly and Elsie
had taken refuge in their rooms, both because they were dead
tired and because there were now quite a lot of drunken
soldiers about the place, and Fifi, who had been doing a
round of the rooms in the hope of being able to steal some
cigarettes, had got embroiled in conversation with a drunken
little officer from Kamieniec Podolski.

"You a Pole?" asked the drunken officer. "I've been in
Poland, and there's one town there I love, but I shan't tell
you which."

"But why not, is it a secret?" Fifi asked.

"Well, no," he finally admitted, with a coy smile, "but it's no longer yours: it is ours now." And then he added: "It's Lwow," and looked slightly ashamed. He blushed and walked quickly away.

Not having got anything out of Victor, I went to see how Jumbo was getting on. I was no sooner there than Alec came storming in, shouting breathlessly, "Mummy's sofa! They've taken Mummy's sofa outside. It's already on a cart. I saw it myself!"

Tacitus said that he had no intention of risking his life for a sofa, and that Elsie could sleep either on Tolbuchin's table or on the floor. Elsie said that, in view of the vermin, she preferred the table. This was an enormous thing that Tolbuchin's staff had fetched from the Manor and which they had used for conferences and for pinning out maps. At that moment the Hero's impresario, the Lieutenant, came into the room and asked whether he might speak to the Master of the house for a moment alone. And would I come and interpret? He conducted us outside. Since he was polite, I suspected no harm. Tacitus walked along resigned to anything. He was sick of everything after that terrible day, to which it would be no more than a fitting end were he now to be shot for sabotage because the bath had leaked. Tacitus, you see, had not yet recovered from the terrible blow of the Russians having taken nearly all his flour and fat and, of course, not returned any of it. The three of us stopped in the yard, which was full of soldiers preparing to move. There, in front of us, was a cart to which were harnessed two young, impatient horses. A wooden platform had been improvised on the cart, and on this we could make out the shape of Elsie's sofa, which was a sort of Madame Recamier *chaise longue* with strong Biedermayer influence.

The question was this, the Lieutenant explained, would the Master consent to the sofa going westward, into victory? The Russians did not steal and so he, the Lieutenant, was

asking as one man of culture to another, whether they were at
liberty to take the sofa. The Colonel's carriage had broken
down: frozen ruts, constant gun-fire, young horses: so they
bolted. Being a Hero, the Colonel could not travel in an
ordinary cart. That was why they needed the sofa.

Tacitus, of course, agreed (how could he have done otherwise?), and the Lieutenant, beaming, held out his hand: "I
knew he would agree. Please tell him that, too," said the
Lieutenant.

"I also knew it," I replied, and there was no hint of irony
in my voice. Then, taking Tacitus by the arm I led him back
to the cold, stinking, filthy house.

Now that it was almost empty, one could see that it would
take at least a week to clean and tidy the house properly.
Tacitus had just started telling the others about the sofa, and
we were all wondering how on earth the Hero would use it:
would he sit on it or lie on it? when the Lieutenant rushed in
again with a carafe of wine and a dish full of pieces of meat
swimming in fat.

"I have come to say good-bye," shouted the Lieutenant,
flourishing the carafe and the plate. Then, having requested
silence, he made a speech. War was war, he said, and he, the
Lieutenant, begged our pardon for the invasion and for making such a mess of our house; but he could assure us that
nothing had been taken, because his men were an honest lot.
He knew them. Now he would like us to eat and drink with
him. We took it in turn to dip our fingers into the fat, each
trying to get the largest piece, but unfortunately for us the
Lieutenant was far the most expert at this way of eating. We
drank the wine out of Rudi's tooth-glass, emptying it at a
gulp before passing it on to the next. The Lieutenant, however, as he said, preferred drinking from the carafe, so again
he got more than anyone else. For all his faults, the Lieutenant was a nice man, and I grew quite fond of him during the
short time we worked together. His love for the Colonel-Hero
was really touching.

After this ceremony I ran to the kitchen, because I was afraid that all the officers would slip away quietly, and we should never get our flour and fat back. Another thing I wanted to try for was some paraffin, so I went out to beg some from the drivers. Returning in triumph to the kitchen, Fifi told me that they had returned the flour but not the fat. Victor had walked off promising to bring it, and had already driven away.

I ran to the Hero's room where he was just getting ready to go, surrounded by the Lieutenant and several officers. "Lieutenant," I said, pulling at his sleeve, "what about my fat?"

"Too late," said the Lieutenant, "the lorries with the food have already left." Then he began to feel sorry, thought for a moment, and produced a small parcel wrapped in greasy paper, "That's my ration of melted butter. My own. Take it!"

Then they all marched out, their footsteps echoing as they strode across the muddy floors of the empty rooms. The last to go was a tall, fat officer. He was slightly drunk. Stopping in the doorway he turned round and said, "You must be thoroughly sick of us, eh? All this mud the boys have brought in, but it can't be helped. There always has to be mud. It can't be helped." Then he held out his hand and shook ours most cordially.

I felt suddenly sorry that in the commotion I had forgotten to say good-bye to the Lieutenant. I ran outside, but he had already disappeared. There in the twilight, outlined against the western sky, was the Colonel-Hero reclining on the sofa, alone but for the driver. The cart looked like one of those allegorical chariots, which were so fashionable in the days of the Renaissance. The driver sat on the box which was covered with a carpet stolen from the little drawing-room. He whipped up the horses, the sofa gave a wobble, recovered its balance, and, looking rather like Pauline Borghese-Bonaparte by Canova, the recumbent Hero disappeared from our sight for ever.

Fifi and I sat down to draw up a balance of the day's thefts. We could list the things we had managed to steal for ourselves, but we had to wait till daylight to discover what the Russians had taken. We counted our booty: a bone with some meat, some potatoes (when peeling them, Dolly had thrown some behind the table instead of into the pail), a few pickled cucumbers (a present), some sugar (stolen with great difficulty by Fifi), a handful of salt, a small piece of pork (what I chopped off during the night), some melted American butter (the Lieutenant's present), some goose fat, and a packet of tea on which Fifi had had her eye all day but was not able to steal till it began to grow dark. Unfortunately Lina and Matilda had stolen nothing at all. They had had every opportunity, but had been far too busy guarding Matilda's bed, and then towards evening when many of the Russians were already drunk, their only concern had been to avoid being raped. However, as it turned out, we were able to add to our list one pot, one lid (unfortunately belonging to a different pot), one spoon, a metal ash-tray and two volumes of Shakespeare plays in Russian.

We went to bed early praying for a quiet night. From the road came a constant rumble of lorries and a grinding of gears, but silence reigned throughout the house. Suddenly we heard Marietta's voice shouting, "My evening dress! My last and only decent dress! Great Heavens, the Hero's taken it. He's stolen it, the mean brute!"

So the Hero had gone and taken with him our sofa, carpet and Marietta's evening dress. What could he want with an evening dress? "He'll probably sleep in it," said Tacitus, in a bored, sleepy voice, "if he can drive up to the front reclining on a sofa, why shouldn't he sleep in an evening gown?"

The day dawned foggy. After yesterday's invasion the garden looked like a battlefield. The lawns were trampled hard, and from them we collected what maize and peas the horses had not eaten. For lunch our invalids had a chicken which we had bought from the peasants, and the rest of us the peas from the horses' table. Then a big, lumbering Russian Corporal, a sailor and two privates, came in asking for billets. We gave them the Hero's room. The Corporal began telling us about his travels. The sailor, who before had never been farther than Odessa, listened attentively and admiringly, though he knew there wasn't a word of truth in what he was hearing.

"When I was in San Francisco," said the Corporal, his expression that of an Eastern story-teller, "in San Francisco," he repeated, because the name embodied all his vague longings and all the poetry in his soul, "in San Francisco I saw a lot of extraordinary things. The houses there are so tall, as tall as the tallest trees, no, even taller! And you see nothing but Americans walking in the streets. Palms grow there and life is easy. You can buy everything, the shops are beautiful and whatever the heart desires you can find it in them. Absolutely anything," the Corporal earnestly assured us.

"How did you get to San Francisco?" I asked.

"Through California," he replied dreamily, and repeated "California," as though the word gave him added importance.

"But how? Why did you go there?" I asked.

"There was a war," he lied unflinchingly, "with the Japanese. We had encircled them, and I was at the far end of the circle."

"When was this war?" I asked.

"It wasn't in the papers," the Corporal admitted, and went on telling us about San Francisco, wallowing in his own imagination as in a wonderful refreshing bath.

So many of the men seemed to yearn for something wonderful, for some promised land, some San Francisco. At one time there used to be a large sect whose only aim was to discover the blessed land of the Rachmanians, a good and just people who inhabited a mythical, beautiful country. The

Corporal talked on and on about San Francisco, and the sailor listened avidly, although he knew that it was all lies.

I had noticed that many of the Russians were hurt and bewildered by the contempt in which the local population so often held them. They could not understand the reason for it. Had not they, citizens of a great power, representatives of the only free nation in the world, educated people, saturated with culture, the flower of mankind from every point of view, come to liberate them? Was there not in Moscow an underground railway, and in the Odessa Opera House mirrors that were ten feet long? And yet it made no impression! Even the most ignorant peasants in oppressed Europe despised them. That hurt. What if some of them did get drunk, shoot people, loot and rape, was that so surprising? Think how much blood they were shedding for the good of the world! And where was that world's gratitude? You could read in every paper how Stalin wanted nothing but justice and intended only what was best. But he would not let anyone cheat him. Stalin was wise. He was not a Tsar from whom one could buy an Alaska. The British thought they were clever, but they were only sly. Stalin had extended the open hand of Soviet friendship to the whole world. Victory had been bought at the price of Russian blood. Russian lands had withstood the terrible onslaught of the enemy. Russian engineering had conquered the most civilized and best organized nation in Europe. And here was a miserable, ignorant peasant, his daughter and his son, laughing at the Russians and despising them.

I often discussed this with the Russians and could see how very bitter they were. There were some in whose minds the light was beginning to dawn, and in a corner of whose brains was a nascent realization of things of which hitherto they had been unaware. They were beginning in a muddled sort of way to realize that the education they received would never make cultured people of them. What if a young soldier-student had been able proudly to tell me who were the world's greatest composers, naming in one one breath "Beethoven, Bach and Molière"? The European peasant and labourer does not go to concerts, and yet there is something about him which makes him the superior of the Russian. Some of the Red Army men were trying to discover what this was.

What in Europe has become a point of honour, with the Russians is ordinary Oriental face-saving. No Russian can stand being laughed at or having his leg pulled. Sometimes when I thought how these Russians were unhappy, bitter and angry at having failed to make any impression, at being despised and laughed at, it made me also wonder what culture really was, and what would be its most concise definition. A capacity for independent thought? That, I think, would describe it: free, independent thought. To develop such a capacity in people takes centuries of struggling for the conditions which make independent thought possible.

Child-soldier and his Chance Protector

18th-19th March

SUNDAY. The sky was almost sparkling, so coldly blue was it. An icy wind blew across the potato fields. At last I was able to go out. There were hardly any Russians left in the village. Was the Commandant's office still in existence, I wondered, and what was Vanyusha doing? How clear the sky was! Fifi and I went to visit the Lieutenant, but he was still asleep. Perhaps he had got drunk the night before? To drink oneself unconscious is not a thing a Russian is ever ashamed of. They accept it as necessary. An epileptic suffers from fits; it cannot be helped. When a man drinks he falls under the table; that, also, cannot be helped; it is the vodka that does it. The present-day European on the whole is just not able to get quite as drunk as the Russian, for if he drinks until all his senses are affected he falls asleep, because his body ceases to function more or less simultaneously with his brain. Not so the Russians. Their minds and cerebral systems cease working long before their fiendish bodies stop moving about. A drunken Russian, whose brain is so fuddled as to be out of action, non-existent, will still have sufficient motive power in his body to be able to shoot his comrade, rape a woman, break the furniture and the window-panes, and shoot a few salvoes into the air, probably hitting his neighbours, before he collapses under the table. He is like a cock that is able to run a few yards after its

324

head has been cut off, and on the following day he will not be able to remember a thing that he did when drunk. They are as innocent as children, and their fellow-countrymen will never hold anything they do against them, in the same way as you cannot blame an epileptic for having fits. Whenever a Russian does something he should not have done, his chief's first question is: was he drunk? If he was, that is a circumstance so extenuating that he may well get off scot free. French legislation invented the *crime de passion*. Jealousy presumably is so comprehensible to the French that it justifies even murder. With the Russians the same applies to drunkenness. A drunken Russian can be very terrible, and I do not advise you to trust even the most angelic of them when he gets tight and starts running around like a beheaded cock. What is running about is not your angelic friend Alexy, but a strong, savage, masterless body.

For want of any other entertainment we went to the school to Mass. Being late, we stood at the back near an elderly Russian Warrant Officer. Individual Russians occasionally went to Mass but not often. I looked at the vacant faces of the peasants, set in the obligatory solemn expression of Sunday boredom, and then I looked at the face of the Russian: rapt and full of faith in miracles. What boundless reserves of faith that nation has, I thought, as I watched the warrant officer. His was the inspired, absorbed expression of the Middle Ages. He did not believe in God out of habit, as did the Hungarian peasants whose faith was age-old and had come to them gently, like a lingering disease. With him it was a sudden outburst, a new experience, miraculous and refreshing. He fell on his knees, pressed his forehead against the dirty floor and remained like that, his brow in the dirt and dust with a kind of life-giving humility. Then he raised his grave face with an imploring look, full of faith that he would be heard. It was obvious that he was praying for something special. What words did he use in his entreaty to God? What did he say to Him, what was he promising? When he

stood up, disentangling himself with difficulty from the mesh
of peasant boots and skirts, he gazed straight at the altar,
crossed himself three times respectfully and intently, his head
bowed. Once more he raised his eyes to the little altar, and
his lips whispered something. What do you want of God, I
kept wondering. I could not take my eyes off him; he radiated
something, and something kept my eyes glued to him. Are
you a good man or bad, I wondered. What are you praying
for, my eyes asked of him. Look at me, just once. I want to
tell you, but only with my eyes, how much I love you. We
are brethren. Do you know what brethren are? It's very
seldom that people understand that word. Blessed are those
who always understand it and feel it. Come on, look at me.
Have I, a disbeliever, to pray to God for that one small thing,
that you should look at me now, for us to be linked by a look
for just the fraction of a second? I need that to complete the
experience which the sight of you began. A sort of com-
pletion, like the word "amen." Do you understand? But he
never looked at me. He could only see inside himself, and his
unseeing eyes were fixed on the altar, like a magician at his
crystal ball.

After Mass we found a number of visitors at home: some
peasants, few former servants, the priest, and an officer, Constantin Piotrovitch, come to read us the latest communique
from the front. March 18th was a turning-point for us. The
nightmare of the front, the nightmare of the Germans coming
back, was dispelled. On that day the war ended as far as we
were concerned. We all spoke in loud voices, laughed and
interrupted each other. Constantin read us the Russian wireless communique: the Russians had pushed ahead all along
the line. For Mora the war was over. The priest smiled
kindly at Constantin, and Constantin smiled respectfully at
the old priest. Everything was turning out for the best, like
the happy ending of a book. However, Fifi croaked dismally,
"Don't let's rejoice too soon, something terrible may still
happen." Dinner was sumptuous because the peasants had

brought us a chicken, some potatoes, and a few carrots. It was Alec's birthday, and I had absolutely nothing I could give him, so instead I promised to romp and play with him after supper. Alec was very pleased with his present.

Oh, what a morning that was! Idyllic. And to crown it, the chicken, the carrots, and the potatoes! We almost sang and danced, so great was the weight that had been taken off our minds. Immediately after lunch a militia-man came for Tacitus, but Tactius had a stye on his eye and was feeling very ill. He was lying on the floor covered with a rug, and announced that he would go nowhere. He asked the militia-man what it was all about, and the militia-man proudly replied that he could not reveal the secrets of the commune. Tacitus would find out on the spot what was wanted from him. Tacitus just turned over on the other side and said that he could not care less. As the commune wanted something from him and not he from the commune, let the commune come to him. The militia-man departed angrily, having lost face.

Fifi and I wondered what pleasant occupation we could find for ourselves, and decided to visit Constantin Piotrovitch. We had been invited. In the doorway we collided with the commune, complete to a man. The Crusoes had come to Tacitus to inform him that they had taken over his land and to discuss the spring sowing with him. Though the land was no longer his, Tacitus knew more about sowing it than the peasants, as they were well aware.

We found Constantin with his Captain, an elderly man for a Russian, for he must have been forty-five. The Captain was very glad to meet us because his wife was Polish. (He had taken her back to Russia with him after the 1920 campaign.) They had a small room in a peasant cottage. A baby was crying in a basket, and a young housewife lay on the bed moaning because she had bad toothache. It was a thoroughly homely atmosphere, enhanced by two hens wandering clucking about the floor. Ever since the Russians had come, the

peasants had preferred to keep their poultry indoors. No officer of any other army would have taken such a billet except as
a last resource, but it was just what the Russians liked best.
Plenty of noise, children running in and out (you could play
with them), a low ceiling, a fire in the stove, everything all
mixed up: it was just like home and that was how they liked
it. The war had been going on so long, and it was dull for
men alone. The Russians' Ukrainian cook, lying stretched out
on the bed, gave us a friendly wave as we came in. The two
officers were sitting by the window carefully cleaning their
automatics.

We began talking about the Captain's Polish wife. After
twenty-five years, her Russian was still poor, of which fact the
Captain seemed to be proud. It was something out of the
ordinary, and emphasised the foreignness and originality of
his wife, for the Russians learn foreign languages with the
facility of children. Many of the Russians already spoke
in a semi-Bulgarian, semi-Rumanian, semi-Hungarian jargon
dressed up in a Russian sauce, and to this German words
would be added when they got to Germany and Austria. The
Captain was proud that his wife spoke Russian badly, as well
as of the fact that she could bake "mazurki," make beef-olives
and many other Polish dishes. The once-famous Russian
cuisine has to-day fallen so low that the Captain's wife was
really somebody to boast of.

"Oh," said Constantin Piotrovitch, interrupting the Captain, "there's something I've been wanting to ask you for a
long time. I've found here a book about Russia, but I can't
read it because it's in the Latin alphabet, though I can see
from the maps it's about Russia, and against the Austrian
army, or something of that sort. Come and help me read it."
He then produced a fat volume and laid it on the table. We
looked through it together. It contained a description of
prisoner-of-war camps during the last war in Russia and
Siberia for officers and soldiers of the Imperial Austro-
Hungarian Army. It was a sort of souvenir book, full of

photographs, drawings and cartoons. The Russians could not understand the cartoons and caricatures. Someone else could make one lose face, but to do so oneself! Why did they print cartoons against their own army in a souvenir book, they asked. I explained that they were making fun of their own army; that they had drawn the caricatures themselves. Some artists among their own officers had done them; they were laughing at themselves.

"But how can one laugh at oneself?" Contsantin wanted to know. He could not believe me and gazed at me suspiciously. "There's no sense in making a fool of oneself. You must be mistaken."

"But I assure you I'm not," I insisted, "the whole essence of humour is to be able to laugh freely at oneself. Those officers made jokes at the expense of their majors, colonels and generals, who laughed and were glad that the caricatures were good and funny."

"But to laugh at one's own superiors, that doesn't make sense," insisted the Russians, "it simply shows that the superiors are no good. How could they ever allow it? And then, if they make jokes at the expense of their superiors, they make a laughing-stock of themselves and of the whole army, because they are part of it. How is a thing like this possible?" and Constantin Piotrovitch showed us a caricature of a dishevelled-looking Austrian general behind barbed wire carrying a soup tureen; he was being chased by a band of thin, ragged soldiers armed with spoons; and on the other side of the wire a pack of wolves was galloping towards him; the general looked terrified. The caption was "breakfast," or something like that. It was quite impossible to make the Russians understand or even see what I was driving at. Self-criticism and our sporting, Western sense of humour, are completely alien to them. The only self-criticism in which they indulge is the repentant self-accusation we know from the works of Leo Tolstoy and other Tsarist writers. But this repentance and grovelling in ashes has nothing in common with our self-criticism and sense of humour. And suddenly it came to me: what made us so completely different from the Russians, what has created the gulf between them and ourselves, is just that they *never* laugh at themselves.

Constantin Piotrovitch laid the book aside. He was convinced that it had been written by some enemy of the Austro-Hungarian Army, but that we were too stupid to understand the German and explain what it was about. Instead, we had told him a lot of nonsense. He handled the book carefully, like a treasure, for it contained maps of Siberia, and Constantin Piotrovitch liked to take it out of an evening and trace with his thick finger the routes of the journeys which as a young mechanic he had once made in Siberia. The conversation again turned to the culinary talents of the Captain's Polish wife, and that led to the subject of famine behind the front and the meat shortage. Constantin Piotrovitch leaned his now beautifully clean automatic up in the corner and suggested that we should go out and try for some hares in the morning. "In March!" I cried horrified at his sacrilegious suggestion. But the Russians have no scruples in this respect and no mercy for the unfortunate pregnant hares. "Well," I thought to myself, "if that's how you feel, it won't matter if I shoot one or two as well; at least we'll have some meat, even though it is cruel murder purely prompted by greed." Then I asked, "Have you a shot-gun and cartridges?"

"No," replied Constantin, "we'll use our automatics."

"But I shall never hit a hare with an automatic," I said, greatly impressed.

"You will, after a little practice, Lida. There's plenty of ammunition. We shan't run short. But we need beaters."

So we agreed to meet the next morning and I was to bring Alec and the gypsy children as beaters. Having smoked to our heart's content, we returned home.

Tacitus was to-day officially deprived of his land. The commune also appropriated the vegetable garden in the Manor park, and had almost finished cutting down his timber.

The war was over for our little corner of the earth, and a new order was coming into being. We had entered upon a new era. Tacitus said that the distribution of the land among the peasants would make agricultural production fall and that there was bound to be a catastrophe, unless the Government introduced collective farms. For Tactitus the expression "collective farm" had no meaning, for he was no longer a landowner. It was now the peasants' turn to spend sleepless nights. But the peasants slept excellently, too stupid to foresee what might come. After supper a few of them slipped in with some bacon and other presents. These were friendly peasants who were sorry for the family of their former lord. Our poor master, they sighed, as they laid their little parcels on the kitchen table, and Matilda raised her arms to heaven and cried, "Providence, holy Providence!"

Jack and Jumbo were asleep. I lit the little lamp, put it on my suitcase and began writing. On the other side of the suitcase Fifi was darning stockings. "The end of the war," I said to Fifi, and, instead of looking into the future, we began delving into the past. What a lot we had been through during those six and a half years! Years full of fear, hope, hardship, and suffering. Great years. They were gone, and what now, my dear Fifi, what now? Now, the darkness of night.

"Do you think people haven't yet had enough?" Fifi asked.

"I don't know," I said, "but they've not changed. Only grown worse, in the old sense of the word bad. It's as if we had all gone back. But it's the same after every war."

"There are too many victors for my liking," observed Fifi.

"Too many victors make another war," I remarked.

"Oh, well," said Fifi, "but what we've lived through is ours, and the finale to those six years is a great ending to great times."

"Actually," I said, "I ought to end my book with to-day."

"God forbid!" said Fifi, in a superstitious whisper.

"There's no knowing what may happen to us yet. Never praise the day before the night."

"But we did well, didn't we, Fifi? Say that we did. I'd love a pat on the back."

"Yes, I think we've nothing to be ashamed of. But it was only training for the future," she added, afraid of annoying those mysterious higher powers who are both malicious and revengeful.

"Good-night, Fifi, my gnome. Time we went to sleep. And thank you for everything during those six years."

"Good-night. And thank you, too. And I don't regret a thing."

"That's funny, neither do I. I would not part with one of our memories of hunger, or of fright; with none of it. It has all sunk into me, belongs to me now, has become one of my branches as it were. Even the fact of there being no cigarettes has its good side. I don't know what, but I feel that it must have."

"Why don't we smoke one of Jumbo's rainy day ones?"

So we stole one, and smoked it together in the dark, inhaling right down to the bottom of our lungs. The tiny glow illuminated first my two fingers, then two of Fifi's, and a part of her face.

"Now it's really good-night," I said, "and congratulations that for us the war is over. Perhaps your husband will now get back from Russia."

"No," Fifi said. "I know that they've killed him there. He won't return. Good night, Lida. And congratulations on the conclusion of the war."

I bent down in the dark and felt for Fifi's face, bent down still farther and kissed her, hoping that my kiss might wipe away all the gravity, hopelessness and boundless sadness of that day.

Fifi and I set out early to go shooting. Tacitus and the rest of the family had sworn that they would never speak to us again if we shot hares in March, but looking at it logically it was immaterial whether the Russians killed them all by themselves or with a little assistance from us. I had decided that I would only shoot at sitting hares, because I knew I would never hit one on the move with just a bullet, but was rather worried by the fact that in March there are no young hares and it is only the young leveret that will lie curled up in terror, and let you walk up close. Imbued with this entirely unsporting spirit, I marched along happily in the frosty air, followed by a couple of small gypsy beaters. The sky was high up and pale blue. We went through the garden, of which hardly anything was left: a few trees on the hard-beaten earth that was almost bare of grass, broken, trampled privet hedges, and some skeletons of motor cars, all of them American, in which a flock of ragged children had made themselves temporary homes. On seeing us, one little boy leant out of his motor car house and threw a stone at us. Then we followed a dilapidated fence, leaping across furrows and over the uneven ground where the dead horses from the veterinary hospital had been hurriedly buried, passed the ruins of a cottage, the wind howling among its clay walls, crossed a potato field badly cut up by tanks, and so reached the house in which Constantin Piotrovitch, his Captain, and their Ukrainian cook were billeted. On the doorstep stood the peasant's young wife, clasping her swollen cheek.

"There's no one here," she called, when she saw us approaching. "They got sudden orders and had to leave. One of them wrote a letter and left it in the room. I'll fetch it at once."

Constantin Piotrovitch had written a farewell letter. He had written it in block letters because he knew that I could not read Russian long-hand. Fifi and I spelt it out together, word by word. With great difficulty we learned that Constantin Piotrovitch was grateful for our friendship and had grown to love us. Also that he was terribly sorry that our acquaintance had ended so suddenly and that he had not even had an opportunity to say good-bye. "A nice man, that Constantin Piotrovitch," Fifi and I kept repeating to each other, "a nice, kind man." And we missed him.

Thus, we never went out shooting, and consequently I was saved from social ostracism.

We spent the rest of the morning packing and unpacking. Jack was still on his back, too weak as yet even to walk. Jumbo directed us from his bed. A minor Crusoe had come to see him earlier that morning and had promised to give us on the sly a pass allowing us to leave, on condition that we ourselves found a horse and cart. We were the prisoners of the village, and like criminals we were not allowed to move anywhere without permission from the commune. It was not only us: no peasant who was not an official Communist was allowed to go anywhere either. Nearly all the Russians had gone, including those from the mill and their Captain Sashka, who left the daughter of the chief Crusoe and headman with tears in her eyes and a baby in her belly. The members of the commune were now the undisputed masters of the village, and there was no Vanyusha to defend me, as the peasants were very well aware. With the village abandoned by the Russians I felt like Samson with his hair cut off. There had been a war, and now it was the turn for revolution. And there were still no instructions from the capital and no proper police. The whole country was in suspense. And there were we, in the midst of the turmoil.

20th-23rd March

THE miller came complaining that the commune would not allow him to work the mill now that the Russians had gone. The commune was afraid that if he were allowed back, Tacitus would recover possession of his own mill. So the mill was to remain out of action until the commune found a different miller from some other village who would side with them against Tacitus. I was sick of listening all the time to this peasant wrangling. Instead I went to fetch the water, a thing I had not done for a long time. On my way back from the first trip, I met Franzi, who had been for a walk in the village.

"The Russians again," he said excitedly.

"What of it? Do you imagine that the whole two hundred and fifty million have already passed through Mora and are parked near Berlin?"

"But these are special Russians. They stopped at the commune offices. The N.K.W.D., I'll bet."

Unfortunately we were soon to discover who and what they were.

Franzi was right. I had not been back long when two N.K.W.D. men rushed into the room. One was a Staff Sergeant, a small, youngish boy with short, bandy legs, the other a Sergeant, with a tremendous mouth and little eyes embedded in layers of fat, a Mongol type. They were both far

too matter-of-fact for hooligans or for mere visitors. The
romantic days of hooliganism were over, and from now on all
looting, theft and assault were to have the official Kremlin
stamp. There was to be a search and, furthermore, the master
of the house was to come at once. What did they want?
Who had informed against us? They were looking for hidden
arms. We sighed with relief; for we knew all that that meant.
I explained that we had been just behind the front for three
months and that during that time the Russians hadn't been
out of our house for a minute, but the Counter-Intelligence
men refused to be bluffed by mere facts. They marched into
the Hungarians' room and began their search. They looted
calmly and methodically, the Hungarians watching their every
movement in silence.

"Hand over those cigarettes!"

"All of them?" asked Marietta, pointing to our last two
packets.

"Of course!"

And Marietta presented them with the sort of smile with
which she would have offered some special delicacy to a prince
of her acquaintance.

In Rudi's room they found a bottle of French cognac.
"What's this? Read it!" the Staff Sergeant shouted to me.
I spelled it out. "B-i-s-q-u-i-t, medicine for the stomach," I
said. "Are you sure it is not poison?" the Russians asked, their
interest aroused. They opened the bottle and ordered Rudi
and me to drink, watching us carefully to see if we should
drop down dead. We tried to drink as much as possible, but
the N.K.W.D. saw through that trick and the bottle went
into their capacious pockets. They scampered all over the
house, taking whatever they came across. In Matilda's room
they discovered an old Austrian military decoration.

"What's this?" they demanded, triumphantly dangling
the medal in front of my nose. "Read!"

"Pro patria," I read.

"Oh yes," said the Sergeant, quite satisfied, as though

Latin were his mother tongue, and the medal went into the pocket of his tunic where it jangled against the orders of Stalingrad and "For Bravery."

Suddenly the Sergeant seemed to remember something. "Where's the master of the house? He's coming with us. Only a couple of steps. Come on, get dressed!" Tacitus, as always, extremely surprised, got up and started to dress. "And this one?" asked the Sergeant, entering the next room. "He's the brother of the lady of the house," I explained. "You too, then. Come on, get dressed!" roared the Sergeant at Rudi.

Tacitus and Rudi had already been hounded outside, when the Sergeant turned round and asked, "Who speaks good Russian in this place?"

"I do," I said naively.

"You're coming with us, then."

Thus, suddenly and unexpectedly, I found myself setting out on a journey. Jumbo watched uncomprehendingly as I snatched our last piece of rainy-day bacon from its hiding-place, and six of the eleven cigarettes we still possessed. "What is it?" he asked and, without waiting for a reply, clasped me in his arms. He was familiar enough by then with these rapid movements and my sheepskin being slipped on while a Red Army man waited in the doorway with a pistol clasped across his belly.

We were to be taken through a number of villages, partly on foot and partly by lorry. By the time we left Mora we were quite a convoy, for they had also arrested the priest, Uncle Joseph (the owner of the five daughters) and another five peasants. The guard was reinforced by a gloomy soldier, suffering from malaria, and a Corporal, a small, thin, fair-haired man with steel-coloured eyes and an impertinent air, a real Prussian type. "Where's your monocle?" I wondered, and looked at his N.K.W.D. uniform. The tail of the procession was made up of myself, an old soldier, Kopeykin, and the official interpreter, Georgy, a Bulgarian in a red beret, with a blue stubble on his jowls and eyes like two juicy olives.

First of all, the prisoners were locked up in a shed just outside Mora, while I was allowed to sit outside and talk to Georgy. I did not know who he was and I was afraid of him. He had a look in his eyes that went right through you, a narrow face and an evil smile. People like that always work for the police regardless of whom the police are serving. Time seemed to be at a standstill. Bored, I peeped into the cottage next door. My friends, the telephone operators, were packing, the ones who always borrowed our mincing machine..

Why had I been dragged here? Where would they make me go? Who had denounced the six peasants, my brother-in-law and the priest? And what for? However, it was no use wondering, and it was doing me no good. I would need all my wits about me. Any sign of nervousness, any hesitation in answering, the wrong tone of voice—and I would be lost. How difficult it is to hypnotize oneself! Experience had taught me that with the Russians you have to be gay, and it must be a natural gaiety that never strikes a false note, and I began to pray that my sense of humour should not desert me. More than that, I needed it to descend upon me, as the Holy Ghost had upon the Apostles, and defend me in my present trials against all evil.

Then Kopeykin lost his gloves and this made it possible for me to let them know at home that we were about to leave for the next village. I told Kopeykin that, if he would allow me to write a note home, my nephew would give him a pair of Russian gloves someone had left behind by mistake. The telephone operators and the guards all gathered round me as I wrote to Jack in block letters, "And mind you write in Russian, for otherwise God knows what you might write, you snake!"

"Yes, yes, look: read for yourselves . . . 'Vaniusha deliver a pair of Russian gloves, *dasvidanya*, Lida,'" they read over my shoulder, and I thought that perhaps those were the last words I would ever write. The telephone operators summoned a peasant child and gave him my note and a pound of lard as a present for my family. After that I felt happier: the child would tell them everything.

The telephone operators walked away and I was left alone on the doorstep of the empty room. I stared at the paper frieze round the ceiling, then at the tangle of telephone wires under my feet, staring intently and long, as you do at your favourite pictures when you go to the gallery for a last visit before going on à long journey. I'll remember that frieze just as well as I remember Peter Breughel's "Ikaros." And the tangle of wires, too. It is a sure sign of loneliness, such intent staring at just anything.

The convoy set off again through maize fields. The spring sun shone brightly and the sky that was smooth and velvety seemed to be smiling. In a flat, treeless country the sky is the main element of the landscape, for it occupies more room than the ground. My interrogation was begun on the march. I was questioned in turn by the Mongol Sergeant and the Prussian, while the others herded the prisoners ahead of us. The Mongol Sergeant's first question was: did I have syphilis? And my husband? No. Had we any children? No. Why not? Obviously I was lying and we did have syphilis. This disease was the scourge of the Red Army and consequently the main topic of the Russians' conversation and their chief interest. The Sergeant was amazed that we had no children; it was incomprehensible, a thing that never happened in Russia. Did we take special precautions, and if so what? "How do you live with your husband," asked the Sergeant, now really intrigued. I pretended not to understand the question, but he just summoned the Prussian and they showered me with a hail of such questions as would have stretched most ladies of my acquaintance senseless on the ground. And I thought bitterly of how they had considered the post-card of Michelangelo's statue pornographic. "You don't want to tell us, you're a sly one," said the Sergeant. "But never mind, we'll soon find out what to do so as not to have children. Do you think you're the only one that knows? Look at her, isn't she clever! They all know here. There aren't many children about."

There was a short pause, because we were approaching a village, then the Sergeant again kept me back behind the others for further questioning.

"What are you?"

"I draw."

"And that village over there, could you draw it for me as a souvenir?"

"Not that," I said indignantly, "that wouldn't be a drawing, but a plan. I can't draw plans."

"Couldn't you try? Go on, just for me, won't you?"

The Sergeant's voice was so coaxing that I had to smile to myself. My poor Bolshie, I thought, if only you knew whom you were dealing with. It took a lot of lying. Although my conscience was quite clear, I had to explain, invent excuses and talk, in order to remain on the surface of that ocean of stupidity, where it was just as necessary to know how to swim as in any other sea.

"All right, then," said the Sergeant, "you can't draw the village. What sort of education did you have?"

"Two years Art College."

"What!" he exclaimed, and almost came to a halt. "Impossible!" and he dashed off to tell the rest of the Russians.

Soon there was a small crowd around me. This was incredible: they had caught a cultured, educated person: an artist! I thought of the Tall Major, because I had never been to an Art College, but by saying that I had aroused their admiration and respect. In no other country is the word "culture" used more often than in Russia, possibly because it does not exist there.

In the next village a halt was called, and we lay in the dust of a roadside ditch, while the Russians vainly searched for their headquarters. It was then that the cart with the porcelain bath passed us for the first time. The bath, as the driver told us, had been ordered a month before by some offi-

cer in the Counter-Intelligence, and he had not yet been able
to find him or catch him up. It looked as though he would
spend the rest of his days on that cart with the bath, calmly
driving on and on as he had been ordered, ever westward. In
the course of our peregrinations he passed us five times, and
never once failed to ask us if by any chance we had seen his
officer.

During the night we arrived at a large village. The prisoners were minutely searched on the veranda of a large house,
any suspicious papers were confiscated, and all others thrown
away. Leaflets were found in the pockets of all the peasants.
Those in Russian were at once thrown away by the searching
officer, who did not even bother to read them: these were
German leaflets intended to undermine the morale of the Red
Army. On the other hand, leaflets printed in German were
scrupulously collected and put away in a leather bag as proof
of the peasants' spying activities; these were Russian leaflets
printed in Moscow intended to undermine the morale of the
German Army. I was glad for the peasants that things had
turned out that way, but on the other hand I was appalled by
the stupidity of the Russians. What help was it being innocent? None at all!

The prisoners were locked up, and I was summoned for
interrogation. However, the officer was playing the gramophone and too busy pawing a plump girl-soldier to take any
notice of me. Suddenly, in the midst of a tango, there was a
deafening cannonade, an orderly rushed in, and everybody
started packing without wasting time on words.

I found myself on a dark road in a cart. The only person
I knew was Georgy. Georgy set me on a Cossack saddle lying
on top of the things in the cart, and we moved off amid much
cursing and swearing. A moment later, breaking through
some fruit trees, we found ourselves in a ditch, out of which
we got with a lot of difficulty. I had no idea where we were
going, nor what had happened to the prisoners. Rocking in
my saddle, I fell asleep. I was awakened by a jerk and in-

stinctively I tried to pull on the reins, but there were none. A small bridge had collapsed under us and the cart was badly damaged. We all got out and it was decided to spend the night in the village. A little soldier took me in the dark to a dilapidated cottage out of which emerged an old Hungarian peasant in his pants. The soldier said that he was just going to his commander for further orders because he did not know what to do with me, and implored me not to run away. I lay down on the ground and fell asleep at once.

I was awakened by the sound of footsteps, and the shadow of a startled rat dashed across the floor. My little soldier was standing in the porch: "Come on, Lida," he said, "you may sleep with us. I'll take you to the unit." We reached the house where our convoy was; the little soldier, humming gaily, disappeared into the darkness, his footsteps resounding in the empty street, and I was left standing on the veranda, lost and sleepy. Then I took off my sheepskin and, wrapping it round me, carefully lay down on the garden table, because everywhere else was covered with mud or ice. I had just gone to sleep, when someone shook me. The guard of the convoy had recognized my sheepskin and were inviting me to spend the night with them. They wanted me to lie down between them in the warm straw, but I insisted that I could only sleep in the frost. Finally it was decided that I should sleep at their feet on the pig-sty door, because the floor was covered with mud. All night the soldiers' bare feet tickled my nose, as two of my senses recorded: smell and touch. What a night that was!

Day began to break, and the prisoners were let out one by one into the garden. Silently we exchanged looks. Some of the soldiers, half-naked, were splashing themselves at the well, rubbing themselves with snow, shaving, wrapping their foot-clouts round their feet; others were heating American tinned foods for breakfast.

"Why are all the labels on your tins printed in English?" I asked, and smiled because I knew what the reply would be.

"So that the Allies can read what the Red Army eats. We know what's in them, so we don't need labels. But the English and the Americans are fools, they can't tell what is bacon and onion and pork, so our factories print the labels in English so that they know what we eat."

"I see," I said, and expressed my admiration for the Russian managers of canning factories who were able to foresee all these contingencies.

We were supposed to leave immediately after breakfast, but were delayed by the sudden appearance of the Sergeant with a Kodak camera which, of course, had to be taken to pieces. Everybody realized that. A few minutes later the Kodak lay in pieces among the half-eaten crusts of bread, bits of bacon rind and black tobacco that littered the table. It now had to be put together again. This was done in a moment. Two screws remained on the table.

"There, you see," said Makarof complacently, "that man Kodak in America, or wherever he is, made a mistake; two screws too many. But the Russians are a clever lot, and we found it out immediately."

I ventured to observe that it might not be possible to take photographs with it now, and true enough, after several attempts it was found that it was no good for photographing. The Sergeant leaned out of the window and roared at a passing peasant child, who stopped, terrified. "Here you are," said the Sergeant graciously, and thrust the camera into the little fellow's hands. The child ran off hugging it, and the Sergeant turned, picked up the two screws from the table and, with a Chaplinesque gesture, threw them out of the window.

The prisoners were now lined up in pairs, and we set out across some marshes to the next village, still in search of Counter-Intelligence Headquarters. The procession had now been reinforced by four more peasants. I walked at the rear with the Sergeant and two soldiers: Shurka, the dwarf, and Makarof. Makarof had the empty leather case of the Kodak,

and he carried it as carefully as though it contained nitrogly-
cerine.

We were walking along a dyke on either side of which
were ponds and bog-meadows. Peewits called despairingly as
they described swift, graceful circles in the transparent, crystal
air. The pale blue sky seemed to be hanging higher than
usual, so flat was the country around us. As we walked along,
the Staff Sergeant began shooting into the pond. Stunned fish
came up to the surface, their bellies gleaming white. I bent
down and pulled out a nice pike. "Throw it away, you fool!"
said the Staff Sergeant. "I'm only testing my pistol, not fishing. I'm cleaning my pistol, do you understand? Do you
want to carry that fish for twelve miles? If we'd been fishing,
it would have been different. But not this way." I could not
understand the logic of that, but he tore the fish from my
hand and threw it away.

We were approaching the railway line. It was working on
this sector and carried Russian reinforcements. The station
we came to was the terminus. "We'll go to the front by train.
Nice and smart," promised the Staff Sergeant. We tried to
explain that the railway went in the opposite direction due
east, but the Russians badly wanted to ride in a train. However, the Russian in charge of the station threw us out and
we found ourselves back on the road.

Beyond the level crossing we were passed by the cart with
the bath. "Brothers," roared the old driver, "have you seen
Captain Metetiuk anywhere?"

"What Captain?" shouted Shurka. "You must go west,
brother. Your Captain's probably in Vienna by now."

We lay down in the ditch for a spell, because the Staff
Sergeant got it into his head that we might get a lift from a
lorry. However, in spite of much shouting and cursing no
lorry would stop. A doctor and a Warrant Officer, who had
been waiting there unsuccessfully since the morning for a lift
to Ruda, came and spoke to our escort. As a result several
Russian deserters were added to our group. We crawled on

along the frozen road in a cloud of dust. The snow had long since disappeared from the plateau, but the frost still held and there was an icy wind blowing. We halted again in the next village, and were told to wait in the ditch, while another search was made for the headquarters. Again they were unsuccessful. We ate our bread in the ditch, and next to us, curled up in the dust like dogs, slept the Russian deserters, a picture of imperturbable brute tranquillity.

Beyond the village, when we were among devastated vineyards, the priest of the village we had just left caught up with us. He was young and came running quickly, his hair dishevelled by the wind and dark against the sky, and his black soutane billowing. He ran up to the Mora priest. The Russians turned their heads away and pretended not to look, occupying themselves trampling down mole hills, peering into craters, and cutting off the heads of plants with the barrels of their automatics. The convoy had halted. As the two priests talked I caught a few scattered phrases borne on the wind. "Yes, for espionage on behalf of the Germans . . . all of us . . . I don't know . . . to Counter-Intelligence Headquarters . . . to the front . . ." Then the young priest lowered his charming face to the trembling lips of the older man, who put his right arm about the young priest's waist and, with his left hand, delicately and with ineffable tenderness pressed the young, dark head against his wrinkled cheek. Then both men kissed. The Russians still stood with their backs to them, busily kicking at the mole hills. When I next turned round, the slim back figure of the young priest was disappearing in the distance of the vineyards so swiftly that it seemed as if his feet were not even touching the ground.

Late in the afternoon we came to another village. It appeared that the Russians in their vain search for their headquarters had described a large semi-circle, and that we were only ten miles from Mora. Again we took to the ditch, while a convoy of tanks rumbled past, shrouding us in an impenetrable cloud. There was no end to the tanks, and all were heading west. The deserters again curled up and went to sleep.

Beyond the village, the now familiar squeak of its axle announced the approach of the cart with the bath. The driver gave us a friendly wave. "Your Captain's in Vienna bathing in Hitler's bath," Shurka told him.

The old priest could hardly drag himself along and the gloomy little soldier had an attack of malaria. We halted in a narrow valley full of leaflets which the wind had blown in. As I ate my bread I picked up one of the leaflets and glanced at it stealthily: Churchill and Roosevelt were holding a large banner on which Stalin was painting the words, "Proletarians of all countries unite with the Capitalists." German planes must have been there.

The Sergeant, while playing with his penknife, had cut the camera case into tiny fragments without realizing what he was doing. Only the strap was left, and the Russians crowded round to discuss what should be done with it. Eventually they tied one end round a tin of American stew, and they dragged that tin along the road all the way to Ruda, pretending that it was a dog on a leash. The soldiers patted it, spoke lovingly to it, or else kicked it and swore at it.

In Ruda there were barricades made of broken-down tanks, the Manor was in ruins and many of the houses had lost their windows. Darkness was falling, and the road swarmed with peasants filling in the shell-holes. Lorries roared as they crept along in first gear; the place was stiff with soldiers. The four peasants who had joined the convoy at dawn began explaining for the hundredth time that they had already been interrogated two days previously and set free. "Never mind, never mind," said the Sergeant. "Don't you like it with us, or what's worrying you? If you're innocent it will be found out: and if it was found out two days ago, then all the better for you."

We were herded into a yard. The Hungarians were sent to the far end of the yard, while I stayed with the deserters and the men of the escort. We sat down on a camp bed. A Warrant Officer began telling us how he became a deserter.

"I got drunk," he explained. "Not badly, but it must have gone to my head, because I woke up in the street. In the meantime my Lieutenant, the swine, instead of waiting for me went off with the whole unit."

"The swine," chorused the others. "Would he have lost the war, that Lieutenant of yours, if he had waited for you? Must have been in a hurry to become a hero."

"Ay-ay," sighed the Warrant Officer. "And here I am."

An hour later we were packed into a lorry which was to take us by a roundabout route to the front, twenty miles away. There was no room in the lorry for the four peasants who had been set free two days before, so to their immense surprise they suddenly found themselves standing alone on the road. We drove into a ruined village. The front was thundering a mile away. The sky was aflame. In the square was the statue of a saint. It stood in a field of wooden stars: a provisional Russian military cemetery. We spent the night all together on some straw in a peasant cottage. The soldiers were tired of looking after me and allowed me to sleep between Tacitus and Rudi. Four of the Russians slept in the only bed. The Staff Sergeant spent the whole night searching for his headquarters and returned at dawn with the news that the officers had just driven off. We were taken to the deserted cottage which had been the headquarters, and half the prisoners were locked up in a pig-sty and a sentry placed at the door. The other half were made to help build a "bania." The "bania" is a sort of Finnish bath. Up at the front it was knocked together with a few planks in a room in any cottage. Then they made a clay oven in which stones were heated, over which water was poured to make the steam. An European using a Russian front-line "bania" would immediately die of pneumonia. An icy wind blew through the gaps between the planks, and the Russians would sit there, stark naked, their fronts as red as lobsters from the steam, and their backs covered with goose-flesh.

I spent the day with the soldiers in the ditch, waiting for the return of their officers. I was horribly bored. I read *Pravda* from cover to cover. My boredom increased. Then I chopped some wood for the "bania" and cut my finger. Old Kopeykin, who was grateful for the gloves, bandaged it for me with cotton wool and gauze stolen from the N.K.W.D., and gave me five of Tacitus' cigarettes to console me. Then I went and lay in the other ditch with the dwarf Shurka, and lazily watched the passing tanks, carts and lorries. The sun was already setting when we heard a familiar squeak: the bath again. "Hey there," roared Shurka, making a trumpet of his hands, "we know where your Captain is, Metetiuk, or whatever he's called. It was in the papers: he's in Berlin. Got through singlehanded."

"What's that? Where?" asked the old driver, pushing his cap over to his other ear and reining in his horses. Then he put his hand to his ear to hear better.

"In Berlin. Got through by himself. He's been made a triple hero. That's why it was in the papers."

The old driver spat furiously. "As if I had the time for such foolery. Go to hell, you Caucasian idiot!" And with that he whipped up his horses and the cart jolted on squeaking mournfully.

At dusk the first of the prisoners was summoned for interrogation; this was the Mora priest. Before he returned a soldier ran out from the house opposite us "for the woman." It was my turn now. I was taken into a stuffy room, where a small lamp, of course without a chimney, was smoking on a table behind which sat a young woman. The surrounding darkness was loud with many rhythmical snores. There was no sign of the priest. The soldier disappeared, shutting the door quietly behind him.

"Please sit down," said the girl politely in Hungarian. Her voice was tired.

"I can't speak Hungarian," I said quickly, and took a good look at my interrogator.

If you were to ask me what she looked like, I could only say that she looked exactly like what the N.K.W.D. up at the front would think a smart European should look like. She had on a Victorian blouse of grey satin with a high ribbed collar and a lace ruffle in front, an ankle-length skirt, a large man's watch on her wrist; and her head was covered with greasy curls, like a poodle. Her shoes had dangerously high heels, and the incongruity was further heightened by her round, apple-red cheeks and typically Russian oval face with high cheek-bones, eyes like narrow slits, and flat, thick lips. Her frequent artificial sighs kept raising her enormous young breasts which anyway were hitched up under her chin. I understood the position at once: you just wait, Dunyasha, I thought to myself, what you should be doing is spreading manure on a collective farm and not tormenting people at night.

"You are not Russian?" I asked her in Russian, pretending to be surprised.

"Of course not," she replied in Hungarian. "A Russian? Me? No, no-o. I am a local girl, in exactly the same position as you. I can't even speak Russian. Oh dear," and she sighed heavily.

Smiling charmingly at each other across the table we began to talk. The girl was perhaps eighteen, and spoke Hungarian with such a strong Russian accent that I could hardly understand what she meant. As I pretended not to be able to speak Hungarian and she pretended not to be able to speak Russian, our conversation was not as easy as it could have been, especially as we had to concentrate on not betraying the fact that we were trying to fool each other.

"You were an interpreter in the German Army, weren't you?" she asked me all of a sudden. "They told me so. *They*," she added, pointing to the door, "*they* know, and that is why you are here. Like me."

"I wonder what language I could have interpreted in the German Army," I said deliberately, weighing every word. "As you see I can't speak Hungarian, and I don't know German."

"There are a lot of German spies hiding behind the Russian lines," the girl remarked casually. "They're lucky," she added, with a tender smile.

I continued to pretend that it was only with great difficulty I could understand what she was saying. This had the added advantage that I had more time to think.

"How can you think," I said, "that after the Russians have been here for three months there could still be even one German spy behind their lines? Not with the Russian organization. Oh no, the Russian Counter-Intelligence service is excellent. You don't know the Russians. But I'm a Pole. I know them. They have the best intelligence service in Europe."

"How did you get here?" asked the girl, trying a new angle, and thrust a German map of Europe under my nose.

"This way, then here, and then that way," said I, drawing my dirty finger along the map.

"A lot of the Poles were on the Germans' side," said the girl, with a smile, looking me in the eyes. "And why," she added, in a conspiratorial whisper, "were you so anxious to escape from the Germans?"

"And where have you been for the past five years, if you don't know why people try to escape from the Germans?" I asked, feeling all my fear leave me, and a hot wave of blood mount to my head. But the girl, with a sly little smile, like a bad chess player who had not realized that he had made a false move, whispered knowingly.

"You know that half of Poland was on the German side and still is. I come from here, I know the European situation."

Very slowly, I rose to my feet.

"You come from here!" I shouted, in the best accent I could muster. "You come from here, do you? Poles on the side of the Germans! After this war! To say a thing like that after this war! In Norway, they had Quisling; in Prague, Hacha; in Yugoslavia, Prince Paul; in Slovakia, Tiso; in Hungary, Szalasy; in Rumania, Antonescu; in Russia, Vlassov; and in Poland, whom? Whom? Give me one Polish name!" I was hoarse with anger.

The girl pushed back her chair. "I can't remember names," she whispered.

"In Poland there are many parties," I hissed, wagging a finger right under her nose, "there are even two Governments: one in Moscow, and one in London. But however much the Poles quarrel, one thing is certain: not one of them has betrayed his country to the Germans."

What a satisfaction there was in being able to shout at an N.K.W.D. woman and know that it would do me no harm, but, if anything, help.

"Do you understand what I say?" I shouted, suddenly bending down over the cowering girl. "Do you understand me? How dare you say such things to me, a Slav, and only a mile behind the Russian front! How dare you! How dare you!"

"Aaa ..." shouted the girl, staring at me as if I were mad, and then she leaped up from her chair, knocking it over. The sleeping soldiers jumped to their feet, the door opened with a bang and in rushed the Prussian and an officer. They had obviously been eavesdropping. The officer gave the girl a hardly perceptible sign with his hand and she left the room. The soldiers lay down again along the walls. The real interrogation now began.

Speaking quietly the officer showered me with quick, boring questions, jotting down my replies on a piece of paper. Then slowly he crumpled the paper into a ball and threw it away.

"Oh yes," he said, as though suddenly remembering something, "do you know the priest?"

"I do."

"He's a Fascist, we know that."

"No."

"But we know he is."

"No," I repeated. "How could a Catholic priest be on the side of the Germans? In Germany religion is forbidden. There's no religious freedom as in Russia," I added.

"But nevertheless the priest used to visit the Manor?"

"Yes, quite often. He was a friend of the owner."

"A close friend?"

"Yes, a very close friend."

"And why did he come to listen secretly to the wireless? Was that out of friendship? Because we know that you used to listen secretly to the wireless."

"When? Under the Germans, or later?" I asked, hiding a smile, because I had just thought of an excellent move. You wait, I thought to myself, this is going to be checkmate.

"Under the Germans, of course," replied the officer, looking contemptuously at me as though I were an idiot.

"Well, under the Germans it was only to Moscow that one had to listen in secret," I replied.

The officer was taken aback, but he did not capitulate.

"And, perhaps, the master of Mora is not a Fascist, what?" he said.

"No," I said.

"Well, then, if they were not both Fascist, why did the priest visit him at night?"

"The priest never used to come at night," I said.

"That's strange," said the officer, suddenly looking me in the eyes, "that's very strange, because only a minute ago, here, on this very spot, the priest told us that he very often used to go to the Manor at night."

"Yes, that's very odd," I replied slowly, returning his look. "Very odd, indeed, that the priest should have said such a thing, because the priest was never once in the Manor at night. Not once."

"Is that true, that you said that the other prisoners are all innocent?" asked the officer, changing the subject.

"Quite true. Three months now the Russians have been in the village. They've taken care of anyone bad long ago. The Russians are too thorough to leave Fascists at large for three months."

"Thank you," said the officer politely. "That will be all. The men will now show you to your quarters, because you can't go home in the middle of the night. You are free. You may return at dawn."

"But not to Mora," said the Prussian, interrupting. "Go wherever you like, but keep clear of Mora," and he brandished his fist under my nose. "I'll go there and make sure, and if I catch you there, you'll soon find out what I'll do to you."

"In that case, please give me a document, so that I may go east, to Budapest. I should also like to write to my husband that I am alive. My husband is very ill."

"You'll get no document," said the Prussian, narrowing his evil, bright eyes. "You speak Russian: that's the best document you can have at present."

The officer stood up with a Pontius Pilate expression on his face, and walked out.

"Good-bye," I said, and went out into the darkness, plunged in the depths of despair. What was I to do? How could I get home? It was forty miles by road and I did not know the short cuts. What was happening to the others? Would I able to see them that night, or in the morning? Where had they taken the priest? Should I be justified in leaving them?

I found my way into the yard. In the flashes that lit up the darkness, I made out the shapes of the escort. "Makarof, Shurka, Kopeykin! I want to say goodbye. I'm free. I can go home at once if I want!" In an instant I was surrounded by the dark figures of the soldiers. They patted me on the back, glad for my sake. "Makarof, is that you?" I asked, touching somebody's shoulder. "Yes, it's me," said Makarof, and I

could tell by his voice that he was smiling. "Good-bye, Makarof, I came to thank you for being so kind to me all the time."
I gave him my hand and patted him on the cheek. Makarof
was very moved and terribly embarrassed. He squeezed my
hand so hard that I thought the bones would crack. Then I
said good-bye to old Kopeykin. They all seemed sorry and I
am sure they were saying to themselves, "She's an innocent
woman and we were so severe with her. But orders are orders,
and how is a man to know beforehand what sort of a person
he has to deal with? And then she comes and thanks us,
Heaven knows what for. Shame." And they were ashamed,
because they were all decent lads.

Then they shouted for the orderly, and when he came running it was my friend Kuznetsof, the one who took our documents the first evening. "Come, Lida, we'll find you nice
quarters, we'll all go with you." Kuznetsof took me under one
arm, Shurka under the other, and we set off through the village, followed by a few soldiers who had joined us out of sheer
curiosity.

We came to the cottage, which was the best billet they
had at their disposal. The room was full of old women and
girls. In a corner burned a bright clean lamp. It was a clean,
warm, pleasant place. The soldiers sat me down in the place
of honour, under the holy picture behind the table, and
signed to the peasants to give me something to eat. The terrified Hungarians, who must have thought from the size of my
suite that I was at least Tolbuchin's mistress, rushed to serve
me. Smoked pork, fried bacon, white bread and black Russian Army bread were set before me, together with a jug of
water, and then they retired to the dark corners of the room,
from where their eyes devoured us as they listened to our incomprehensible talk.

The soldiers wanted to know all about the interrogation,
so I gave them my version. Then I accused the Hungarians,
all and sundry, of making false denunciations to the Russians,
and ended up by telling them how I was not allowed to re-

turn to my own village and to my sick husband. At this point
I tried very hard to produce at least two tears, but I just could
not manage it. It was infuriating. If I go to a film and see a boa
constrictor strangling some stupid monkey, I burst into a flood
of tears, even if I am told that the monkey is not real, but
stuffed. Yet, when my own existence was at stake I could not
produce even two miserable little tears. All the same, the soldiers were very moved by my tale. They kept offering me
food and water and beautifully even pieces of newspaper with
tobacco. They were so considerate and friendly that I could
see the respect of the Hungarians in the room increasing
every minute. The girls gazed at me in awe, and if I happened to glance at them, at once lowered their eyes.

"Well, off to bed now, my dears," I said to the soldiers,
"I'm tired too." Our farewells were those of good friends and
comrades. "I'll come back in the night," whispered Kuznetsof, "and tell you why they won't let you go back home."
Then they left, telling me not to be afraid and assuring me
that they would think up something before the morning, and
that I would be able to go back to Mora and not on foot,
either. When they had gone leaving me with the inhabitants
of the cottage, an old peasant, whose presence I had not even
suspected, emerged from under the feather-bed, and gazed at
me with interest and respect, but ready to dive back under the
feathers at the slightest provocation. "Listen," I said, in my
best Hungarian, "I'm the sister-in-law of the master of Mora.
I was dragged here as an interpreter. The master of Mora is
also here, and so is the priest, whom you know because he
used to be in your parish. And there are six peasants, all of
them denounced as Hitlerites and German spies." At this the
women clutched their heads in unison. There was something
theatrical in that simple gesture.

"You can spend the night in the next room," said a
gloomy voice from the depths of the bed, "there's no room
here." Thus the only man there was afraid to have me in the
room. The women were ashamed of him. Now that they

Comes the Comrade!

knew who I was, they were suddenly overcome by pity. Till then my unkempt hair, dirtiness and filthy rags had made no impression on them; I had just been part of the Russian Army, which was what I looked like. But as soon as they found out who I really was, they at once noticed how shabby and miserable I was and pitied me. I had ceased both to be the Soviet spy and to impress them. They patted me on the back and promised to give me a shake-down on the floor, but the man was suspicious and unrelenting: he did not trust me and wished to be rid of me. There was an unheated room with a straw bed across the passage, he said, and I could sleep there. The women protested, wailed and wrung their hands. "Poor lady! Such a frost! There are no panes in the window there and no stove. She will freeze. She shall sleep here with us, on the floor." But the man was adamant and the women gave in. "You will not be afraid all alone?" they whispered.

"The Russians won't do anything to me," I replied proudly, "but what I must have is a lamp or a candle."

I threw myself down on the straw and covered myself with my sheepskin. The women placed an old ink-well on a little table at the side of the bed and filled it with oil in which they put a wick. I laid a box of matches beside it. Then there was a lot of whispering, and I could hear them barricading the door into their room. Then there was silence.

I opened my eyes: the moon was looking in through the broken window, casting a tranquil, liquid coating of light on the worn boards of the floor, the corner of the bed and the edge of my sheepskin coat. The guns had started up when the moon rose, and the whole front was in an uproar. Every now and again an explosion would turn the sky white-hot, and at times the rosy light of a fire would extinguish the lazy, unearthly gleam of the moon. Occasionally a shell would fall quite close and seem to shake the whole village. What was I doing in that stinking straw, strung up and taut like a watching animal, my head swept clean of thought? I had only instincts left, and they were not in my head like thoughts, but had crept into every corner of my body. I was afraid of bombs, I was afraid of drunken soldiers in the night, I was afraid for the prisoners. My whole body ached with all that fear, for besides being exhausted, my muscles were kept braced as I endlessly listened for footsteps, or curled up whenever a bomb or a shell went off with a hollow bang. Would the soldiers come during the night? What would I do if they should want to sleep with me in return for the lorry which they were going to try to get for me? Kuznetsof would keep the others off. He would come alone, but was I smart enough to keep him at bay? There was still a long time before dawn.

I lit a cigarette. The hand in which I held it went numb with the cold almost at once. I could hear footsteps outside. And then again a long-drawn-out whistling sound, a bang, a burst of white light, and the fiendish rattle of anti-aircraft guns. Shouts, the running of many feet, guttural calls of Russian voices. What had happened? But I was too tired to look out of the window. If there had been more cloud I might perhaps have risked trying to escape from that confounded village, but what would happen to the others? If I were caught there would be no doubt I was a spy, for why should I run away in the night if my conscience was clear? It was quiet now, but I could hear someone's footsteps approaching. The cottage door squeaked. This was it.

Was it Kuznetsof? The door slowly opened, and for an endless second I lay with every muscle tensed unbearably, frantically clutching the box of matches that was my only weapon, and ready at any moment to leap from the straw and make for the window. I told myself not to be afraid of shots. He would certainly shoot into the air.

"It's I, Kuznetsof," said a quiet voice. "Smoking? Why aren't you asleep? I've come."

"So I see. I'm very glad. I'm ill, that's why I can't sleep. We'll have a chat." I quickly struck a match and lit the miserable wick in the ink-well.

"It's cold in here, my dear," said Kuznetsof, "and that

lamp of yours won't warm us. Let me get in under the sheepskin. And you can put out your lamp."

"I can't," I said seriously. "I'm frightened. I'm afraid of
ghosts. And the bombs. And I'm worried about my sick
husband, and I'm ill myself. I've caught a chill."

"Let me warm you," Kuznetsof suggested politely, "you'll
feel better straight away. You might let me in under that
sheepskin. You can see I'm freezing."

Again the deafening clatter of the anti-aircraft guns, and I
leapt to my feet. Kuznetsof quietly sat down on the bed and
drew the sheepskin over his shoulders.

"I am terribly afraid of bombs," I said, hoping to rouse his
pity and make him unselfishly sympathetic. Then, sighing
heavily, I, too, sat down on the bed.

"Our fellows will shoot him down in no time," said
Kuznetsof consolingly. "They got one a short time ago.
There were only two about."

"What do you do when you're at home?" I asked. "Are
your parents alive?"

"Only my mother," he said. "She's a doctor on a collective farm. I always go to her for the harvest."

Then he went on, "You, Lida, will return home to-morrow
like a countess, on a lorry. I've already told the boys. They'll
fix everything. And to hell with the officers. When we get
home after the war we'll show them. They think that if
they're officers, they can order us about. And now, Lida, let
me get in among the straw and we'll go to sleep. I honestly
mean sleep. I wouldn't think of any tomfoolery. Don't be
afraid."

"Why should I be afraid of you, Kuznetsof? You're so
nice and cultured. Only I'm not sleepy."

"That's right!" Kuznetsof's face lit up. "I am cultured,
aren't I? Exactly. You appreciate that. You, too, are a cultured woman. Now come and lie down beside me."

"First give me a cigarette."

"All right, but then you must lie down next to me. I

shan't do anything. Or are you afraid, eh? But I tell you, I'm cultured. We'll do a little love-making, and to-morrow you'll return home like a countess. I also told those fools to set the prisoners free, said they were innocent."

"Thank you! You're a good boy."

"I've been good to you all the time, haven't I? And you? You should be ashamed of yourself."

"Tell me, instead, how you were wounded," I said, and he began talking about the front, explosions and wounds. But still the dawn did not come. We cowered together under my sheepskin, with our feet buried in the straw, and slowly the ink-well lamp died down. What else could I do to keep Kuznetsof amused?

"Oh! Perhaps you think I'm ill?" he asked suddenly, delighted at having found the obvious answer. "I'll never be ill," he said proudly, thumping his chest with his fist, "because my mother is a doctor and I know how one catches syphilis. And I know that if you once catch it, it doesn't matter how much vodka you drink, it doesn't help. Others only found that out during the war. But I knew all the time, and took good care."

"Kuznetsof," I said, in a matter-of-fact tone of voice, "I must go outside now, but don't be afraid, I'll be back in a minute."

His face paled and twisted in a grimace. Aha, I said to myself, now you're beginning to lose patience; another minute and you'll fall into a rage and the unequal, tiresome struggle will begin, and my arms will be twisted, and I'll throw the ink-well at you and scream. Then I laid my hands on his shoulders, and, looking him straight in the face, said, "Kuznetsof, I give you my word of honour that I shall come back."

He calmed down at once, and smiled.

"I believe you," he said, adding with a mischievous smile, "and I shan't even look out of the window."

There was no one outside, not even a sentry. The sky over

the front was pink with the glow of new fires, like a false dawn. But in the east it was still dark.

When I got back I had to fight Kuznetsof, as I had expected. I jumped backwards and forwards over the bed, put the chair in his way, exhausted all the tricks of American slapdash comedy in fifteen awful minutes. I was frightened to hit too hard in case bad pain should make him really furious. I tried laughing and shouting, "Kuznetsof, you're crazy! Be quiet, I'm tired. Enough of this, let's sit down and have a cigarette." Then I screeched at him, "Fool! Fool! Did you say you were cultured? Let me go or I'll kick you so that you'd even prefer syphilis." But all my screams and screeches brought no one to the rescue, and the peasants only reinforced the barricade behind their door. They evidently knew my Kuznetsof. Then at last Kuznetsof caught me, and so I began to whimper, "I shall cry. Oh! how my hand hurts. Oh! how miserable I am! I'll do anything, but not if I'm bullied. I'm cultured, but you? You're like a wild animal. You don't know the first thing about culture. I hate you. Oh, how miserable I am. I shall cry in a moment. Of all the things, to attack an innocent woman. What have I done to you? You're worse than a German!"

Kuznetsof was young and let himself be taken in. "Don't cry, Lida, please don't cry! There, there, quiet now . . ." he said. We sat down on the bed as before, and started to smoke. However, Kuznetsof's youth also had its drawbacks. We had only taken two or three puffs, when he suggested that we should smoke lying down because he had pins and needles in his leg. I racked my brains for some other excuse, some other way of putting him off. Then, suddenly, I could hear somebody calling, "Kuznetsof! Kuznetsof!" first from a distance, then nearer and nearer. He leapt from the bed and ran outside. I could hear a whispered conversation and then three Russian heads in sheepskin caps appeared in the window, blocking out the pink sky. "Here, Lida," it was Kuznetsof whispering, "our attack has started. It's going well, and at dawn we are to be in the next village only a couple of miles away. We're leaving immediately. We'll be back again to say good-bye. Meanwhile you go to sleep, you poor thing." Then they disappeared.

I threw myself on the straw and immediately fell into an uneasy sleep. I don't know how long I had slept when I heard a sound and realized that there was someone in the room. I did not even have the strength to sit up. "Don't wake her, the poor thing's asleep. Don't wake her, you fools." That was Kuznetsof's angry whisper. A little soldier walked up and leaned over me. It was the dwarf, Shurka. I smelt garlic and felt a hand stroking me gently. "I shan't wake her," said the dwarf, "I'm only saying good-bye." Then another came up and gently patted my shoulder.

"What is it?" I called out, waking up completely.

"Nothing, Lida, nothing. It's only us. We came to say good-bye. We're going to the front. Our chaps are attacking."

"I told you you would wake her!" shouted Kuznetsof angrily. "You are all free now, get home as soon as you can," he whispered, and then they all stumped out.

I went to sleep again, but I don't know for how long. It was a dark, deep sleep, like death. Again someone was touching my shoulder. It was dark in the room, I could scarcely see anything. "Kuznetsof?" I asked, getting ready to leap up.

"Please don't be afraid, it is I," said a voice in French, and there was Rudi standing over me, smiling. "We must leave at once. They let us go. God knows why. One of them just came and said, 'We're leaving. You're free, but get home as quickly as you can.' Hurry up! Hurry up!" urged Rudi, smiling down at my terrified uncomprehending face. "It's after five already and it'll soon be light, and then it may be too late."

I leaped to my feet. Beyond the cottage I found the priest, Tacitus and the peasants, all standing waiting. I was shivering with cold. Everything was white with frost. We shook hands, and without exchanging a word, set off in Indian file along the backs of the cottages. The priest knew the village and led us along a path between the hills. It was quite quiet in the west.

We climbed on in silence. Then we could see the village below us, the ribs of roofs, tumbled walls. Dawn was breaking, and we walked on, still not speaking, just glancing or smiling at each other occasionally. Two Russians appeared on another hill, and we all bobbed down. Not till we were over the crest did we begin talking, the words bursting out as suddenly as the twittering of the birds at sunrise.

"Nothing unpleasant happened in the night, I hope?" enquired the old priest, with great delicacy.

"No, father," I said.

"How lucky we were to hit on that kind boy," said the priest, thinking of Kuznetsof.

"A grand lad," I agreed, and gave Rudi a whispered description of my nocturnal acrobatics. "Just like Harold Lloyd in the 'Thief of Baghdad,' " I said, and Rudi laughed.

Even if we used the normal short-cuts we had twenty miles to go to get to Mora. However, after conferring among themselves, the peasants thought of an even shorter way: straight through the vineyards, which meant keeping to the crest of the hills the whole time.

The sun flooded the whole country. It was a lovely spring day, fragrant, blue, immense, enveloping the whole world. Larks began singing high up in the sky. We scrambled through the dry vines, and along narrow, winding paths. Every time we saw a man, we dropped to our knees. If it was a peasant, one of ours would go up and make sure that we were on the right route and find out if there were any Russians about. We passed many shot-down planes, mostly Soviet ones. About nine o'clock we stopped and, squatting in the sun on some brushwood under cover of the vines, we shared what remained of our provisions. Everybody pulled what he still had out of his pocket and put it on the grass in front of us. The priest said grace and we began to eat. The peasants pulled out their pipes, we joked, and laughed at the slightest provocation, mostly because everything had ended so well. Then we set off again.

From the next pass we could see the chain of hills behind which lay Mora, and the peasants quickened their pace so that the old priest could hardly keep up. It grew hot. About noon we reached the boundary of Mora. At the cross the priest stopped and made a short speech in Hungarian. After the speech, first Tacitus and then Rudi came up and kissed me. Then the peasants came one by one and shook my hand and thanked me. Evidently the priest had said something nice about me, but I had not understood. Then the priest went up to the cross and in a loud voice thanked God that everything had turned out so well. We crossed ourselves, and then began the race home.

I was the youngest and the strongest. I ran, cutting across the fields and little valleys, straight for home. Mora lay in a hollow before me. I ran on, stopping once to pull some pussy-willows, then there was Teresa's patch of potatoes and our garden. I could see Jack chopping wood in the yard, shouted to him, and in a moment he was beside me. I threw my arms round his neck and lifted both feet off the ground, and Jack swung me round and round, kissing me all the time.

"Enough, enough," I shouted, laughing. "I was doing physical jerks half the night! Has anything happened here?"

"No," Jack said, "but where are the others?"

"They're on their way, all of them. But I wanted to be first."

I almost strangled Jumbo. Then, with an elegant gesture, I presented him with the pussy-willows: *"Le premier tribut du printemps."* It was not till I was sitting with my feet in a basin of hot water that Rudi and Tacitus arrived.

Oh, it's well worth having terrible adventures, I can tell you. How, otherwise, could one be so happy? Alf almost howled with happiness. He whined, whimpered, uttered quite un-canine sounds, and kept jumping up in the false hope that he could get at my face.

Our conversation was the incoherent, staccato conversation of happy, excited people. Everyone talked at once.

We carried on like that until our late lunch. After lunch I went to sleep, and then Fifi came and told me all that had been happening at home during those few days. We were alone, for all the others were in the hall with the priest, discussing the situation. Communal elections were to be held the following day, which was why they had wanted to get rid of us. It was the Crusoes' work all right. They must have promised the Counter-Intelligence men good loot from our house, if they would take us as German spies. We were lucky to have got off so lightly! Perhaps Kuznetsof was decent after all.

After supper, Fifi filled a tub with hot water for me, and I washed, standing in it naked and singing. Jack talked to me while he supported the screen which kept threatening to collapse. When I went to sleep, the edge had already been rubbed off my happiness. What Fifi had told me filled me with a fresh feeling of hopelessness, and as I lay there I decided to do everything in my power to emigrate with Jumbo to Tasmania. I could not think of anywhere farther away.

Fifi told me that after we had left, a small red-haired N.C.O. arrived and turned the whole house upside down. He was ostensibly looking for arms, but he took everything: all the money, the "rainy-day" cigarettes, cigarette cases, what remained of our jewelry, and anything else that took his fancy. From his collection of stolen treasures, he selected a comb and magnanimously presented it to Jack, because he was a Pole. When he left, he promised that he would return in the evening with his Major to make a final clean-up of the bloodsuckers' den. Thus the thefts were an official punishment imposed by the Russian civil administration. Poor Major! After the N.C.O. had finished, there was not much left in the house for him. Before he left, the Russian admitted to the two Poles that, although he had not found any arms, Tacitus would be disposed of on the following day. Bloodsuckers had no right to live. Neither Fifi nor Jack dared repeat that to anybody. As it was the Hungarians were in the depths of despair, for this was no longer war but Russian civil administration. Being law-abiding Europeans, my husband and his family just could not understand it; they were amazed and utterly appalled.

At midday, the following day, Elsie and Alec had set out on the dangerous enterprise of walking to Budapest. With their sack of soya flour, torn rucksack and miserable little suitcase tied up with string, they had looked like a pair of tramps. That sack of soya flour and a few rags was all that Elsie had in the world. She had felt that she could not stick it in Mora a moment longer. She just had to go, even though it meant going on foot. Yet there was now no escaping from Mora on foot, for Mora stretched from the Oder to the Aleutians. Poor Elsie! Our numbers were dwindling, and there were only six at table for lunch.

Summer Uniforms

24th-28th March

GLORIOUS weather. Spring burst upon us suddenly and overwhelmed us, filling us with false hope. What a spring! The first for seven years. And now I understand why the Russians are so intoxicated by such words as San Francisco. I've caught it myself. We'll go to Tasmania, won't we, Jumbo? Does anyone know the Russian poem, "Granada, Granada, my Granada"? It was written by a Russian who, instead of "San Francisco," used the word "Granada." The Russian millions are always longing, always dreaming, and now I understand them. Never again will I laugh at Russians when they tell wonderful tales about San Francisco. Never again. I know what it means. As I sat on a stone in the ruined rock-garden and stared up at the damask spring sky to keep my tears from falling, I thought of San Francisco and Tasmania: my Granada! If only I knew where the Rachmanians lived! If only I could find the way to their country! And millions of others want to know. Millions from the Volga once set out to join them, thousands of villagers abandoned their homes and rushed off blindly, but they never reached them. In the Tsarist days it was Rachmania they searched for, now they talk of San Francisco.

Fifi said that on a day like that we ought to pick violets, so the two of us went to the Manor park. We said nothing to the others, for we wanted to be alone. How many weeks was it since we were last in the park? What a sad sight it was! Littered with papers, some of them ancient priceless documents from the family archives, and some worthless old bills. You could hardly see the grass for them. The marble lions were broken. Why? The bronze statue of Marietta's brother who was killed in the last war, lay on the ground close to the entrance. An atmosphere of neglect, destruction and sadness. The last chapter of the book of the Eastern and Central European nobility.

"You see," I said to Fifi, "Marietta's brother has fallen for a second time."

We strolled farther into the park where the destruction was less noticeable. It was quite quiet with only the birds singing, and our feet sank deep in the dead leaves, left lying since the autumn.

There were no Russians left in the village and the place had suddenly begun to teem with animals: dogs, cats, geese, hens plastered to the neck with their own dirt, and a few ducks. Only now had the peasants dared to let them out into the sun.

Lunch was eaten in an atmosphere of suspense, for the communal elections were in progress. We were just finishing when the news came that all the main Crusoes were out. The newly elected headman was a peasant of the Small-holders' party, and the whole village was triumphant, including the Hungarians. We told them that they were rejoicing too soon, because the Crusoes would take a terrible revenge, especially as they had the support of the new Soviet administration. But why, protested the Hungarians, surely to lose an election was no reason for taking personal offence! It was difficult to argue with them. After dinner we were about to sit down to a game of cards to celebrate the elections, when two Russians were reported in the kitchen and I had to go and charm them. They were insolent, knowing that they were the only people with arms in the whole village. They demanded cigarettes, but we had none, so we had to talk and talk with them. They settled themselves comfortably and smoked some tobacco given them by a peasant who had come to the kitchen to discuss the elections with Tacitus. The conversation turned on the wages of factory workers. It seems that in Russia there is an enormous discrepancy between the different rates of pay. The difference between the earnings of an engineer and an ordinary labourer is reminiscent of the times when the Pyramids were being built. Or perhaps those soldiers were lying, just trying to boast of the huge income of an engineer or factory director in the Soviet Union. Yet, many other Russians had also boasted about that. They did not seem to realize what bad propaganda that was for their system. Why, I wondered, didn't they call themselves the land of high officials and technicians instead of workers and peasants?

When they had gone, the house began gradually to fill; peasants came, emboldened by the result of the elections; then the miller, hoping that now he would be able to start up his mill; and the priest to discuss village affairs. It appeared that the elections were all very well, only the Crusoes had announced that they would keep the militia in their own hands and would not hand over the Soviet arm-bands issued to them by the Russians. This caused consternation, because the militia-men were the dregs of the village, and the militia was the Crusoes' main weapon. The identity cards issued to the militia-men by the Russians were not handed over either, and the newly elected members of the commune were defenceless and trembled at the thought of the militia.

Sunday I decided to go to church and see for myself what the village was like after the elections, but on the way I ran into Jack coming back from the well with the water. The well, as in Biblical times, was the main source of our information. Puffing and panting, Jack said that the former commune, after conferring all night, had set out in a body at dawn, headed by the former headman, for the nearest office of the Russian administration to have the election invalidated. The Russians by now had branches of the civil administration of the Army of Occupation in all towns and larger villages.

After Mass it was like a bee-hive outside the church. The weaker element were too frightened to do anything, but the stronger characters gathered round the priest, Rudi and Tacitus, to discuss further action. The new commune offered Tacitus and Rudi a cart and horses if they would consent to go to the Russians as delegates of the village. As the Crusoes had slunk away before dawn on foot, so as not to attract attention, the idea was to overtake them in a cart. Within a minute or two the horses drove up. Tacitus climbed into the cart, grunting and very annoyed at having been given such a mission. Then Rudi jumped in, looking stubborn and naively determined, and the party was completed by the village schoolmaster, a sly and slippery opportunist, whose only worry was that, not knowing the future, he was constantly obliged to change his political allegiance. They were to go first to the mayor of the neighbouring town under which Mora had come before the Crusoes had declared it independent, hoping to get him to go with them to the Russians.

After lunch I went to the garden. Dolly and Marietta had clipped the faded, battered box hedge, swept the lawns and raked up the rubbish, straw and maize leaves into huge heaps. The water-meadows behind the house were already sprinkled with small glistening yellow stars. The sky was stretched smooth, without a crinkle, and hung like a huge blue cloche over the earth. There was such a lot of sky and only a narrow strip of earth, then a few hills, like mole hills, then more sky, nothing but sky. The sun was hot and a mild wind blew off the fields, smelling of earth. The mud had dried and the snow all gone, as though it had been spring for weeks.

That night we were one fewer. Honono's nerves had been unable to stand it any longer and she had gone off dressed as a beggar woman with one of the village lads to try and get to

Budapest. People seemed to think that Mora was the only place where there was injustice and violence, and that somewhere beyond it the world was still normal and law-abiding; and so, all who could, escaped. Jumbo, too, lying in bed with bronchitis and a temperature, was racking his brains how to get away. He at least had the consolation that the new commune would give him a pass to leave the village, which would have been almost impossible with the Crusoes in power. We felt as if we were on an island, and each one of us had in his order-loving soul, the deep-rooted, but entirely unjustified, belief that Mora was just a terrible exception.

After supper the moon again tempted Fifi and me out into the garden. It hung high in the heavens silvering the lazy, heavy, sleeping bodies of the hills. There was such peace in the air that it seemed as if even the oldest inhabitants would not be able to remember when last there had been a war. And yet no more than twenty miles away the greatest war in history was still in progress. We gazed at the flat spotty face of the moon and breathed the air off the water-meadows with its smell of damp mould.

"How marvellous," Fifi said. "How absolutely marvellous. And how good that we're alive. So many people have been killed, more or less under our noses, and we've come out of it untouched. We've seen deaths and births, terrible wounds, mutilations and dreadful illnesses, and yet we've come through all right."

"You know, Fifi, that I'm writing a book about it all, keeping my notes beside me. I'm so afraid of giving the wrong twist to anything, or of over-simplifying and generalizing, or departing from the truth. I'd rather it were dull, but true to the point of exaggeration. I'm not writing about the Russians, but about each individual Russian."

"Do you like them?" Fifi suddenly asked. "I mean the people, of course, not the regime."

"Yes," I said, and because human nature is more apt to remember the good side of events than the bad, I suddenly thought of all "the Alioshas," as we called the good Russians, and added, "I like them a lot."

"So do I," Fifi admitted. "But I'm afraid that nobody else will, now. I think it will be better not to say one does."

"Isn't it strange," I said, "that most of them don't even hate the Germans: where do they get that unswerving faith in human goodness, that inexhaustible patience, that self-denying, cow-like obedience? First the Tsar was holy, now it's Stalin. That's their misfortune. Slogans need no cover in Russia."

"But they are not all like that," Fifi said. "They have one thing in common: they can't think independently. Half of them are dangerous brutes. And then there's the vodka. You haven't forgotten that?"

"Well, what do you think of them?"

"I've told you already: I like them. I'm also frightened of them; I hate them and they disgust me, and I would rather never set eyes on them again, despite all the Alioshas."

"You're right. They have so many sides to them. Nearly every one of them describes a complete circle, as far as human possibilities are concerned: from a ferocious brute to St. Francis of Assisi. That's why you can't describe them in a few words. Just as it takes every attribute to describe the absolute, so to describe the Russians would take every known adjective. I like them, I don't like them, I adore them, I hate them, they move me, they frighten me, I admire them, they disgust me . . ."

This was the day when a Russian Major was to come with the mayor from the neighbouring town. The priest and the village teacher had gone to fetch them at dawn. There were no horses for ploughing, but when it came to politics they were available at once. I was summoned to go and interpret.

When I walked into the low-ceilinged room, the Major was sitting behind a table with the mayor and his own interpreter. One glance at my wretched appearance was enough and I was told that I should not be needed for the time being, but should go and wait outside the cottage. Outside I was met by the smell of hot cake coming from the neighbouring cottage and an irresistible force drew me towards it. By the window, his generous figure shutting out all light, stood Franzi, stuffing himself with poppy-seed cake made with sugar-beet syrup, while the housewife and her girls watched him, laughing. Franzi blushed. "Is that how you chop wood, you poor delicate thing?" I greeted him. Then I was given a piece of the cake and completely forgot about the Major. In fact, I never went back, but went a round-about way home. An hour or so later, Tacitus and Rudi came back, radiant. What a man, that Major! An excellent fellow! He had cursed the former headman, told him that according to Stalin a prince and a peasant must be treated the same, that that was the essence of the new justice, and if he did not know it, he was a bad Communist.

"Victory all along the line," said Tacitus. "To-morrow at dawn, Rudi and I are going to see him. He invited us both, we are to discuss everything with his Colonel." And the girl who had been slapped in the face by the former headman, because she told him that his daughter was a whore, was to go and lodge her complaint personally. Justice at last. That girl was the only person in the whole village who had had the courage to lodge a complaint against the ex-prefect. The suspicious peasants, scenting danger even where there was none, and actuated by some age-old instinct, had withdrawn their complaints against the chief Crusoe.

I cannot possibly describe here the whole of the background against which we then led our lives; but there is one thing that must be mentioned. As soon as it became quite clear that the Russians were going to win, their attitude towards the Western Allies changed completely. I don't mean in their Press, which I often read, but among the soldiers. How did it happen? I don't know. But I'm sure that the idea that the British and Americans were their enemies did not occur to the Russian soldiers of itself. Perhaps they attended special courses, or lectures, or the word may just have been passed from one to the other. However it was, I did notice a very definite change in the attitude of the Red Army towards the Allies. I no longer dared admit that I had friends in England, nor that my brother-in-law was a political refugee there. That had come to be a sin. When I first met the Russians they had merely laughed at Britain as the "land of lords," while the United States they treated as an equal of the Soviet Union. Now that the war was almost won, Britain became the obvious enemy, despised, ridiculous and prostrate, and the United States a sort of competitor for world domination. The peasants in Mora, like peasants the world over, felt this at once and reacted to it.

Where was the Sahib? He was gone. Perhaps he fell in Singapore or Tobruk? I don't know, but in any case he had disappeared. How long was it since I had been teaching Victor Klimof English? Only a few weeks. And in that time this giant, which is led by a single hand, had turned completely round in the opposite direction. We did not want to believe it at first, yet our instinct told us not to talk English together. Not that the Russians could tell one European language from another, but the Hungarian peasants might always have denounced us as Anglophiles. The change had come almost overnight, and we were appalled. Where was our place in the world? When at last would we be free from fear? And, above all, where was justice?

The peasants were constantly bringing back some of the things they had stolen, so as to keep on the safe side, but only some: one shoe, a clock case without the clock, parts of stolen dresses, odd gloves and a few pictures, the ones that did not appeal to them. Others came with complaints, because they thought that Tacitus was well in with the Russian Major, seeing that he was to see the Russian authorities on the following day. The house buzzed with the voices of our visitors.

We implored Rudi to try and get the Russian authorities

to give us permits to go to the capital, when he saw them in
the morning. Freedom of movement was impossible. Tacitus
was still full of hope, and we Poles felt sincerely for him. To
us the war seemed almost wonderful in comparison with such
a peace. The war had been like a difficult confinement, which
everybody had hoped would produce the longed-for heir. Instead, a monster had been brought into the world. What was
going to happen? What was there still in store for us? Oh,
this cursed, thrice-accursed peace! And we began talking
about the great times of the war as if it had been the Golden
Age. This only after a few days.

After dark the sound of a lorry could be heard in the village. Jack and I went out into the empty courtyard and
walked towards the gate. In front of the former headman's
house a huge Russian lorry was trying to park in the narrow
road. We knew that lorry only too well. The ex-prefect must
have sent his militia-men for help, and Sashka's men had
faithfully answered his call. What would to-morrow bring?
However, being still rather naive, we refused to believe that
Sashka's men would take a hand in public affairs. We knew
the Russians, but not their regime.

The next morning I got up at dawn. It was still dusk when
Tacitus and Rudi had set out to see the Major, still hopeful,
stubborn Europeans that they were, and believing in the
victory of so-called truth, justice, personal freedom, *neminem
captivabimus, habeas corpus,* etc. Fifi and I went to fetch
the water. There had been gunfire since early morning, and
quite close, but ever since we had noticed the change in the
wind which blew the Soviet official sails we had grown cynical.
We had only one desire and that was—to live.

And people like that are the worst of all. You cannot
build a new world with them, because they won't have anything to do with it. They have grown accustomed to think
only of themselves, of their own little world, because the big
world has let them down and they are finished with it. And
they will bring up their children as little pocket cave-men,

whose only care is that there should be meat in their particular cave. That's where mankind came in, and that's the point to which after much circling we have returned. Perhaps there are luckier countries in Europe? But not in our neighbourhood. And our neighbourhood is pretty big.

It was hot. There was no sun, but there was a brightness in the air, for the clouds were no more than a thin veil. We did our washing in the yard, outside the kitchen door. The gunfire sounded as close as ever, but we knew that the Germans would never return. And that was what worried us now: what was going to happen seeing that they were not going to come back? The American-made Russian lorry was again roaring outside the former headman's house. Fifi noticed the chief Crusoe fussing round it at midday, when he should have been with the Russian Colonel that Tacitus had gone to see. What was he doing still in Mora? Franzi brought the explanation when he came back from the village. Sashka's men had promised to arrange things with the Colonel. That put an end to all our hopes. Poor, silly Tacitus, we said. Our Polish grandfathers had ended up in Siberia, and it now looked as though it were the turn of the Hungarians. Except that after this war nobody will be willing to risk Siberia. There have been enough martyrs, and people will prefer to be cynics.

As yesterday was Dolly's birthday, we Poles made her a present by doing all her work for her. There was to have been black coffee for lunch, but we postponed having it until dinner when Tacitus and Rudi would be back. Looking forward to black coffee was about the extent of our future hopes. After lunch the four women sat down resignedly to a game of rummy. In the armchair Jumbo was reading his eternal *Richelieu*, and Jack had stretched out on the sofa and fixed his eyes on the engraving "Le Bal chez Monsieur de Villemorin," that so many Russians had looked at in wonder. Our little room looked very odd with the huge table on which Tolbuchin had planned his campaign, the broken Venus, and chairs from which the hide had been literally taken off. And we, too, looked odd, carefully groomed paupers.

Franzi returned from another trip to the village. (Since he had recovered he was always going there to pick up odd bits of food, for he had grown thin on our diet.)

"More Russians," he announced. "They've just arrived. Not troops on the way up: occupation forces."

We no longer cared. I went over to the window to have a look at my Watteau. The sun was setting: against the *vieux rose* background of the silky sky the outline of the great stone jar was black and distinct. The old elm had put out some leaves. The winter and the war were over.

Suddenly, we all jumped to our feet. A motor-car had driven up the drive.

"What's wrong with Lina and Matilda?" someone said. "Why aren't they shouting: 'Lida! Lida!' "

At that moment Lina came in with the lamp.

"Madam," she said to Marietta, in the voice of one who no longer knows good tidings from ill, "they have sent a car from the capital for Madam's brother-in-law. The firm has sent it. He can go at once. They have all the papers."

Jumbo threw down *Richelieu*.

We left the next day after a long quarrel about whether Alf was to stay behind or not. However, he jumped in himself and on to our knees, our only valuable piece of luggage. We drove off, feeling like the first people on their way to the moon.